CHRISTINA AGUILERA

CHRISTINA AGUILERA

CHLOÉ GOVAN

OMNIBUS PRESS

London / New York / Paris / Sydney / Copenhagen / Berlin / Madrid / Tokyo

Cover designed by Fresh Lemon
Picture research by Jacqui Black

ISBN: 978.1.78305.039.0
Order No: OP55286

Exclusive Distributors
Music Sales Limited,
14/15 Berners Street,
London, W1T 3LJ.

Music Sales Corporation
180 Madison Avenue, 24th Floor,
New York,
NY 10016,
USA.

Macmillan Distribution Services
56 Parkwest Drive,
Derrimut, Vic 3030,
Australia.

Every effort has been made to trace the copyright holders of the photographs in this book but one or two were unreachable. We would be grateful if the photographers concerned would contact us.

Typeset by Phoenix Photosetting, Chatham, Kent
Printed in the EU

A catalogue record for this book is available from the British Library.

Visit Omnibus Press on the web at www.omnibuspress.com

Contents

Contents

CHAPTER 1

Born On Beats

Shelly Loraine Fidler, Christina Aguilera's mother, was born in 1960 to a North American father, Lowell, and an Irish mother, Delcie, who'd emigrated from County Clare, and her future was full of hope and promise. A straight-A student, talented violin and piano player, she'd longed to make it in music. Yet destiny was derailed when, at just 12 years old, she lost her father to leukaemia. His premature death left her bereft of a male role model and her longing for love and protection would soon lead her into the arms of a father figure 12 years her senior with whom marriage turned out to be anything but a bed of roses.

In her mid-teens, she enjoyed a little transient freedom, travelling the world as a musician with the American Youth Symphony Orchestra, but her success was short-lived as she would soon be swept off her feet by her dubious lover.

Just like Shelly's mother, Fausto Wagner Xavier Aguilera was a migrant, hailing from Guayaquil, the largest city in Ecuador. By reputation, it was also the most violent and dangerous. In the country overall there was a history of bloody military conflicts – the Ecuadorian War of Independence, in which citizens resisted Spanish rule, an eight month long invasion by the Peruvian Army and near habitual civil warfare. Yet even when the country at large was at peace, Guayaquil was a terminal war zone. It was one of those places that, by necessity, invested more in war and weaponry than social welfare – and it showed.

As poverty took its toll, a popular mugging technique on the streets was to creep up behind an unsuspecting passer-by and strangle them, choking them unconscious before grabbing their bags.

As gruesome as it might seem to a Westerner, for many it was a matter of survival. The city was packed with slums, shanty towns and derelict high-rise flats, with millions living on the breadline. With unemployment at an all-time high in the overcrowded, underfunded city, one of the few sources of income was manual labour on a cocoa or banana plantation. These were often owned by wealthy foreigners, who expected cut-price labour – the work was long, hard and blighted by the baking hot sun.

Times were hard and, despite Ecuador's strong tradition of Catholicism, many had abandoned the notion of God altogether. When Mormon missionaries had first arrived in Fausto's city in 1965, when he was an impressionable young teenager, they symbolised the change he'd been looking for. When he acted on his desperation to escape, emigrating to the United States, he took his new-found Mormon values with him.

That was when Fausto and Shelly found themselves at the Brigham Young University in Provo, Utah together – although Shelly had been Protestant by birth, she had deferred to his beliefs. The two were like chalk and cheese – Shelly was an educated, middle-class teenage musician with an aptitude for languages, while Fausto was a rough and ready descendent of a working-class city. There was also a large age gap between them; she was just 19, while he was 31.

Then there was Mormon culture. Fausto and the university belonged to the Church of Jesus Christ of Latter Day Saints division, a sect that permitted polygamy. The university's founder, Brigham Young himself, had had a grand total of 55 wives. While Fausto himself didn't subscribe to the idea of multiple lovers, there were other religious demands. All drugs were forbidden, under a strict definition that included coffee and tobacco. There was also an expectation that the majority of students would take a two year break from their studies to become active missionaries and recruit new members for the church – a challenge that neither Fausto nor Shelly ultimately took up.

The religion banned passionate kissing – in reality, anything more than a peck on the lips – along with any activity likely to cause sexual arousal, even if fully clothed, until matrimony. With this set of rigid, suppressive rules, it was perhaps little surprise that Fausto and Shelly were in a rush to get married. They did so at the Church of Latter Day Saints Chapel in Washington D.C. and, when Shelly fell pregnant, they both dropped out of school.

Fausto joined the army to support his family, moving to a military base in Staten Island, New York – not far from Shelly's mother, Delcie's, home in Pittsburgh. Giving birth to their first daughter, Christina Maria Aguilera, on December 18, 1980 at Staten Island University Hospital, was a joyous occasion – but Shelly joined in the celebrations with a heavy heart.

A fluent Spanish speaker, she'd originally wooed her husband with her extensive knowledge of his mother tongue and, while he found her stumbling accent endearing and appealing, she found his background equally exotic. They'd revelled in the mysteries of each other's cultural worlds. Plus, as someone who'd lacked a significant male presence in her life since the death of her father, Shelly had thrown herself into the relationship wholeheartedly and with almost reckless abandon. Yet things had started to change when she took on Fausto's name. Previously the perfect gentleman, all of the niceties with which he'd won her over rapidly disappeared.

While the couple regularly attended church together with their new arrival, Shelly's depression was apparent. "They were both very quiet and kept themselves to themselves," one fellow Mormon told the author, "but Shelly was like a little mouse. She never looked anyone in the eye and always seemed really subdued and withdrawn."

Unbeknown to outsiders, Fausto was becoming increasingly unpleasant towards her. Fortunately for him, however, they moved before his wife's unusual behaviour could arouse any stronger suspicion.

By now totally isolated from family and friends, Shelly joined her husband at army bases in Texas, New Jersey and Sagamihara, a city bordering Tokyo in Japan. To her detriment, the latter would immerse her totally in military life. The army operated private buses to transport children to school or families to social events, a service which was not just convenient but essential. In a world of indecipherable symbols, anyone who hadn't mastered Japanese was as dependent as a child. The language barrier would leave Shelly heavily reliant on her husband and ever more vulnerable to his rages. As Christina would later recall, "The military police would come, but a lot of them were doing the same things [to their wives]."

The first chance she had, Shelly grabbed Christina and a few meagre possessions and fled. However, within days, she'd be back. "There was a period where we were going back and forth a bit," Christina recalled. "She would leave and he would talk all his Spanish about how he would treat her like a china doll. He knew how to romance her like that."

The question on most people's lips might be: why did she weaken and turn back to him? However, there was more for Shelly to contend with than common sense. First there were reasons of faith: the Mormon religion taught that every human action was forgivable, with the exception of murder. It also placed a high value on working at a marriage, no matter how impossible it seemed, instead of resorting to divorce. She'd vowed that Fausto would be her partner "until death do us part", responsibilities she took extremely seriously. As outrageous as such self-imposed entrapment might seem to modern, secular sensibilities, a religious lifestyle was what Shelly had chosen. As a romantic teenager, her marriage contract had seemed a legitimate covenant of love, but in reality she felt she'd signed her life away to servitude and slavery.

Besides her moral obligations, there were financial reasons for continuing the union. In Japan, she'd taken a job teaching students English, but the wages were low and, inevitably, spent as quickly as they were earned on Christina. Fausto's wages were modest too – even if Shelly claimed child support in the aftermath of a break-up, how could it be enough to house herself and her child? Her own dreams of becoming a bilingual Spanish translator or a musician were now long forgotten and the last vestiges of her self-esteem, which had once given her the conviction she was capable of these professions, were shattered into pieces by the beatings.

She desperately wanted to find a way to make it work – so much so that she was willing to delude herself. Fausto was manipulative, skilful and persuasive – every time she reached the end of her tether, he would sweet-talk her into believing that he'd change. He'd insist that Christina both needed and deserved a two-parent home and that they were stronger together than they'd ever be apart. Seduced by his lavish promises and truly wanting to believe them, she succumbed to staying. It was all against her better judgement, but she saw little other option.

Besides, Shelly might even have found her husband's outbursts flattering – and when they alluded to possessiveness, it could have seemed like proof that she was desirable. She was also sympathetic to the fact that Fausto seemed to come from a background of violence. As someone who'd grown up exposed to violence in the streets of his dangerous home city, he'd become desensitised and had learned to see it as normal. She realised her husband's background wasn't his fault but a product of his environment.

However the biggest tug on Shelly's heart-strings was that she was in love – and that could be an open prison in itself. She'd given so much of herself to the relationship that her identity was tied to Fausto – she didn't know who she was any more without him. This love affair, as toxic as it was, was more addictive than any Class A drug.

Yet Shelly ignored the nagging voice in the back of her head which told her she deserved better. She did, however, have a backup plan. "Each place we'd go, I'd get a phone book and write down the number of the local woman's shelter," she recalled. Yet for the most part that number would stay safely folded in her jacket pocket, unused.

Christina, an unusually precocious child, drowned her sorrows by socialising with another army child – and sometimes a little more. "I was an early maker-outer," she confessed, "not really knowing what I was doing, but kind of like when you play house when you're little… my mom caught me on the front porch with this kid that lived a couple of houses down. It was very cute and flirtatious, but it wasn't no little peck. It was a make-out session!" She'd been just five years old.

At around the same time, she was also being consoled by a mystery apparition she believed was her guardian angel. "My mom and I were playing hide and seek one time and I ran up the stairs," she recalled. "My mom was saying, 'I'm going to get you, I'm going to get you.' All of a sudden I looked up and stopped dead in my tracks. There was this guy and he was in an all-white outfit, just kind of glowing. He had a white beard and was looking down at me calmly, very peacefully."

Whether Christina really was receiving spiritual protection or simply indulging in an infantile fantasy, no one knew, but few little girls were more in need of a guardian's watchful eye. Faced with constant fights at home, she had two choices: succumb to misery and cry her eyes out, or disassociate from reality altogether. It wasn't long before she opted for the latter and distracted herself with movies – she would watch her favourite, *The Sound Of Music*, over and over on repeat.

The play, detailing a nun-in-training's escape from the confines of a convent and eventual freedom, racing over the Austrian Alps with her lover, depicted concepts that were elusive and alien to Christina – happiness, safety and liberation. Yet it was the soundtrack that captivated her the most – when she closed her eyes and sang along, it was pure escapism. "Music was my release to get away from it all," she would enthuse later. "I would seriously run up to my bedroom and put on that *Sound Of Music* tape. [Heroine] Julie Andrews [who plays Maria] was free and alive and she was playful and rebellious against the nuns. I know it sounds really cheesy, but that was my escape. I would open my bedroom window and I would just imagine the audience. I would just sing out."

She would fling a window open, singing her heart out to unsuspecting passers-by – little did they know, of course, that they had witnessed one of the earliest Christina Aguilera concerts. When no human ears were vacant, she'd simply line up her stuffed toy collection as a makeshift audience and sing to them instead. "I wanted to share this with somebody," she would explain, "because it was where I wanted to be, running up those hills, free and alive. Julie couldn't fit in, just like me."

Living in Japan, of course, it was inevitable that Christina was never going to blend in – but it wasn't just that life as a travelling "army brat" had meant uprooting herself several times in her short young life already. Every time she made a friend, she had to leave them behind to follow her father to the next military base. She was lonely and envious of those who were settled, but the soundtrack became her one constant fixture in a chaotic world. Singing became a way to release negativity and restore balance – and not only was Christina healing herself, but, as she hummed along in her mother's arms, even Shelly felt that the tension was broken. On one of her rare visits to her mother's house, Mrs Fidler would exclaim to Shelly in excitement, "There's more to this than playing around – she's going to make you rich one day! She was born to be a singer."

Shelly laughed it off incredulously, dismissing her words as the bias of an overzealously proud grandmother. Yet Christina's impromptu concerts continued. She would spread a towel out on the floor to represent a stage and then grab a shampoo bottle which she would lisp, by way of explanation, was her "'icaphone". Yet like all addictions, her singing masked an inner pain. "Growing up, I did not feel safe," she would reiterate later. "Feeling powerless is the worst feeling in the world. I turned to singing as an outlet – the pain at home is where my love for music came from."

That pain showed no sign of receding and by 1986, a heavily pregnant Shelly saw her chance to leave when Fausto was relocated to an army base in Philadelphia, just a short drive from her mother's house in Rochester, a suburb of Pittsburgh. Shelly, a six-year-old Christina and her newborn sister, Rachel, fled while he was at work and "never looked back".

Life with her grandmother was idyllic, especially as she encouraged Christina's musical leanings, but the memories of the past were slow to fade – and she soon found herself drawn to the blues. Spending weekends rummaging through Pittsburgh's vintage record stores, she discovered singers like Etta James and Billie Holiday and related to their honesty, agony and raw emotion – unlike modern music, in which natural voices were often rendered unrecognisable by special effects, these heartbroken divas seemed to mean every word they sang.

"It just had grit, heart and emotion," Christina reminisced. "As soon as I got an old record, I'd run up to my room, pop it in, learn every lyric straight away, come back down and say, 'Grandma, I learned it' and act it out for her in our dining room… I related to the pain in that music. Although I was only six or seven, I had already dealt with a great deal… and witnessing all the chaos in my home, so there was something I got about that music."

Combining old-school tracks with a more modern repertoire, she began to put on full-length concerts at home. "B.B. King's 'The Thrill Is Gone' was one of my standards," she recalled. "Then there were more modern things like Bob Seger's 'Old Time Rock And Roll' and Whitney Houston's 'I Wanna Dance With Somebody'." Christina would belt out the latter at her school's first grade talent show.

Soon her grandmother arranged for her to perform at block parties, pool parties and record stores, believing she had a real talent to be harnessed. Onlookers were initially sceptical, however. "I was known around town as the little girl with the big voice," Christina explained. "Once, when I was seven, this guy couldn't believe I was singing, so he unplugged my microphone in the middle of my song, which freaked me out. Then he was like, 'Oh my gosh, she's really singing!'"

That same year, she received news symbolising freedom at last – the divorce between Fausto and Shelly had been finalised. Shortly afterwards, Fausto was relocated to a station in Colorado – it would be the last time Christina saw or heard from him for over a decade.

In spite of their estrangement, Shelly had been keen to ensure that her daughter didn't abandon her Latin roots. The marital home had been a predominantly Spanish-speaking environment, with English spoken only between mother and daughter, but Christina had blocked out every foreign word she'd learned as she associated their sounds with her father.

Instead of language lessons, Shelly would honour his culture with cookery, preparing traditional South American dishes such as encebollado, a fish stew prepared with boiled cassava and pickled red onion rings and served up with slices of avocado and banana chips as a side. Accented with spicy chilli sauce, it had been one of Fausto's favourites. She'd also regularly prepare one of his favourite cinnamon-infused drinks, with oatmeal and pineapple, for Christina and she even observed his Ecuadorian family tradition of eating a huge feast at midnight on Christmas Eve instead of waiting until the following day. With all of these touches, she kept the Latin side of Christina alive.

Meanwhile, as a converted Mormon living in an Irish Protestant household, Shelly tried not to label or categorise her daughter's religious experiences but instead strongly encouraged general spirituality and a belief in God. She would even tell a young Christina that her voluptuous talent for singing was God-given, recalling, "I kind of learned real quickly that this was sort of out of my control, that she was going to be a singer, that God was kind of guiding everything."

That was exactly who she held responsible when, without so much as a single singing lesson, Christina's amateur home audition tape stood out among tens of thousands of entries to win a place on TV talent show *Star Search*. The contest had a reputation for singling out undiscovered youth talent – Justin Timberlake, Britney Spears, Aaliyah and even an early version of Destiny's Child would first become known to the world this way.

In fact, before the days of *The X Factor* and *American Idol*, it was the only way to publicly compete for a recording contract, with the chance to win over the nation in the process. Christina's tape, which saw her belt out Whitney Houston's 'Greatest Love Of All', would lead to two further auditions and, when she passed those with flying colours, an invite to the show's LA studios. The show organised an all-expenses paid trip to Hollywood, a seven-night stay in a luxury Beverly Hills hotel and a minimum of $1,000 in prize money regardless of how far she came in the competition – which, for an eight-year-old back in 1989, was a small fortune.

However, the level of competition was intimidating – most of the other young contestants had vocal coaches and talent agents, whereas Christina's gift was raw and unpolished. As her proud grandmother would tell the media, "She's never had a lesson in her life. What she's learned, she has learned up in her room. It's all on her own." Getting this far on innate ability alone was a clear coup – but would her lack of formal training put her at a disadvantage when it came to competing?

In addition, the show had a reputation for undemocratic rules; in fact, three years later, it would pit a preteen Beyoncé and pals against competitors twice their age – a battle even the most talented child performer seemed doomed to lose. A similar fate would ultimately befall Christina.

On the day of reckoning, just a month before her ninth birthday, a nervous Christina donned the blouse her mother had worn in concerts during her days as a violinist for the Youth Symphony Orchestra, for good luck. However it had been comically voluminous on a child of her tiny stature – unusually slim and petite even for her age – and it had to be belted and worn as a dress. She was also trying, metaphorically speaking, to fill oversized shoes. Her soulful rendition of Etta James' 'A Sunday Kind Of Love' did captivate the audience – but it wasn't enough. The judges' votes tied her with a 12-year-old boy – both performers had earned three and a quarter out of a possible four stars – and, when it came to a deciding audience vote, her competitor scraped through to the semi-finals by the skin of his teeth. An overwhelming sense of injustice rose in Christina like an electric shock and, for a few momentous seconds, it looked set to spill over into a full-on tantrum. After all, her rival had been several years older and more experienced – to an eight-year-old, it simply wasn't fair.

Yet Shelly had instilled humility in her daughter, as well as the necessity of being a graceful loser, warning that arrogance didn't pay and that her "God-given" talent could at any moment be snatched away on account of bad behaviour. With this threat in mind, a devastated Christina, tears pouring down her cheeks, shuffled over to her rival, hesitantly shook his hand and managed a muffled "Congratulations! I'm really happy for you!" All the time, she later recalled, she was thinking, "Not fair!"

This introduction to the ruthless nature of showbiz was a cruel awakening and her tender age only accentuated the agony. However, while she might have been down, she certainly wasn't out – her performance had stood out sufficiently for a Pittsburgh newspaper, *The Beaver County Times*, to write a full page feature on the rising star.

The journalist would write admiringly, "She sings the blues like a young Billie Holiday and pop like a fledgling Janet Jackson. Clutching a microphone with one hand and motioning with the other, Christina's face shows pain and yearning during a song about heartache – a heartache she hadn't yet experienced at her age."

Little did they know that, as atypical as it was for the average child, heartache was an emotion with which Christina was very familiar. In fact, it was the memory of the helplessness of her early years that was spurring her on.

The two matriarchs of her household had already noted Christina's need to be independent and always in control. Yet these were not organic traits or signs of a healthy predisposition to leadership; rather, they were the signature of someone who was deeply insecure and emotionally wounded. For Christina, who trusted almost no one, staying in control was a way to ensure she was safe, whereas she associated a loss of control with dangerous vulnerability. Like Michael Jackson had done before her at the hands of his own father, there had been times when she had vomited in fear. Yet unlike Joe Jackson, Fausto's behaviour had not been motivated towards turning his children into better performers. Somehow though, Christina had managed to turn a negative into a positive and link the two. Shelly recalled that after witnessing life in the home, she'd grown up "determined that if God blessed her with her dream of fame, she'd use it somehow to help people in that situation". This pioneering spirit was the driving force behind her desperation for fame.

Of course, there were also other perks. At one house party where she'd performed, an impressed neighbour had humoured Christina – hoping to boost the child's self-esteem – by asking for her autograph. The rush this single request induced was a defining moment for her – and from then on, her search for adulation and recognition would become addictive. She would later joke, "I was signing autographs when I didn't know how to write joined up and I barely knew how to spell my name!"

Another person wowed by her was Jude Pohl, a theatrical producer and founder and director of Pittsburgh company Pohl Productions. He was running his own version of *Star Search* locally and, although he had high expectations, when he saw Christina's tape, he was stunned into silence. "It wasn't that she had a big voice," he would explain. "She had an *adult* voice. We could have had her compete in the adult female vocalist contest if she had been behind a curtain."

Unfortunately he'd already selected the performers for that year's event, but he called Christina nonetheless and invited her to be a guest vocalist at the finals. There, she terrified one young performer so much that she hid in her dressing room and refused to go on stage.

This was Christina's first taste of just how intimidated people would be by the quality of her voice and the strength of her ambition. At school, other children struggled to relate to her focus and drive and because she stood out as different, perceived her as a threat. Resenting the attention she received in the spotlight, they would react with such barbed aggression that it even shocked Shelly.

"Christina would cry every time her name got in the local paper because it meant more fear at school," she revealed. "We had threats of slashed tyres and her getting beat up. She would be late to school because I had to time leaving the house so that there wasn't enough time for them to do things to her."

To make matters worse, she had few friends to defend her. "As soon as I would make one," Christina recalled sadly, "the other girls would steal her away."

As someone who'd already moved six times in as many years, the concept of friendship was almost alien to her anyway. She'd never lingered in one place long enough to force lasting friendships, so she was already awkward around her peers – and her classmates' complex hybrid of jealousy and confusion only added to her troubles. "We were very confused [ourselves]," Shelly would explain "because it was OK if she was out doing little league or cheerleading or something, but fame seemed to flip them out because apparently it threatened them."

In fact Christina had been a cheerleader, briefly becoming a part of their "clique" but for a meagre week, before dropping out when it emerged it would clash with her singing commitments. While school sports was something that every child could share in, the sheer scale of Christina's ambitions inspired an inferiority complex and the inevitable, age-led immaturity of her peer group meant that they had no other way of expressing their feelings than jeering at her.

It wasn't just the children, either. "As soon as *Star Search* happened, a lot of my mom's old friends, other parents, wouldn't talk to us any more," Christina explained. "Sometimes teachers [also] made it difficult because I would be off with the flu and I would return to school and the teachers would be like, 'Oh, she wasn't out sick, she was out singing somewhere.'"

With animosity from all sides, it was hardly surprising that she would recall "constantly feeling like an outsider growing up". However, just as she had allowed growing up with her father to shape her positively as a person, she used the bullying as a learning experience too. "I got the cold shoulder a lot merely because of what I loved to do and who I was, so I completely relate to anybody that feels they ever have to confine anything about themselves to please someone else," she would assert. "I knew at a really young age that I would never do that. Though I would feel helpless in many ways, I would always be courageous and stand up for what I believed in. That drive was instilled very young."

So Christina soldiered on – but the misery would build in her subconscious and many evenings would see her wake from nightmares screaming in terror. The escape route she hankered after finally came when her mother fell in love with Jim Kearns, a paramedic, and remarried on May 12, 1991.

This would lead to the family switching school districts when they relocated to the nearby town of Wexford. It was a more affluent suburb than Rochester and, while she was still teased and alienated, it was considerably easier to cope.

Her stepfather came with baggage: a seven-year-old son, Casey, and four-year-old daughter, Stephanie, from a previous marriage. However, two years her mother's senior, Jim was the total opposite of Fausto – gentle, kind and softly spoken. Ultimately his presence was positive for Christina, teaching her not to paint all men in the same colour. Without Jim in her life, she might have grown to distrust all adult men.

Christina again turned for solace to the one thing she felt would never let her down – the healing effect of music. To the bemusement of her new classmates, she shut down and focused on visualising herself on the stage. By the time she finished high school, she vowed, she'd have graduated not just in education but in music and would have an award-winning album on store shelves. "A lot of times, I didn't want to talk about just boys, I didn't want to talk about cheerleading practice," she sighed. "I wanted to be fully into music."

Christina's harrowing early life experiences, as distressing as they were, had bestowed upon her focus, drive, direction and a maturity that none of her peers could match. She couldn't relate to the superficial amusements the other girls indulged in – for her, it was all about her future.

Yet big dreams had to start somewhere and Christina – whose room was adorned with hockey sticks and posters of her local team, the Penguins – started to sing the national anthem at matches. In fact, in 1992, every time the team won the Stanley Cup at a home game she had been present singing the 'The Star-Spangled Banner' and she soon began, albeit jokingly, to attribute her presence to their success. Singing at sporting events was also the way that Taylor Swift would find fame but, at that time, Christina was the youngest anthem singer in the whole of North America.

To her disappointment, there was something else for which she had been not just unusually young, but prohibitively young – a coveted presenting slot on the national TV show *The New Mickey Mouse Club*. The programme, which provided comedy skits, music, dance choreography, acting, celebrity guests and all-round children's entertainment, was a favourite on the Disney Channel. Producers had been looking for "triple threats who could do it all" – in other words, those who could effortlessly dance, sing and act. While she clearly stood up to scrutiny on every count, becoming one of the favoured final few at the auditions, there was one curve ball – she had been too young. The average age of a presenter on the show was 12, while Christina had been just nine when she auditioned – and, according to insiders, had looked more like seven or eight at the time. Show bosses would recall that she was "astoundingly, breathtakingly talented", but that she simply failed to correspond with the average age of the show's viewers. She was gutted – again, she felt as though she'd been rejected on a technicality.

By 1992, the setback had been long since forgotten – but, unbeknown to her, the audition tape she'd provided had been kept on file and now that she was approaching the ideal age, Disney wanted to see her again. Shrieking with excitement, Christina ran up to her bedroom and pressed play on Whitney Houston's 'Vision Of Love' – the rehearsals were beginning again.

When she auditioned the second time around, she was instantly accepted. Along with six other new stars – T.J. Fantini, Tate Lynch, Ryan Gosling, Nikki DeLoach, Britney Spears and Justin Timberlake – Christina would join an existing cast that included JC Chasez and former *Felicity* star Keri Russell. All of them had the same burning ambitions that she had spent a lifetime being ridiculed for – now, finally, she fitted in.

CHAPTER 2

The Note That Changed A Life

The New Mickey Mouse Club would give a previously unknown Christina a new lease of life. "It was a great way to grow up," she would enthuse, "working with a cast that truly enjoyed performing and saw it as a future career choice as much as I did." Indeed, it was here that Justin Timberlake would meet 'N Sync bandmate-to-be JC Chasez, while Britney and Christina shared one thing in common before they'd even met: both had been initially rejected from the show for being too young. Even now, they remained the youngest, with other cast members ranging from their age to 18. "We were the little girls of the show," Christina reminisced later, "so we bonded."

Envious of the seemingly effortless maturity and glamour of the older girls, they took comfort in each other's presence. "I know she's going to kill me for saying this," Christina would later announce mischievously, "but me and Britney wanted to get our periods so bad. There were some already developed older girls that we looked up to and we were 11 and 12 – still at the [bra] stuffing stage. Thank God for Britney on that show, because we needed each other."

Even the pair's mothers became close – Shelly had relocated to Orlando, Florida for a large part of the year to look after Christina in their Disney-sponsored apartment, while Louisiana resident Lynne

Spears had made the same sacrifice for Britney. "[The two girls] were inseparable," Shelly would explain. "I mean, literally. Lynne and I lived at each other's apartments practically, with these girls back and forth. When you have a child like Christina or Britney, I saw the same thing in her, they have this passion about what they love doing."

The pair would even study together, with three hours per day of compulsory schooling part of the Disney contract. Christina was a perfectionist, maintaining a straight-A average and fascinated by English and science. She also had a keen interest in psychology, pondering even at the age of 12 whether she should study the subject in college. However, the real focus was music – and anticipating the thrills of becoming a teenager would come a close second.

Christina's longing to be older was nevertheless apparent. "We totally looked up to [16-year-old] Keri Russell," she would later confess. "She was a Barbie doll to us... She was the first one to fray her jeans, which was cool at the time – and she was beautiful, we were just in awe of her." On top of that, Keri was the first of the girls to have a car and a boyfriend. Christina would fawn over her, clamouring to hear her secrets and constantly touching her hair in admiration. Keri would display an equal fondness for the girl she grew to regard as her baby sister.

However, when Christina returned to her regular school during breaks from the show, things couldn't have been more different. "Whenever I'd come back, people would either welcome me or they would shun me and say, 'She thinks she's better than us,'" she would sigh. "And that was totally not true. It was really hard for me because all I wanted to do was be a part of everyone else and be a normal kid. But a lot of times, people wouldn't allow me to be that way because of how they perceived my lifestyle."

Suddenly it became like primary school all over again. Other girls would gossip, taunt her and hide her bag and even kick balls in her direction, hoping they'd hit her. "Once, this jeering group of girls came up to her and threw two balls they'd been hiding behind their backs straight at her body," a classmate told the author, "then they'd grab them back to kick at her. It must've really hurt, but she was strong."

Although bullying might knock the average child's confidence, Christina hadn't judged her self-worth in terms of her popularity with her pre-teen peers. Instead, she revelled in the knowledge that she'd beaten over 15,000 aspiring hopefuls for one of just seven "Mouseketeer" slots. As much as she longed to be normal, she knew in her heart that she'd always be anything but – and, if it meant she could fulfil her dreams, all the better for it. "[The bullying] was why I became so introverted and focused on my career," she would reflect later. "My dream of becoming a recording artist kept me going."

Ron Fair, Senior Vice President of A&R at RCA Records and the man who subsequently signed Christina, concurred that her insatiable drive was the most important factor in her subsequent success: "It wouldn't have happened at all if she didn't work at it," he claimed. "If it's your dream, you also have to have the discipline to support that dream. That means when the other kids are going shopping, going to the mall, going to the movies, you're working on your dream. You're practising your vocals, you're singing in the mirror with a hairbrush, you're learning the songs, all the words…"

She worked tirelessly on her routines, her efforts eventually reaping rewards – for example, when her idol Whitney Houston guest-starred on an episode of the show, she was able to meet her in person.

There were other networking opportunities, too – one season, talent scout and famed "PR whiz" Ruth Inniss was at the Disney studios to promote R&B girl group SWV, who toured with an early Destiny's Child. While she was there, she spotted Christina singing and immediately demanded to know where her mother was. When a sheepish Shelly came forward, convinced her mischievous daughter was in some kind of trouble, she was open-mouthed to see Ruth standing there, pressing a business card into her hand and urging her to call. Christina was going to be a star, she insisted, and she wanted to be part of the journey. Christina was locked into a five-year contract with the TV show but, as it happened, Shelly was able to make use of her card far sooner than she'd ever anticipated.

In February 1994, as Christina prepared for her third series of *The New Mickey Mouse Club*, she received a letter explaining that the popular show – on air since 1955 – was coming to an end with immediate effect. She and her fellow Mouseketeers were no longer required and it was back to the mundane minutiae of everyday life in Wexford. By that time, Christina had swapped school for home education to allow her to focus on the show – an initiative that now appeared futile. However, she didn't feel deflated for long. Ruth, using her contacts, referred Christina to New Jersey-based producers Roberts Alleca and Michael Brown. She'd worked with them previously when they'd produced tracks for SWV, so it seemed only natural to introduce the young singer to them.

As a result, Christina recorded an album of demos with the duo, *Just Be Free*. Unfortunately these efforts were almost entirely fruitless, so Ruth set up a meeting with the highly influential music business lawyer Normand Kurtz. How exactly Christina's management deal progressed from there was a matter of some contention and, later, legal wrangling.

The road to success was progressing frustratingly slowly. Within months of *Micky Mouse* ending, Justin Timberlake and JC Chasez had attracted attention from a label, joining boy band 'N Sync. By 1995, they'd released their debut single, 'I Want You Back' and the following year Britney – who'd been squirrelled away in a Philadelphia studio recording demos, like Christina – would sign a deal with Jive Records. Christina, on the other hand, was still unsigned and simply marking time. "I would watch *Total Request Live*," she recalled mournfully, "and see all their videos and go, 'I can't wait 'til I'm a part of that.' But I had to work on my patience a little at that point."

It was possible that she was a victim of the trend for groups that prevailed during the nineties. Several industry executives had turned down Britney before she was signed, claiming that it was the teen eye candy of the Backstreet Boys or the female empowerment anthems of the Spice Girls that the public truly craved. They didn't need another solo artist. In fact, one label had even told Britney's manager – by way of explanation before rejecting her – "There'll never be another Madonna." Even worse, some labels didn't bother to give a reason. The industry was not just intensely competitive but bitingly brutal, and for a self-confessed "sensitive" soul like Christina, the perpetual rejection was far from easy.

In June 1997, she performed at the Golden Stag music festival in Braşov, Romania, with a set which included covers of Sheryl Crow and Diana Ross songs. Here, Christina's diversity was shining through, with soul and popular country music now part of her repertoire. Yet when she competed in the festival's Singers Contest, she failed to win over the audience or the jury and left empty-handed.

A duet with Japanese artist Keizo Nakanishi, 'All I Wanna Do', would meet with an equally lukewarm response. Keizo, who had been extremely popular in his home country but almost unheard of abroad, had sought an American singer to kick-start his career stateside and expand his fan base. As Christina had a natural affinity with all things Japanese due to her time spent residing there, the decision to take part was an easy one. She'd even travel to Tokyo for promotion and two concerts in the city, which would see her duet live with Keizo. However, the public didn't share her enthusiasm, largely perceiving the ballad as insipid and criticising its "cheesy, uninspired" lyrics.

Meanwhile, the clock was ticking on Christina's dream to release an album before her high school years ended. She had begun to regularly cry in frustration, sobbing into her pillow, 'Will I ever be discovered?'"

Finally, after years of waiting in the wings, it all started to happen at once. When RCA Records' Ron Fair received yet another demo with a note attached insisting the singer had "talent" and "quality", he fought the urge to roll his eyes dismissively. Every day he received dozens of demos with equally persuasive handwritten notes promising exactly the same thing – and they rarely lived up to the hype. What could possibly be different about this one?

Nonetheless, he felt obliged to go through the motions and invite her for an audition, because this tape had the seal of approval from his boss. Bob Jamieson, the label's president, had initially received the tape from Normand Kurtz. When Ron pressed play, Christina did little to ignite his curiosity. The fault lay predominantly with the material, which consisted mainly of tracks from her demo tape, *Just Be Free*, which *NME* would later sneer "combines lame 'dance' grooves with lyrics that would disgrace a Hallmark card". Ron concurred, muttering "Excellent singing but the material's not really strong." Then he heard the final track, a cover of Whitney Houston's 'Run To You' – and he was won over.

Christina was summoned to his office, together with Steve Kurtz, the son of Normand, and he decided to put her to the ultimate test: whether she could pull off the same sound in an unforgiving acoustic live context. "I took a meeting with Christina and said, 'OK, sing!'" Ron explained simply. "It was in a very, very small office, with three or four people crammed into it, but she basically got into that performance zone and sang a cappella, with a complete sense of self-possession, with perfect intonation. She was very determined and extremely professional. From a musical point of view, her chops were way beyond her years and it was obvious that she had the potential to become a major vocalist. I went to my boss and said, 'This girl's the bomb, let's sign her!'" As an afterthought, he took the note he'd received from Bob bragging about Christina's star quality and affixed it to his wall for posterity – he had the feeling it referred to a future legend.

The ink had barely dried on Christina's draft contract when Ron received a call from an associate at Disney asking for a performer for a song called 'Reflection', which would appear on the soundtrack of *Mulan*, the company's next major film. There was one condition: he wasn't interested unless she could hit the notoriously difficult to reach note "high 'E' over middle 'C'". Instantly, Ron thought of Christina. The synchronicity was undeniable – the track seemed made for her. She assured him she could produce the implausibly high note and he urged her to send him a tape of her singing it "tomorrow, by the latest".

Of course, in the internet age, it would have taken a mere click of a button to transfer the files, but the reality in the nineties was that Christina was facing a race against time – and she didn't even own a tape deck. Springing into action, she ran out to buy a cheap karaoke recording machine and set it up in the bathroom right next to the shower to emulate the echo effect of a real microphone. Her lack of technology made her cringe, feeling that the sound was "so cheesy and so tinny". In fact, she would stay up half the night, ever the perfectionist, to achieve the right sound. "Since it's not like in a recording studio where you can do take after take," Christina grumbled, "if you're halfway through a song and you mess up, you have to stop and rewind and play it all over again. So I must have been up until like four in the morning trying to get the perfect recording. It was crazy!"

She sent in her track, another rendition of Whitney Houston's 'Run To You' and within 24 hours she was on a plane to LA for a face-to-face audition in front of Matthew Wilder, a Grammy-nominated film score composer and producer of No Doubt's *Tragic Kingdom*. She passed with flying colours on the strength of one note – "the note that changed my life".

Within the same week, the young singer had landed both a starring role on a soundtrack and a record contract – and, in keeping with how quickly her career was moving, Ron upgraded the terms from a demo deal to the guarantee of a full-blown album. "I was ecstatic," a 17-year-old Christina recalled of the twin deals. "They took a huge chance, using an unknown like me." Indeed, the role would earn her a place in the unofficial Disney Vocalists' Hall of Fame alongside Celine Dion, who'd sung on *Beauty And The Beast*, and Vanessa Williams, who'd appeared on *Pocahontas*. Both had been platinum-selling artists before they were hired, which made Christina's breakthrough as an "unknown" all the more satisfying.

It was now, of course, that the hard work would really begin. She received her first vocal lesson to nurture her talent and polish her vocals, and then sang the *Mulan* track 'Reflection' non-stop for five days, until it met with the producers' approval. She also filmed her first ever music video at Disney's Epcot Center in Orlando, a typically fantastical affair with doves and Chinese-themed furniture to honour the heroine of the film and her nationality. "It was a long day for me, having to wake up at 4.30 a.m., be there at 5 a.m. for hair and make-up and start shooting at 6.30 a.m.," she recalled of her first taste of the ardours of fame. "They wanted to begin early to capture the sunrise. My favourite parts were getting to release the doves – which wouldn't keep still in my hands – and filming inside the Chinese Pavilion, where they'd set up smoke machines, big gold pots with fire lit inside and I was completely surrounded on a table by a hundred candles. It was really, really cool to be in the middle of it all."

After filming, she then begged for her time in LA to be extended an extra day so she wouldn't miss hearing a 90-piece orchestra record the accompaniment for her song. She would later gush that the experience had brought her to tears.

Yet it was the *Mulan* storyline that meant the most to Christina. The film depicts a Chinese girl who cunningly disguises herself as a warrior to prevent her elderly father from going to war with invaders. All the while, she struggles to discover herself and allow her true identity to surface. Although she hadn't found the courage to confirm it to her record label yet – on the contrary, she was still experiencing sheer relief at having won a deal – this theme secretly replicated Christina's emotions in real life. She too was disguising herself, posing as the saccharine-sweet pop artist her bosses wanted "purely to get my foot in the door" and earn a contract. When the recording for her debut album began, it quickly emerged that she would have to compromise hard to please her label and producers – and bury a large part of her identity in the process. In the studio, she was constantly chastised for ad libbing and "over-singing", reined in to fit in with the strict brief of a mainstream pop CD. All of this meant, in Christina's eyes, that she was denied a chance to showcase the true range and diversity of her voice. When 'Reflection' reached the number one spot in the charts just four weeks after its June 8, 1998 release, the success was overshadowed by her sheer frustration.

Her conflict was never more apparent than on her debut single-to-be, 'Genie In A Bottle'. The track was a catchy pop number about a girl urging her boyfriend to treat her right if he wanted to see her release her inner genie. As much as her heart and body wanted to be intimate, her head was commanding commitment and respect first.

The song's theme was part of a cunning strategy to garner universal appeal: the raunchy undertones and easily identifiable sexual inferences would make it a hit with the boys, as would Christina's breathy voice and nubile teenage physique, while it also had a moral message about not giving up one's body too easily. The entire premise was to introduce the singer to the world in a way that would appeal to as many different audiences as possible – and so, unsurprisingly, but to Christina's horror, the sound had to be equally mainstream. "I was held back a lot from doing more R&B ad libbing," she revealed later. "They clearly wanted to make a fresh-sounding young pop record and that's not always the direction I wanted to go in. Sometimes they didn't get it, didn't want to hear me out because of my age." For example, when she first came across 'Genie', she had tried to incorporate her own style into it. "I was a little unhappy with the rough beginnings of the song," she admitted, "so I put my own flavour into it. Before that, it was too keyed into the pop sound that was happening at the time, which often has no soul. I put some ad libs into it, spiced it up and the R&B drum pattern, changed it."

While some of her ideas were met with condescending smiles and shakes of the head and, often, outright rejection, she thought she'd slipped a few great ad libs past the censors to express her voice's versatility. Yet while producers might have humoured her experiments initially, in the formal recording they quickly edited them out. "When it came to recording her performance for real," clarified the song's co-writer, David Frank, "we tried to choose which of her ad libs we used, so that it didn't sound too bluesy... we intentionally said that we really didn't want to use that [style]... because Christina delivers a really committed performance every time she opens her mouth and we'd tried to get her to sing a little more subdued." He wanted to coax out a soft, sensual voice, whereas her enthusiasm to show off her vocal strength and scales had given the track another vibe altogether – and the battle of egos that ensued was drawn to a close by the authority of her label.

"In our business," Ron Fair explained, "it's more important to start off with a number one record on a debut act than it is to start off with a great song – but it's still great sugar candy."

In the end, Fair got his wish and his vision came to pass. After its release on June 22, 1999, 'Genie In A Bottle' hit number one on the *Billboard* chart, where it remained for five consecutive weeks. It also made the number one spot in the UK and Canada, while in every country that it charted, it made the Top Five. Due to financial difficulties at RCA Records and the need to perfect her debut single, the track hadn't arrived quickly enough to capitalise on the success of *Mulan* – but as her breakout success showed, that hadn't mattered.

The quest for world domination was going to plan, but while Christina was delighted at such prolific exposure, her joy was overshadowed by her ambivalence towards the song. She also felt she hadn't been appropriately credited for her role in creating one of the hooks, where she declared that she was a genie in a bottle and asked her man to come on and let her out.

Christina also struggled to come to terms with the emphasis on her body rather than her voice. She'd filmed the long, arduous video shoot on Malibu Beach in uncomfortably cold temperatures, "greased up in baby oil, [wearing] a little cut-off top". Ever the professional, she'd smiled seductively for the cameras, later commenting that she'd pulled off "faking warmth" by suppressing her shivers. Yet her experience was bittersweet, eroded by the injustice of her half-naked state in "freezing" weather, while everyone else on the shoot was comfortably enveloped in winter coats.

In addition, she increasingly suspected that displaying such sex appeal on a debut single might detract from people's ability to take her seriously. "I'm not just another bimbo," she would fight back in indignation. "I've got a brain and a heart and I'm not gonna let my body distract people from that fact." While she would subsequently flaunt a sexual image to extremes, there'd be one vital difference: it would be on her terms, her own self-expression.

Yet every time dissatisfaction rose up within her, she swallowed it, silenced by the conflicting emotion that she was lucky to be a success at all, living her dream of the world hearing her voice. Her repressed anger would come out in short bursts instead. "The producers were like, 'Hold back, hold back, hold back'," she told *All Pop* in one unusually candid moment. She added, "I didn't want to release 'Genie In A Bottle' as my first single. I made my company well aware of that. We went back and forth a couple of times because I thought that maybe people would get the wrong idea, that I was all about being what pop music is all about right now. I think it's really sad that pop music right now happens to be a lot about gimmick, a lot about a package deal, a lot about a song that's very easy to remember, catchy, and that's not what I wanted to be about."

A more immediate concern for her was that one aspect of the carefully crafted pop star master plan hadn't been executed quite as intended. Rather than seeing the track as a "no nookie" female empowerment song, as Christina referred to it, detractors would accuse it of brimming with thinly disguised eroticism and inappropriately sexualising a barely legal teenager. After all, when Christina had recorded the video she had just turned 18.

One of the most notable critics was former pop star Debbie Gibson, whose 1987 debut album, *Out Of The Blue,* had sold over eight million copies. These figures would place her on a par with Christina when it came to career success, but she made a point of insisting that, unlike the stars of modern music, her clean-cut image hadn't relied on scandal or sex appeal.

Fast forward to 1999 and Debbie's unsolicited media moniker at that time was merely "the Britney Spears of the eighties". Perhaps disgruntled at this none-too-subtle reminder that her career was past tense and that many new girls were now coming up in the ranks ready to steal her crown – or, perhaps, genuinely disconcerted that a young pop star might have been exploited – Debbie vented some of her anger on 'Genie'. "It terrifies me to hear an 18-year-old sing 'Come on in, let me out' with some conviction." Granted, the demand for someone to rub Christina the right way seemed a clear reference to clitoral stimulation, but Debbie had misheard at least one of the lyrics: the word "in", which she'd quoted, had actually been "and" – this one-word alteration transformed it from slightly sleazy to ambiguously innocent.

Regardless, critics could debate indefinitely – several writers and producers, a record label and of course Christina herself had all tried their hand at tweaking the track, so in reality its true meaning was probably lost to a diluted hybrid. Nonetheless, Debbie would claim that it "frightened" her to see Christina "live and breathe the sexual image". Fear, as opposed to mere disapproval, was a curious word to use – did it suggest a sincere concern or simply that Debbie was intimidated by Christina's body confidence and toned physique and consequently wasn't able to feel comfortable in her own skin?

Also, the underlying objective of Debbie's words seemed to be attaining moral and artistic superiority (not to mention publicity), implying that if she could achieve four Top Five singles and a multiplatinum album without any references to sex, why couldn't Christina?

A crestfallen Christina, who believed in the concept of sisterhood and female unity, would take it badly. She perceived that Debbie was trying to stifle and suppress her, suggesting she should limit what she performed purely because she was a young woman – and coming from a fellow female, that hurt.

"The last person Christina would have expected to criticise her was another woman," an insider told the author. "She felt girls should stick up for one another in a male-dominated industry and try to further their cause, getting more freedom from society's double standards. She'd thought the oppression came from men and she was really disappointed to see a fellow woman – a fellow artist, for that matter – joining in."

Yet she was forced to keep a lid on the multitude of emotions both Debbie and the public had inspired and simply recite calmly her pre-rehearsed comments defending the song. "If you listen to the words 'My body's saying let's go but my heart is saying no'," Christina asserted, "my heart is saying no. So it's really a song about self-respect and treating me the way I want to be treated before I just give my love away to anybody." She added, "The song is *not* about sex. The words 'rub me the right way' are not literal. It's more like, 'C'mon, treat me right.'"

She would tell another interviewer, "A genie has always been portrayed as a man's slave [but] now it's 'I'm not coming out of my bottle unless you please me the way I want to be pleased'. It's a total girl-powerful song."

So the genie was staying firmly in the bottle – and, unfortunately, so did Christina's dormant creative freedom. Even with a number one single – and maybe even *especially* with one – the right to look and sound the way she pleased was one liberty that was still painfully far away. Just about the only freedom she had was financial – that summer she would purchase her first apartment in New York, while jetting backwards and forwards to record her album in LA. "Right now," she would joke, "I'm bouncing back and forth across the country like a ping-pong ball!"

However, the circumstances in which she was doing so highlighted a key theme in Christina's life: a desperate striving for elusive control. With her father, she had felt powerless and now with her record label, she'd started to feel the same. The label had unleashed upon her a team of stylists and make-up artists, to the point that she barely recognised herself. "Every time I see myself in magazines, it never looks like me," she had complained, referring to an excess of cosmetics and the ubiquitous trend for airbrushing. "I like my hair better curly, but the record company wants it straight... they tell me how they want me to look. And it's like, 'Excuse me, it's my body!'" She'd even been asked to change her name – label bosses claimed it was too exotic, would alienate American fans and would be too difficult to pronounce. That was one of the few battles Christina won – she was too proud of her Latin ancestry to consider ever disguising it behind a generic Caucasian replacement.

Perhaps keen to overcompensate for the negative press Christina had accumulated due to the sexual connotations of 'Genie', the label also thrust a sweet, virginal image upon her. Hence she found herself preaching, "It is important to me to be a positive role model. Parading around in my bra and a pair of hot pants will not inspire confidence in other girls. That would just make me one more person pushing them to feel like they have to be something they're not." Yet ironically, behind the scenes, it was Christina being pressured into becoming something she was not. Behind the defensive moral disclaimers, she yearned to be more daring about her fashion choices. She might not want to be known purely for her body, but she didn't want to be portrayed as a picture of innocence either. Yet for now, experimenting with her sexuality was strictly forbidden.

Yet she couldn't escape her media image, the ditzy blonde Barbie-esque teenager. In interviews, she would giggle coquettishly like a sound-alike from a show such as *Girls Of The Playboy Mansion*. Unable to suppress her mischievous side, she'd talk about her celebrity crushes or the "little seductive walk" she used to capture a man's attention and yet, time and time again, flashes of a more mature Christina would come shining through.

"Being 18 in this business and surrounded by people who are a lot older and more experienced than me... that's fine," she told the same interviewer, suddenly adopting an intense and serious demeanour. "I respect that. But they have to respect a newcomer who has fresh new ideas. Sometimes you feel like you're not being heard. You're a puppet on a string sometimes." She would later elaborate, "I never went to proms or dances and I wasn't around kids my own age. I was thrown into this world of adults who share my musical love and visions but who may want to talk about, like, politics, while I want to go to a club. But at the same time, I don't feel a part of the teenage world. I've always been older than my years. I'm basically a [teenage] businesswoman."

That dichotomy summed up Christina's dilemma: she was trapped in a no-man's-land between the bimbo stereotype and the adult world to which she related but didn't yet belong.

In the teenage world, she was a social outcast. The one and only prom that Christina attended was a total disaster. Although she'd known the music business was the right path for her, it hadn't stopped her heart from sinking a little when she saw a former classmate's yearbook, its photos depicting fun and lyrical teenage college experiences, rites of passage that she would never go through. Attending a high school prom seemed like the obvious way to indulge her curiosity. Plus, a signature of the shameless sexuality and irrepressible quirky nature she'd recently felt obliged to hide behind her pop princess image, Christina took not one but two dates with her – a blind date *and* an existing boyfriend.

She recognised many of the girls she'd known in middle school, but they took little interest in her. The boys, unsurprisingly, were very friendly, but only two girls exchanged the briefest of pleasantries before going to find their boyfriends and holding them in a vice-like grip for the rest of the night.

The ultimate kick in the face came when 'Genie' was played and the girls left the dance floor en masse, many of their boyfriends obediently trailing behind them. The irony was all too clear: a number one single and a deserted dance floor. Her looks, talent and fame were, yet again, a threat. It would have taken a dose of self-worth and confidence far greater than the average teenage girl possesses for her former middle

29

school compatriots to swallow their inferiority complexes, smile and simply pat her on the back. In the end, everyone lost out. "It was kind of sad," Christina lamented, downplaying the bullying. "All I want to do is be normal, but really, it's other people who won't let me be that way."

On the other side of the coin, her age-incongruent maturity almost seemed like a curse when it couldn't be redeemed for career credibility points. Her Disney image didn't help – when 'Genie' songwriter David Frank had first heard Christina's voice on 'Reflection', he hadn't been convinced that she was even fit for a teenage audience, let alone an adult one. "Although she had a good voice," he began, "I didn't know if she could sing in a more hip-hop oriented style too. The tape sounded a bit too much like you'd expect a song from a Disney film to sound!"

For that reason, he'd initially been reluctant to hand over 'Genie' to Christina at all – there was already a bidding war for the track and he was inclined to believe the new kids on the block, a short-lived girl group which Britney Spears had nearly joined by the name of Innocence, would be a better match. Yet here was one of the kings of cheesy pop, someone who'd been involved in the creation of S Club 7's 'Don't Stop Moving'. Meanwhile one of his co-writers on the track, Pam Sheyne, had worked with novelty act Right Said Fred. If Christina couldn't be taken seriously by him, who *would* give her the time of day? Moreover, as a bubblegum pop artist, how could she hope to diversify into the more serious R&B, rock, soul and blues sounds that were really capturing her heart?

She felt obligated to challenge the myriad preconceptions people had about her, but barely knew where to start. RCA had already spent close to $1 million on writers and producers that mirrored their vision for her development, with seemingly little regard for her own opinions. However, one part of the package would prove beneficial to her: singing lessons. These would give her a chance to hone her potential and shape it.

"Before I was never trained enough to know when is too much, what's going to blow my voice out," she admitted. "Since then, I fell in love with technique, how to make your range go even further, how to place notes, all these things I never knew about, rather than just singing and listening to my favourite vocalists and going on instinct. I never would have been able to hit the notes I'm hitting now a couple of years ago."

That said, she wasn't getting to show her virtuoso tendencies off. Ron and his team would arrange showcase after showcase for Christina, where she'd sing a cappella for TV and radio bookers and the media, with nothing more than a grand piano to accompany her. Yet when it came to recording the debut album – entitled simply *Christina Aguilera* – the material reverted back to safe, tried and tested pop tracks. She had little or no creative input in most of them.

There were just two exceptions – 'So Emotional' and 'Obvious'. The former had an R&B and soul tinge that Christina revelled in – not to mention that it also served as a welcome blast from the past. "When I was seven or eight, I used to take B.B. King guitar tracks and just riff over them," she recalled nostalgically. "I was [also] really into Billie Holiday and gospel and I think those influences really show in 'So Emotional'." Coincidentally, the title also shared its name with a 1987 Whitney Houston song.

As for 'Obvious', there was an amusing anecdote that tied in with the song's title. According to a persistent rumour, Christina had made fun of a bellboy in a Chicago hotel in early August for failing to recognise her. When he politely enquired, catching sight of her casual attire complete with a midriff-skimming top, whether she was on holiday, she laughed back, "I only have the number one single in the country!" Wasn't it *obvious*? Where had that bellboy been?

Joking aside, the track – a poignant piano ballad – struck a chord with Christina that was far more meaningful, as it tapped into her struggle, even when it seemed the whole world was listening, for her true self to really be heard. "I really related to that song while recording the album because… in this business, it's very hard," she mused. "You do have your own opinions and your own views of yourself. Then all of a sudden, when you're signed to a record company, it's almost like you become this product and you're pushed in all different directions… it's almost like, can't anyone see how obvious it is that I'm feeling these emotions? It's a moody song. It'll put you in a serene kinda mood. I really like it. It'll make you think." She would also add, with a sense of melodrama that punctuated just how difficult stifling her own creative instincts had been, that the lyrics had "really helped me get through the experience".

Although, overall, the kitsch song collection made Christina cringe, the public was hungry for more. By mid-August, Steve Kurtz had a triumphant call from RCA's sales manager informing him that the album had already shipped two million copies – and there were still ten days before it was due to hit the shelves. "Multi-platinum before it's even released!" he would exclaim. "This is it."

Sure enough, the eponymous *Christina Aguilera* would debut at number one on its release date, August 24, 1999, selling more than double the copies in its first week than Britney's debut had managed in the same timeframe.

There was a subtle rebellion the following month when Christina teamed up with Tommy Lee to present Best Rock Video at the MTV Video Music Awards. When the petite Christina handed over the trophy to KoRn – a group of long-haired metal artists – for their track 'Freak On A Leash', it was a comical sight, yet perhaps proof, as she would tell the band, that "the rules of rock aren't written in stone".

In November, she'd rush to capitalise on the success of the album by releasing the festive classic 'The Christmas Song', a tester from the *My Kind Of Christmas* album that would arrive the following year. The track had previously been covered by a variety of artists, new and old, since its conception in the forties – Tony Bennett, Aretha Franklin, Celine Dion, Whitney Houston, Frank Sinatra, the Supremes, the Jackson 5, Bob Dylan, Aaliyah and 'N Sync to name just a few. However, Christina was the first artist since it was originally recorded in 1946 by Nat King Cole to see her version reach the Top 20 in the US charts.

The track's official promotional video interspersed home video footage of a young Christina opening her presents in front of the family Christmas tree with shots of her in the studio as an adult. At one point, delirious with excitement, a pre-teen Christina was depicted twirling round in circles ballerina-style, a broad grin etched across her face all the while. Her facial expressions in the footage seemed to be convincing evidence that, even in the days before *Star Search*, she was already building on an innate, strange presence, deliberately flirting and acting up for the camera.

Hot on the song's heels was 'What A Girl Wants', released on November 28. The video was set in a high-school common room, which was ironic as a home-schooled Christina had never set foot in one. The plot was simple: she commanded a boyfriend to close his eyes, before putting on an impromptu performance as a token of appreciation for giving her exactly what she wants in a man. The performance was interspersed with a scene of Christina reclining elegantly on a chaise longue, tiara on head and Victorian-style concertina fan in hand. When she lifted up her long, billowing skirts to reveal a glimpse of stocking-clad thigh, her maids – who doubled as dancers – blushed, fanning themselves and dabbing the perspiration from their faces. She would then put a hand over her mouth, smiling teasingly.

Perhaps the Victorian-era costumes and the maids' prudish reaction to her flashing the flesh was her way of surreptitiously poking fun at the moralist brigade, those who'd chastised her for her previous single and would surely infer that, as the man in her current track was giving her "what a girl wants", she'd relaxed the rules and let the genie come tumbling out of the bottle. If it was a middle-finger salute, it was a subtle one – and a good bit of kitsch dress-up, too.

As the video hit TV screens, Christina performed for President Bill Clinton and a myriad of other VIP guests for a nationally televised show, *Christmas In Washington*. The show aired on December 12, with proceeds going to the Children's National Medical Center. While Christina didn't meet Clinton, she did have the opportunity to rehearse with fellow performer B.B. King, one of her ultimate idols. In fact, she would allegedly come under fire for breathily announcing backstage that she'd far rather have met him than the president any day.

The continual exposure, however, was pushing Christina's career towards meteoric heights. That month, her album sold half a million copies in one week alone and by mid-month, the total sales tally had passed four million. By now, she had three tracks in the *Billboard* Top

20 – in fact, all her commercially released singles thus far. However, it was 'What A Girl Wants' of which she was most proud. The track was a triumph for Christina as she'd managed to surreptitiously inject it with some slightly blues-infused ad libs – as well as a few extra lyrics that she'd co-written – for the remix of the track, which was formally released as the single.

"Some people do want me to stay in the pop scene," Christina announced rebelliously, "[but] I want to grow from there." As her track crept closer and closer to pole position, it seemed that 2000 might just be the year that she achieved that goal.

CHAPTER 3

The Illusion Of Freedom

Christina started the new century just as she had ended the previous one – leading a bout of Aguilera mania. 'What A Girl Wants' became America's first number one single of the year and, at 0.01 a.m., she was the first female artist MTV viewers would see on their screens after counting down the seconds to 2000.

All of the hype closely preceded her first ever full-length stint on the road – a support slot on TLC's Fanmail tour. However, there was a hiccup in New York when she made her grand entrance in front of thousands of already sceptical TLC devotees by falling on all fours. Already close to tears, she'd face further humiliation when the backing track started to skip, forcing her to sing an a cappella version of 'Genie In A Bottle' – not what she'd bargained for. Incidentally it was also the first show where her estranged father, Fausto, was in the audience. Had his presence jinxed what had otherwise turned out to be an enormously successful tour?

Regardless, it was a momentary blip as she'd soon be celebrating the release of the Disney song 'Celebrate The Future Hand In Hand', a duet with Enrique Iglesias. With lyrics that promoted world unity, the track was performed at the half-time show of that year's January 30 Superbowl, alongside a choir and full symphony orchestra.

By now, Christina fever was in full swing. During one mini-concert and CD signing at a Target store in Chicago, nearly 30 police officers were called upon to forcibly evacuate the venue. The demand for Christina had been totally unprecedented – Target had accounted for around 2,000 fans but in reality they were faced with more than double that number. Although Christina had been virtually unheard of a year earlier, people were now camping out in their vehicles to be first in line to see her. One woman was even hit by a car in her desperation to reach the store. When Christina took to the stage, the crowd surged forwards forcefully, knocking fellow concert-goers to the ground and destroying thousands of dollars worth of merchandise in the process. As shelves crashed down and CDs rained into the audience like bullets, Christina issued an urgent plea for calm. "It is seriously getting to the point where they are going to close this down," she warned. "I really, really, really want to sign your autographs, but I can't do it if you are all over the shelves." Her reasoning was to no avail and, as fans received treatment for injuries and excitement-induced asthma attacks, the store was closed down halfway through.

That wasn't the only sign of Christina mania – she also had her own customised doll. It was clad in the same outfit she'd donned in the 'Genie' video, with accessories including a boombox, mobile phone and miniature hand-held microphone. The biggest part of its appeal, however, was an internal song cartridge meaning that at the touch of a button, the doll would break into song. Unfortunately, Christina almost pulled out of the deal when she discovered each cartridge was removable and could be mixed and matched with those of other celebrity dolls. This cunning feature meant that a Britney doll could sing 'Genie' while her own could end up serenading someone with '...Baby One More Time'. With her trademark lack of diplomacy, she admitted she would "cringe" every time she saw one of them because they were "not that cute".

Maybe so, but the doll sold in its thousands. With this level of hype preceding the February 23 Grammys, the only surprise when she netted an award came from Christina herself. Her hopes had been far from high – after all, only one of her singles had been released before the cut-off date for eligibility to be considered for an award. Could she really clinch a Grammy on the strength of just one number one single? She doubted it. In fact, she'd even been rehearsing her "loser's face" for the cameras. When her name was called, declaring the Best New Artist of 2000, she was "in utter and complete shock".

The expression on her face was not a seasoned performer's look of defiant triumph, or blasé nonchalance, but one of raw ecstasy and gratitude. She had dreamed of this with desperate longing since seeing, on her TV screen, Mariah Carey win the same accolade many years earlier. She was endearingly new to the protocol, even murmuring "Rip off!" to herself when she had to surrender the award to be shipped to her later.

When she arrived backstage, she exploded. Recalling incredulously that her album had been out for less time than those of any of the other nominees, she marvelled, "I was completely blown away. Shocked, overwhelmed and thrilled. I thought there was no way I would get it. I was rambling off the top of my head – my knees were shaking and I'm still floating on air!"

A lifelong dream achieved, Christina was now looking to even loftier heights. "My long-term goal," she told an interviewer on the night of the show, "is to become an all-round entertainer. I look up to great performers such as Madonna who've taken on the stage, the studio and the screen and been successful in all three." The genie of the fairy tale world had the power to grant three wishes, so perhaps her luck was in.

Indeed, that same week Christina's track 'Don't Make Me Love You ('Til I'm Ready)' appeared in a film starring Madonna, *The Next Best Thing*. The movie told the story of Abbie, a woman who ill-advisedly gives birth to a child following a one-night-stand with her gay best friend. The pair decide to raise their son together as platonic parents, until Abbie finds a heterosexual lover and plans to leave the state with him, prompting a bitter custody battle. While Christina lacked an acting role in the film, it was early days – and she was confident that her moment would come.

However, alongside all the success that came as her star rose, rumours bearing her name began to fly and became increasingly ludicrous. When she wasn't on the receiving end of lewd jokes courtesy of unkind radio and TV presenters, she was the subject of all manner of outlandish accusations. One of the most comical fictions placed her at the heart of a supposedly torrid love triangle consisting of her love rival Britney Spears and, of all people, Prince William. Thankfully, the prince came to her rescue to put a stop to the untrue claims that the pair had been catfighting over him and competing to see who could send the most lavish gifts.

However, one of the rumours concerning Christina really was true. The day before the Superbowl, it emerged that she and TV presenter Carson Daly had controversially been spotted in Atlanta lap-dancing club the Cheetah, where they'd received a private moment with one of the dancers in a behind-the-scenes booth. This came in addition to the rumours that she and Carson had been dating. However, it seemed that these were the actions of a young woman partying with her showbiz contemporaries and experimenting with new things in the process, rather than anything more sordid.

Nonetheless, as a celebrity, her life was an open book and consequently Christina found herself chastised in the media, accused of being irresponsible and setting a bad example to young fans. Not one to take a perceived injustice lying down, she instantly hit back, accusing the nation of sexist double standards and rhyming off a list of male celebrities who'd been there that night, but whose reputation had remained unscathed. "Carson's there and Joey from 'N Sync," she ranted indignantly. "That's the shady part – nobody says anything about 'N Sync being there. We had 98 Degrees, we had a couple of members of Backstreet [Boys]." While she acknowledged that she was "totally tattling", she claimed to be doing so to raise awareness of a gender-based double standard.

Thankfully, however, while the gossip columnists seized triumphantly on stories of her alleged romance, they had been largely oblivious to the true issues that dominated her private life – such as her bid to mend the broken relationship with her biological father. Until January, that relationship had been non-existent, but after watching his daughter perform in New York, Fausto had become desperate to reconnect.

Shelly had been touched by his desire to make amends, admitting, "I'm quite impressed. I have seen a tremendous amount of healing take place, which is a blessing in itself. He's become very supportive, has made major amends and is quite supportive of her being open with everything in order to help those still in such a situation... That takes a lot of work. I'm surprised and feel I must hand it to him."

Christina would muse that he was a virtual stranger to her. There had been no contact for years.

Nevertheless, it couldn't have been easy for Fausto. The longing he might have felt to be reunited with her, the pride he probably had, might have been intermingled with grief when he saw her reach dizzying heights in her career, but from afar. And the aching disappointment that he had not been there personally to see her make the big time. Each time he saw his daughter from the anonymity of a TV screen, instead of being by her side to cheer her on, it may have been a direct reminder of what he had lost with an accompanying jolt of pain to the heart.

Meanwhile for Christina, the situation was clear-cut – due to her religious upbringing, her instinct was to forgive. It was early days, but if there was any mileage in their relationship, it would surely soon emerge. For now at least, she was able to work on repairing their bond from behind a cloak of anonymity – the unsuspecting media was more interested in snippets of gossip relating to her affair with Carson Daly.

Another drama that had rocked the world of print – and, in this case, Christina herself – was a painful rejection by Mariah Carey. At *Top Of The Pops* in March, Mariah had refused to be photographed with her. "It was actually hard for me to take at first because I have idolised her for so long," a devastated Christina had lamented, "and I just wonder why?" Certainly, she had made no secret of the fact that she idolised Mariah, even name-checking her as an influence directly after accepting her first Grammy. On several occasions, she'd told the press, in a tone of hushed reverence, that she'd longed to "follow in her footsteps" ever since she was an eight-year-old child watching her collect the Best New Artist award at the ceremony. This backdrop of saccharine praise made Mariah's snub all the more puzzling. Yet now Christina's vocal acrobatics, no longer in the realm of childhood fantasy, really *did* rival her idol's.

On the April 2000 edition of VH1's annual music show *Men Strike Back*, Sting joined the Backstreet Boys for harmonies on 'I Want It That Way', Tom Jones paired up with D'Angelo for a revitalised rendition of 'Sex Machine' and Nick Carter, Enrique Iglesias and Sisqo added their vocals to the mix, too. So far, so predictable – as its name suggested, the show was a line-up of purely male performers. But then there was Christina, waltzing in, clad in an androgynous trouser suit and bowler hat, Michael Jackson style, for – among other tracks – a rousing rendition of the Etta James track she favoured for live shows, 'At Last'.

"It's really cool being the only female here," she would enthuse backstage. "I chose to do this one because I wanted to hang out with the boys." Indeed, Christina now had the bizarre distinction of being the only female performer to feature in the show's entire history.

Each year, VH1 ran a Divas show concurrently, to represent the female side of the talent pool. This year, a formidable line-up had been scheduled of Destiny's Child, Diana Ross, Faith Hill – and Mariah Carey. TV bosses saw offering Christina as an opportunity to lift the lethargic viewing figures for the men's show. This, of course, worked on the assumption that sex appeal was a more important factor in viewer choice than singing talent – something which an embittered Christina would later discover was often all too true.

In time, the issue of Mariah's rejection would intensify still further, with Christina revealing to *GQ* that she had "never been cool to me". She would go on to explain, "One time, we were at a party and I think she got really drunk and she had just really derogatory things to say to me." Mischievously, she then took a vengeful dig at her formal idol's hospitalisation for "exhaustion" after a series of increasingly bizarre TV appearances, adding, "But it *was* at the time that she had that breakdown, so she might have been very medicated."

While the comment outwardly seemed to make excuses generously justifying poor behaviour, it was – as Christina probably knew – akin to a red rag to a bull or a gust of oxygen to a flame. Mariah's response? "I had hoped that Christina was in a better place now than the last time I saw her, when she showed up uninvited at one of my parties and displayed questionable behaviour. It is sad, yet predictable, that she would use my name at this time to reinvent past incidents for her promotional gain."

Not that Christina needed the publicity. In any case, as it turned out, snubs from Mariah would be the least of her worries – the other thing that would blight her career was unsavoury entanglements with the opposite sex. She had previously insisted, "All my life, my career has been my number one focus, more so than boys ever were... I really don't want anything to get in the way of that."

Her endless stream of crushes and dance-floor kisses, however, might suggest otherwise. Christina was a red-blooded Latino woman and, as such, passion was practically hardwired into her DNA – no amount of cajoling from her concerned record label could persuade her to disguise it. Although she was still a teen, she was married to her career but didn't try to hide that she had "fun on the side". In fact, as her star rose, she made her way around the party circuit with rebellious abandon.

"My manager was giving me a hard time," she would sigh to *Interview* magazine with barely concealed exasperation. "He was like, 'What was up with all the partying you did at such and such a place?' and I said, 'What were you doing at 19 years old? You were in college having your frat experiences. This is *my* college experience.'"

Despite her forced submission during childhood – or perhaps even because of it – Christina was keen to call the shots when it came to her own life. Among her nightclub clinches was duet partner Enrique Iglesias. While the likes of Britney might have issued a blushing denial aimed at preserving an illusion of absolute chastity, Christina was straight-talking – she and Enrique had maintained a special "friendship" ever since the Superbowl.

Yet her tutting management team was keen to maintain the family-friendly Disney image their protégé had cultivated over the years, presenting her to parents of teen and pre-teen audiences as an icon of family values, a responsible role model and, above all, a safe investment for their beloved daughters to buy into. Yet outspoken Christina didn't exactly feel the same. "How do [I] feel about being a role model?" she

41

would ask incredulously. "It's *impossible* to parent America." She would add, "No matter what I do or say, someone is going to have a problem with it."

Insightfully, the *Edmonton Post* would later comment that she was "a bad girl trapped in a good girl image" – and, as if to prove it, Christina had argued, "I think my personality is fighting to come out, fighting with the image that everyone has of me."

During these dark days, Christina suffered from the recurring dream that she was prey, pursued by the bestial will of paparazzi photographers, and felt trapped. Fame? Musicianship? This was *her* dream – but she wasn't even a willing participant in it. It was someone else's puppet show and she could only stand by as someone else pulled the strings. After all, not only did her Disney image pacify the conservative southern belles, the Republican-voting parents of middle-America and the chastity-ring brigade – a significant subsection of society – but her untouched image also made Christina all the more alluring to men. She was young, sweet and, at least seemingly, innocent – assets which only enhanced the public's perception of her beauty. The tease of elusive unavailability and their vision of Christina simply drove male audiences to distraction – exactly the effect her financial strategists had hoped for. Sex sold.

Britney had proved that when her debut single, '...Baby One More Time' – the video of which featured her in girlish pigtails and a school uniform – had made it to the number one spot across all five continents. The track had been a good piece of pop, with an obligatory karaoke-friendly chorus, but so had many others of its era. Why had it stood out? Cleverly, it appealed to teenagers by portraying their world – or at least one to which they could relate – while simultaneously it was drawing in those from the darker side of life: youth-starved older men clinging forlornly to slightly sordid schoolgirl fantasies and perhaps reminiscing on their own lost boyhoods in the process. The fresh-faced, untarnished and blissfully untroubled youth of someone like Britney was, to the average middle-aged American, probably an escape from the stresses of married life, a distraction from the wife who nowadays nagged more often than she seduced and who, exhausted by the burdens of parenthood, was perhaps more excited by the prospect of a nap or someone else doing the vacuuming than of her rapidly diminishing sexual needs being satisfied.

The dynamite moment for the record label was finding within Britney a fantasy image that spoke to these disillusioned everyday Americans. All of this complex psychological plotting might have seemed a little comical when lived out through the coincidental innocence of an oblivious teenage girl, but it was a reality. Critics might disapprovingly have described her as a paedophile's wet dream – but perhaps the notion was no more cynical than the profit-fuelled vision with which the image had been created. As ludicrously implausible as Britney's damsel-in-distress routine was, the unrealistic notion that a young, beautiful girl could ever be lonely tugged on the heart-strings of the public, and then their purses.

In Christina's case, the tastemakers at her label had observed the trends diligently. Millions had been invested in her burgeoning career, so there was no chance of changing the tried and tested formula now; indeed, to do so on a whim would have been veritable career suicide. When she'd said she was married to her career, she had meant it – and the vows "'til death do us part", which had been undertaken with naïve, heady enthusiasm, were now little more than shackles that unjustly bound her and repelled her freedom. Against the stifling backdrop of overbearing patriarchs commandeering her career, it was little surprise that Christina was no longer so sure.

Just one of many flies in the ointment of success, her inherent teenage zest for life was barely containable – and she was loathe for this vital aspect of her personality to be buried or, even worse, pinned to the desires of a male audience. It was as though she was squeezing her soul into an outfit ten sizes too small – while the restrictive corset might have held together in the short term, it was only a matter of time before it would burst and the buttons which had haphazardly held it in place would cascade loudly and defiantly into view.

Just as Britney's own career trajectory would eventually indicate, repression could only continue for so long before it was all unleashed at once in an undignified explosion for which no one was quite prepared. The first subtle rebellion came with the tell-tale single 'Not That

Innocent', followed by tales of drugs and debauchery good enough to grace a primetime soap opera, and finally culminating in a full-scale meltdown, as her true self exploded in a bid to break free. With a wisdom that belied her teenage years, Christina realised such issues were better resolved sooner than later and she simply had to let her hair down sometimes, regardless of the wrath it induced in her investors.

Her celebrity crushes were numerous and well-documented – Enrique, Robbie Williams and Sugar Ray star Mark McGrath to name just a few. Yet of all of these, Eminem was perhaps the most ill-advised. What had started out as a harmless infatuation would end with Christina taking a starring role on an album which sold over six million copies – for all the wrong reasons.

Eminem first became known in 1998 with the controversial, crass, yet – to many – humorous and irresistibly appealing debut single 'My Name Is'. Hot on its heels was *The Slim Shady LP*, an album which begged to be plastered in parental advisory stickers. It featured the rapper's satirical take on topics such as suicide, rape, murder, assault, drug addiction and homosexuality – and it was far from clean. Depending on the listener's viewpoint, the fiery rapper was either holding up a mirror to the ills of society and wittily parodying them to raise awareness – providing a dose of black humour in the process – or he was merely a hateful misogynist, whose lyrics were obscene, bawdy, mean-spirited and, above all, gratuitously offensive.

What was more, the colourful language and casual insults that characterised his interviews were sometimes even more inflammatory than his songs. Of particular concern from the viewpoint of Christina's wellbeing was his attitude towards the opposite sex. To Eminem, all women were "hoes". In fact, his portrayal of the woman who gave birth to him on his first single was deemed to be so offensive that she even launched a $10 million lawsuit against her son for slander. If he was willing to treat his own mother with such wilful disregard, that said little for how he might treat Christina, a symbol of the teenage pop world he openly resented and deplored.

There was another elephant in the room, too – his provocative track ''97 Bonnie And Clyde'. Christina had been enraged by the elaborately staged fantasy about killing his partner, Kim. Eminem wasn't content with a bog-standard murder, either – in his fantasy he was not just killing her but strangling her and cutting her throat before drowning her in a river with the assistance of the couple's infant daughter, Hailie.

It was a brutal track, one that sizzled with audible fury – and its tale of seemingly boundless sadism was disturbingly imaginative. While a tiny sick minority of society might fantasise about being killed themselves – and subsequent films such as 2010's *The Killer Inside Me* seemed to grossly over-exaggerate the bizarre fetish's appeal – for the vast majority, being strangled was decidedly *not* what a girl wanted.

A popular theory is that there lies a fine line between genius and insanity – and many surely felt that Eminem's twisted creativity, as witty as it sometimes might have been, was symptomatic of an as yet undiagnosed mental illness. In fact, critics called for psychiatric intervention on hearing the song, claiming he was more deserving of a straitjacket than a place in the charts. Perhaps Eminem was aware of these views, but if so, he remained defiant. On subsequent song 'The Real Slim Shady', his call to arms was that his imitators should be proud to be out of their minds and out of control.

It didn't get much more out of control than fantasies of murder and "97 Bonnie And Clyde' hardly seemed the best way to acknowledge and pay tribute to his childhood sweetheart of 11 years, the woman who had also mothered his child. And yet Kim – full name Kimberly Ann Scott – was undeterred. A year after the track's release, she went on to marry him. Such a public and harsh betrayal might seem impossible to forgive – after all, this was no drunken rant that could quickly be forgotten, but in contrast, a song that had been indelibly broadcast to the world. However, Kim's lover had an inexplicable magnetic hold over her and, when Christina pursued him, it seemed she was under a similar spell.

Rumours quickly began to circulate of her crush and, when the news reached Eminem's ears, he wasn't slow to act upon it. He saw his chance at the 1999 EMAs, when Christina presented him with the prize for Best Hip Hop Act. With his trademark disregard for "teeny bopper" prize ceremony accolades, Eminem brazenly announced that he'd rather take the presenter home than the award. What was more, when he walked offstage, he set about showing her that he wasn't a man of empty promises.

"I couldn't hear him from the way the sound was onstage, so I didn't even know about it until after I got offstage," a star-struck Christina would later tell *Rolling Stone*. "On the way down, he was like, 'So baby, we gotta talk', but we never really had our moment because the next thing you know, I'm headed off to the press room and he's being pulled in another direction."

Judging by the stream of insults that would later come flying her way, it seemed Christina might have had a lucky escape. In any case, Eminem had been bubbling under with barely contained rage all of that night – despite his well-documented hatred of bubblegum pop, he'd found himself up against the likes of Jennifer Lopez, the Vengaboys and Westlife in the Best New Act category, before losing out to, of all people, Britney Spears.

To add insult to injury, Eminem had expected to snare Christina – a constant supply of groupies had lulled him into thinking he could have almost any woman, and the pop singer, who'd openly admitted to fancying him, had seemed like a dead cert. Yet he'd interpreted her busy schedule and consequent disappearance as a sign of disinterest and, according to Byron Williams, a former member of his security team, he was ill-equipped to cope with rejection. "He tried to approach Christina to see if she was interested, but she didn't give him the time of day," he claimed. "He was trying to get her attention with small talk, but she didn't pay him any mind and I guess he took that as a rejection. He gave her a kiss on the neck on national TV, but she didn't like it. I could tell he was upset."

"Upset" was an understatement – the unignited passion had begun to fester and, when the spurned rapper saw an MTV interview with his crush criticising his lyrics and questioning his marital status, those emotions quickly morphed into hate. As part of the channel's *Christina: What A Girl Wants* TV special, she'd been quizzed on a number of artists and, despite being complimentary about Eminem's voice and even choosing one of his music videos to screen on the show, she made it clear that there'd never be a romance.

"What happened was, I was asked, 'Do you still have a crush on Eminem?'" she recalled to *Rolling Stone* later. "I said, 'He's cute and everything, but he's got too many girls after him. Besides, he's married, so I'm going to stay away from that."

It didn't stop there. She was also adamant that she couldn't condone domestic violence. "That song ['97 Bonnie and Clyde'] is disgusting," she would continue. "Jeez. Slicing up your baby's mama and stuffing her in a trunk and shoving her in the ocean with your daughter watching. That's disgusting. I'm sorry, but I think the majority of the world think that's disgusting."

According to Byron Williams, this was the moment that "turned his crush into anger". "No! You didn't just say that, bitch?!" he'd exclaimed in disbelief, before adding, "Why did she pick my video if she was just going to pick it apart?"

It wasn't in Eminem's nature to let a perceived slight go by and it was a mere matter of months before he delivered a sneering public reply. By April 2000, radio stations around the world were playing 'The Real Slim Shady', a track which would give the rapper his first number one single in the UK and, in America, a respectable peak position of number four. Unfortunately for Christina, however, the lyrical content was anything but respectable – and much of it was aimed squarely at her.

In the track, which referenced bestiality, murder and necrophilia, Eminem also mocked Pamela Anderson and hinted that friend and fellow rapper Dr. Dre was lying dead in his basement. If this was how he serenaded his friends, what of his enemies?

Christina was about to find out. In the video, set at a simulated Grammy Awards ceremony, he rapped that he wanted to sit next to TV presenter Carson Daly and rap metal performer Fred Durst instead of Christina so that he could hear them fight over her. In the face of existing rumours that she'd been romantically involved with both men, his jibe was made all the more embarrassing. However that was just the beginning. Storming that she'd said, "Yeah, he's cute, but I think he's married to Kim – hee hee!", he went on to accuse her of all sorts of untruths. There could be few revenge-fuelled humiliations more public than that. These lies hurt her. While the song was a work of fiction, Eminem's weird imagination must have hurt Christina.

As Harry Allen of hip hop group Public Enemy would exclaim, it was "like watching someone lose their head on Jerry Springer". Never had a psychopath been so glorified in pop culture, the cries of the critics came, but Eminem, unsurprisingly, was far from repentant. With comically affected self-righteous indignation, he justified himself by explaining he'd had "nothing but respect" for Christina until her mention of him on MTV, after which – no pun intended – she'd "blown it". Not, of course, in the way that he had first hoped. "She went on MTV talking about my personal business," he raged, adding that his shout-out had been "an eye for an eye". "She heard a rumour that I was married and then she started trashing my video, talking about 'Doesn't he have a song about killing his daughter's mother?'"

That marriage rumour turned out to be a fact, although Eminem might have hoped to shroud it in secrecy lest it have a logistical impact on his army of eligible groupies. Christina, likewise, might say that he too had blown it; after all, the lyrics weren't an ill-advised Facebook post that could be wiped away – the entire English-speaking world had heard them. They were an indelible black mark in the memories of their listeners, but for Christina – barely 19 years old at the time – they were particularly hard-hitting.

However, when it all got too much for her, she'd simply zone out, tapping into an alternative frequency, a self-protective higher plane far from the horrors of reality. After one harrowing interview with *Rolling Stone*, where duty called upon her to discuss the Eminem fiasco – something she was keen to point out was "disgusting, offensive and above all, not true" – the media would catch its first glimpse of her doing just that.

"Christina sits in the back seat and stares out the window in silence for the entire ride to La Guardia Airport," the magazine reported. "Her Discman headphones are over her ears, but no music is playing. She is simply shutting off. Whenever she can, she will stare out a window or off into a fireplace or at the sky and her mind will drift off somewhere. You can yell her name, tap her on the shoulder or set her shoes on fire and chances are she won't respond. She's lost in her world – and if you ask her what is going on there, sometimes she'll return glassy-eyed and calm, with an answer from the dark and thorny heart of teenage hell."

"When she was growing up, we called it zoning out," Christina's mother, Shelly, would rationalise. "She literally gets lost in thought and doesn't hear you. This happened from childhood in seventh or eighth grade and people would think she was stuck up because she wouldn't answer them." Confirming the potentially dark nature of her daughter's all too frequent tendencies to detach herself from the world, she added, "I think she's got a lot of baggage… I wouldn't be surprised if that was why."

Indeed, according to psychological theory, children who have experienced intense trauma often react to painful situations by a process of disassociation – a coping strategy that enables them to detach and become dead to an event to avoid feeling the pain. Under this type of self-hypnosis, the image of her father's behaviour towards her mother became a film that she wasn't interested in watching – someone else's nightmare, someone else's pain – and if she let her eyes glaze over, she could render herself blind without even closing them, drowning out the curses with the pleasure of imagining she was on a stage somewhere, singing her favourite tracks from *The Sound Of Music*. "I'll think about really crazy things," she would confess, "like being on top of that pole over there – or I'll get a lot of different weird visions. It is my own little world. My life just revolves around giving and giving, so whenever I get those five minutes in a van or limo or wherever, those are special moments to just zone out and think and dream."

Regrettably those moments were fleeting – and it was soon back to business in the quest to clear her name. "No female should be talked about like that," she would assert. "I'm not gonna laugh it off and say, 'Haha, it's a funny song, heehee.' That's just not gonna fly with me, so I just had to speak my piece. I had to be honest about it and speak for all women. It's like the girl who, you know, the guy boasts the next day at school about getting laid or something, when it totally didn't happen and the girl's all meek about it. Screw that! I'm not trying to be meek about it. If I have something to say about it and someone offends me, then I'm gonna say it."

She would add to *All Pop*, "[Domestic violence] is a sensitive subject… since it was the reason that Eminem supposedly got so mad at me in the first place, speaking my mind about it, I had to come out with it and say what I really thought. If I can do anything throughout my career to help better this problem that's so private and in the house and kept hush-hush, then I will definitely do what I need to do to get it out there more and become more public with a problem that so desperately needs to stop."

If publicity for her cause had been her goal, then by all accounts, she'd achieved it – and the constant stream of vitriol from Eminem in response was helping to fuel the fire. Sneering at the prospect of legal action against him, he adamantly hit back, "No. I believe I should be able to say what I want on a record. She wants to sue me and I don't care whether she does or not. By the time my career ends, I'll have no money left, thanks to all the lawsuits. I'll be broke!"

Eminem appeared to have missed the irony of his own words – if it was his right to say what he'd wanted, surely the same liberties applied to Christina. Just as his free speech entitled him to make jokes about domestic violence that most would find distasteful, she too had a right to express an opinion on his depiction of it.

While patronising stereotypes might have dictated that her trademark fragile beauty disqualified her from having an acid tongue and being unafraid to use it, merely looking angelic was no guarantee she would turn the other cheek. "I was just making a remark about domestic violence, which is something I feel strongly about," Christina would defend to the *Edmonton Journal*. "He feels strongly about dissing pop music and if anything, it's contradictory of himself because he can dish it out but he can't take it."

Perhaps Eminem hadn't expected her to be quite so vocal about fighting back – not to mention that her argument had employed a degree of sophistication and quietly assertive maturity of which, some might say, the rap genre was often devoid.

However, paradoxically, there was one thing this unlikely pair *did* have in common. In 'The Real Slim Shady', Eminem had voiced his contemptuous hatred of "mindless" teen pop, vowing that he'd been sent to "destroy" the likes of 'N Sync and Britney Spears. If the competition had been based on a war of words, perhaps he'd succeeded, but the lyrical sadism did nothing to quell the public's passion for those he dismissed as "little girl and boy groups".

While the puzzle piece that was Christina might have fitted that jigsaw, she – just like Eminem – was feeling increasingly uncomfortable among her peers. Despite earning her place in the Kitsch Hall of Fame by virtue of the dolls that bore her name, she was keen to distance herself from that tag, telling *Launch,* "my artistry is really important to me too and I want to make sure that people take it seriously as something that's not just a come-and-go thing. That's why I want to fight a little bit being categorised with a lot of pre-manufactured teen acts."

Sounding wise beyond her years, she'd even turned down requests to star in films because she was waiting to lend her name to an edgier role than casting directors were at that time willing to give her credit for – one the world would least expect of her.

Eventually, what had once masqueraded as a polite, subtle tinge of irritation at being branded a here-today-gone-tomorrow teen pop act transformed into something much more blunt. In one interview with *Rolling Stone*, she admitted, "To tell you the truth, pop music is what I listen to the least... I never wanted to be a straight pop artist myself."

Perhaps her background, with all the attendant pain of being misrepresented and misunderstood, inspired Christina's surprising sympathy for the man who'd ridiculed her. "I see where he's coming from," she had mused, "in the sense that you take this guy who wants to be respected as a serious rap artist and all of a sudden he is in the world of MTV and TRL. I can see why he would get a little mad and want to rebel against the Britney Spears, 'N Sync, Backstreet Boys world of teen music. And if he has to do it that way and be that immature about it, then fine, be that way – I'll just answer it on my next record!"

She had her work cut out for her when a spoof by a mystery female rapper, entitled 'Slim Shady, Please Shut Up', invaded cyberspace. The track alleged that Eminem's outburst had arisen when Christina had turned him down for a date, finding a balance between humour and provocation, without being offensive. It was originally claimed that it had been released by Christina herself, something which she found very amusing. "It's just hilarious!" she told MTV. "The girl is so white, it's not even funny. I don't know who out there did this, but it's funny and obviously it's in support of me... I appreciate that."

It came in stark contrast to Eminem's original song. However nine out of 13 tracks on *The Marshall Mathers LP* depicted the gory murder of women in some form – a breathtaking tally of choking, stabbing, shooting, drowning, throat-cutting and head-splitting – so perhaps, as ludicrous as it seemed after his verbal assault, Christina really had got off lightly. One thing was for certain – she wouldn't be going on that date anytime soon.

However, the song would expose another near-miss with an inappropriate suitor – this time, Limp Bizkit's Fred Durst. They'd forged an unlikely friendship – much to the horror of her management – and for once it seemed that they'd been right to forbid Christina to take him as her date to an upcoming award ceremony. "They were like, 'No, no!'" she would later laugh in memory of their fervour, "but in the future, I'll probably do something like that." Yet it wasn't to be – and the reasons for that would all too soon become horrifyingly clear.

Fred had a flawed track record from the beginning – his lyrics were widely seen as lewd, crude and misogynistic and, behind the thinly veiled metaphor of a "chocolate starfish", he had dedicated an entire album to the "delights" of anal sex. That alone seemed enough to wipe him off the dating stratosphere – but there was more. At the Woodstock 1999 festival in New York, fans had allegedly feared for their lives as his rousing brand of rap metal incited extreme violence. During a rendition of his popular single 'Break Stuff', revellers were doing just that, even tearing plywood from the walls. When not engaged with that, they were breaking each other. There were bloodied noses, violent mosh pits and worse. The scenes were everything a violence-conscious Christina would have spoken out against. Fred might have legitimately dodged blame had it not been for his provocative remark: "People are getting hurt... but I don't think you should mellow out" – delivered before launching straight into another song. He later denied that he'd been aware of violence altogether, defending to the media, "How do they expect us [the artists] to see something bad going on?"

Fred's reputation was far from savoury, and as soon as she saw the video for 'The Real Slim Shady', an enraged Christina would find that he'd double-crossed her, too. To her horror, the man whom she'd befriended and given her trust to was complicit in her humiliation. For in the faux Grammys scene, there he was pictured alongside Carson Daly, playing a tug of war with a blow-up doll crudely modelled in her image. The two battled with her until she went flying into the audience while Eminem – dressed as Britney Spears – stood at the sidelines, reducing the video to a pantomime-style charade. Yet there was no disguising Fred's involvement.

As Christina herself would point out, pulling her apart like a piece of meat for TV entertainment was not the way to woo her. "Fred is crazy," she told *Rolling Stone*. "Fred, man, how dumb are you, if you're trying to get with somebody and then you are going to appear in a video that flat-out disses her?"

He would swiftly change tactics after the incriminating scene was aired, telling MTV, "Christina's amazing. I really like that girl. She's an amazing singer. She's gonna have longevity. She's gonna be one of those amazing icon women. I'm really attracted to her, I like her and I've talked to her a couple of times and that's that. I haven't had any type of relationship with her."

So far, so gentlemanly – at least, by the low standards of the average rapper – but it was too little, too late, in view of his appearance in the offending video. Their relationship – if there'd ever been the potential of one – had burnt out long before it had even ignited.

Christina, who, just a couple of months before the video was released, had suggested she'd "learnt to be a very good judge of character", was now left eating her words. The embarrassing publicity also had a knock-on effect on her personal life – Enrique Iglesias, with whom she'd been having fun at the time, publicly withdrew from the relationship in June, claiming she was "too forward". Admittedly, a front cover photo shoot for that month's *InStyle* magazine, featuring Christina's hand provocatively draped directly over his crotch, did little to counter that line of reasoning – but was it more the fallout from the Eminem video that had deterred him?

CHAPTER 4

Reviving Christina

Fortunately, Christina didn't have much time to scrutinise what prompted the death knell of her romance – by June 13, her attention was diverted to the more worthy cause of promoting her third single, 'I Turn To You'. This followed an enormously successful performance at Party in the Park the previous month – her first ever UK appearance. With it, she'd set a world record, seeing all 100,000 tickets sell out in less than seven hours.

Her efforts on the new single would also pay off, as the song would spend four weeks glued to the number three spot on the notoriously uncrackable American *Billboard* chart. Intriguingly, she also excelled in countries where there'd been very little promotion – including reaching number one in Argentina – indicating a word of mouth phenomenon.

The video, which depicted a girl involved in a car accident, celebrated the warmth of a relationship between a woman and her mother and the latter's role of confidante in times of trouble. The scenes of Christina walking down the street clutching a brolly predated Rihanna's metaphor of an umbrella as a protective object by seven years.

The video was directed by Joseph Kahn, who would also work on Britney Spears' 'Stronger' and Destiny's Child's 'Jumpin', Jumpin'' and

'Say My Name' the same year. He'd also go on to work with Eminem – and his participation in 'Without Me' would earn him a Grammy. However, it was the 2011 collaboration between Eminem and Rihanna, 'Love The Way You Lie' (which tackled the thorny subject of domestic violence via a woman who claimed to enjoy it) that would prove to be one of his most dramatic works with the rapper. More than a decade earlier, of course, Christina could have known none of this – she was simply enjoying the fruits of yet another chart-topping song.

As yet another single – her third so far – successfully romanced the charts, it seemed as though her first headline tour was desperately overdue. By July, Christina was ready to give some of the almost two million fans who'd purchased a copy of 'I Turn To You' exactly what they wanted.

Onstage at the Milwaukee Marcus Amphitheater on July 2, Christina's vulnerability saw her instantly stand out as the new girl. "God, you guys!" her quaking voice rang out over an intimidatingly large stadium – one she seemed barely to trust to carry her weight. "This is my first headlining tour!" In that moment, addressing the 17,000 strong crowd, she sounded about as awestruck by her position as the fans whose ear-splitting screams echoed around her. But then the music started, and she showed why she had been elevated to the star so many teenagers dreamed of meeting. As she embraced the true escapism that her onstage sanctuary provided, her supporters would argue that she sang like a diva decades her senior.

Meanwhile, her female fans seemed confused by whether they wanted to look like her, or just to look. Placards clutched by hysterical teenage girls reading "Christina – what a girl wants" were teasingly ambiguous, but suggested she might have become a bisexual icon, even back in the days when bisexuality was barely recognised, let alone fashionable.

To her audience, she was a jaw-dropping work of art, but while looks certainly helped, they barely scratched the surface in critics' evaluations of her potential. One reviewer commented, "The show struck a balance between style and substance, suggesting that Aguilera wants her fans to focus more on her music than on the teen-dream spectacle she created since the release of her album."

Audience members would punctuate that point too, with one unlikely fan – there to escort his preteen children – admitting sheepishly, "That girl can SING! She just needs better material." As it would soon emerge, Christina, of course, felt exactly the same. She would emphasise that by spicing up the set list with a bluesy rendition of the Etta James classic 'At Last' as well as an unexpected cover of the authentic 1970 rock hit 'All Right Now' by Free. As the first chords of that song rang out, some of the bored parents instantly perked up and became visibly more animated, nodding their heads and pumping their fists to the music. This was her chance to show a versatility that could appeal across the generations – could Britney really claim the same?

The question hung in the air, ever present for debate, as the tour continued. In her hometown of Pittsburgh later that month – where she invited her mother and sisters onstage to join in on 'All Right Now' – another reviewer echoed, "What separates the Genie from the other pop Lolitas of the moment is the voice – an awe-inspiring instrument she uses like a girl who spent her childhood dreaming she could one day be the next Mariah Carey. And today, of course, she is."

A third reviewer, on hearing Christina's 'At Last' cover, lamented that "an artist who possesses the potential to become a true blues legend has chosen to conquer the pop world." She added, "What a few discerning critics in the crowd want is for Christina to lend her talents to better songs instead of settling for the ballad-for-hire tripe that should be reserved for lesser lights who don't deserve better material."

All the publicity would prove a coup for her sponsors, the popular brands Sears and Levi's. Sears was particularly supportive, placing a dedicated Christina boutique inside 650 of its US stores as part of the deal. The arrangement gave her a stratospheric level of exposure – her T-shirts, CDs, dolls and even stationery were now on the doorstep of the average American.

However, the lucrative multimillion dollar sponsorship would place something of a stranglehold on her creative freedom. Modest, clean-cut and above all family-friendly, Sears had previously sponsored tours for the likes of the Backstreet Boys – and this set the restrictive tone for Christina's expected behaviour. There'd be no dates with Fred Durst and certainly no more late-night strip-club visits but, more concerning, there was additional tension over her hopes of recording a song with DMX. The rapper – yet another of Christina's hormone-fuelled crushes – had released songs laced with profanities and homophobic content. These were not values that Sears – or Christina herself for that matter – would want to be associated with.

As the proposed duet hung precariously in the balance, Christina would comment that her sponsor was "straight-laced" and that, for now at least, she was "trying not to do anything too drastic". While that might have been the right decision where DMX was concerned, Sears' other criteria were more suffocating, its brief stating that nothing could take place unless "it was done in good taste and it was fun and cool and something kids would enjoy". This set a difficult precedent, as it obligated Christina to grow into an adult woman while still taking care to act as innocently as a child – all in the name of avoiding the wrath of her sponsors.

Incidentally, her other sponsor, Levi's, had previously worked with Lauryn Hill, a God-fearing gospel artist who gave lyrics about religion, karma, morals and the Ten Commandments starring roles in many of her songs. It was clear that, like Sears, Levi's wanted to endorse nothing less than safe, conservative family values. Christina's early flickers of irritation would be just the beginning of her urges to break away from her Disney image. Nonetheless, as she announced cheerily and none too diplomatically, her sponsorship deals would be over anyway by the following year.

As the tour – which spanned from July to October – continued, support acts such as the Moffatts, Sygnature and Destiny's Child joined her. The last named, of course, was a far more formidable prospect than some of the other unknown acts that fleetingly shared the bill with her.

Destiny's Child had already sold over three million albums, despite being almost as new to the business as Christina, while their in-group dramas threatened to overshadow Christina, the night's official main attraction. The comparisons would also prove hard to take – one review sniped that "unlike Aguilera, the group writes its own lyrics, which lends songs such as 'Independent Women' a valid sense of

youthful, fresh faced Christina in 1999—back then a picture of innocence—smiles for the camera in the dawn of a life-changing
cord deal. BRIAN RASIC/REX FEATURES

A demure nine-year-old Christina belts out a tune on breakfast show *Wake Up With Larry Richert* in 1990. ITV/REX FEATURES

A young Christina waves to the camera in 1993 as a helper perfects her hairstyle backstage at the TV series *The New Mickey Mouse Club*. MOVIESTORE COLLECTION/REX FEATURES

n the set of *The New Mickey Mouse Club*, Christina strikes a pose with co-stars, including Ryan Gosling, Justin Timberlake and itney Spears. Mum Shelly would claim she and Britney—the babies of the show at just 11 and 12—were "inseparable".

A pensive Christina seems to carry the weight of the world on her shoulders as she poses in a bright red bandana in 1999.
MICHEL LINSSEN/REDFERNS

istina wears a fringed Las Vegas crop top for her first
essional visit to Sin City in 1999. REX FEATURES

Christina shows off her Best New Artist Award at the 2000
Grammys—an award she had dreamed of winning since she saw
Mariah Carey take the title back in 1991.
JOE THOMAS/GETTY IMAGES

bid to fend off rumours of bad blood between them, Christina and Britney stroll on stage together hand-in-hand at the MTV
o Music Awards in 2000. SIPA PRESS/REX FEATURES

Christina and fellow singer Enrique Iglesias perform the Disney song 'Celebrate The Future Hand in Hand' at the 2000 Superbowl Atlanta. The appearance would lead to a brief relationship between the two. JEFF HAYNES/AFP/GETTY IMAGES

Christina didn't share the same sexual chemistry with Ricky Martin – back then secretly gay. One assistant would recall how the bashful pair had to be pushed together during the video shoot for their duet, 'Nobody Wants To Be Lonely'. Here they perform the track at the 2001 World Music Awards in Monte Carlo. NIKOS/REX FEATURES

istina steps out with first love Jorge Santos in 2001, the friend who would inspire tracks such as 'Infatuation' and ving Me For Me'. REX FEATURES

Clutching an award in each hand at the 2001 Blockbuster Entertainment Awards in LA, Christina demonstrates the start of her love affair with edgy styling. STARTRAKS PHOTO/REX FEATURES

critics didn't believe Christina could pull off a Missy Elliott-produced track, but as she, Pink, Lil Kim and Mya triumphantly the Best Video of the Year Award for 'Lady Marmalade' at the 2001 MTV Video Music Awards, the musical and stylistic formation is proved to have paid off. CHARLES SYKES/REX FEATURES

During the 2001 Wango Tango concert in LA, Christina performs 'Lady Marmalade' in stocking, suspenders and the red velvet gloves from the video shoot. SIPA PRESS/REX FEATURES

empowerment". Words like these would induce a crippling sense of frustration in Christina, who felt sure she could write, but, under her current circumstances, lacked the opportunity to showcase it.

The mention of "empowerment" was also an undeniably sore point for Christina – she'd told *Cosmo Girl* that she was "all for empowerment" in the "very male dominated business" that was music. She also went on record to say that one of her long-term goals was to emulate the "power" exuded by more mature artists such as Madonna and Janet Jackson who, to her, were "dominating as women and not vulnerable". With these ambitions in mind, being slighted as a more junior artist in comparison to peers of a similar age must have wounded Christina, had she made the arguable mistake of reading her own press.

Yet the same review that had chastised her offered the prospect of redemption, asserting that while Destiny's Child merely "made the best use of its resources", Christina's set "suggested her finest work is yet to come". Indeed, unbeknown to her critics, when she stepped offstage each night, she would return to the enviable position of having two new albums in the making – and all would be revealed soon.

Yet while Christina divided herself between the studio and the stage with a seemingly tireless enthusiasm, other curve balls arose to distract her from her focus. This time it was a court case over her management and, while the threat of legal action loomed, another setback occurred, this time on September 7 at the New York VMAs. It should have been a moment of elation – despite being virtually unknown a little over a year earlier, Christina was now in the running for five awards, overshadowing even Britney. Plus, to prove the critics wrong in their baseless gossip of bad blood between them, the two former Mouseketeers would walk onstage hand-in-hand, in matching black gowns with thigh-high slits, to introduce their idol Whitney Houston.

Yet Christina's wins were conspicuous only by their absence, while Eminem netted awards in three categories, two of which honoured the video that had ridiculed her. With a self-satisfied smirk that enraged her stepfather into threatening to get on the next available plane and "kick his ass", Eminem – who had been chased outside the venue by demonstrators protesting against his "sexist, homophobic, misogynistic and discriminatory" lyrics – chuckled, "This is the one night where you can fit all those people I don't like into one room." He added, in a thinly veiled dig at Christina, that no matter how many people "slammed" him in the press or threatened to sue him, its only effect was to add to his notoriety or "sell more records". When the mischievous rapper added, "I really want to thank you people for making my record as big as it was", he definitely hadn't been referring merely to his fans.

Later that night, he would perform the now award-winning song, and Christina would silently simmer in her seat as he repeated the offensive lyrics about her. To add to the overall cringe factor, the seating plan positioned her directly in front of Fred Durst and right next to Carson Daly – the pair of love rivals alleged to be fighting over her. She then received another betrayal at the hands of Carson, who gave Eminem a high-five as he came offstage.

It added insult to injury when Christina also failed to triumph over Eminem in the Viewers' Choice Award, an accolade for which they were jointly nominated. As Eminem had already prophesied himself, his none too subtle taunts about other artists had done little to dent his popularity. Why should he be penalised for having a tongue-in-cheek reaction to the world, his growing fanbase argued, when he poked fun at himself just as readily as the next person? He would later taunt Amy Winehouse, a few months before she died, for her rehab efforts – but he'd struggled with drug addiction and rehab battles himself. To him, life was a comic strip, with real-life wounds all part of the storyline. It seemed that nothing was off-limits, no matter how offensive, self-denigrating or close to home.

As Christina would later recall that her label had advised her, there was no such thing as negative publicity, but Eminem's treatment of her stung all the same – and the worst insult was yet to come.

Perhaps playing into the scandal and turning an embarrassing episode into a profitable one, her team had arranged a live collaboration with none other than Fred Durst. Despite a star-studded line-up including 'N Sync, Janet Jackson and the Red Hot Chili Peppers, all eyes were on this ludicrously mismatched duo – and their attentions were well spent. Christina looked sensational – gone was the mature and sophisticated long black dress, replaced instead by skintight red leather and flowing hair with jet-black streaks. While she sang 'Come On Over Baby (All I Want Is You)', Fred stormed the stage, rapping a portion of his own track 'Livin' It Up'. To add to the drama, Rage Against the Machine bassist Tim Commerford later gatecrashed the stage by climbing atop a 15ft crane while Fred was performing, hollering at him all the while. Limp Bizkit's formal response was to request that the uninvited guest "gets his head checked soon".

Yet the stormiest anger of all was directed towards Fred, traditionally a rap metaller with an intense distaste for pop. In the wake of the duet with Christina, furious fans labelled him a "pop-loving piece of frozen dog shit" – along with other responses that had made Eminem sound about as diplomatic as the Queen. His peers echoed the insults, with Filter frontman Richard Patrick speaking on behalf of the rock camp to claim he'd "embarrassed us all". Slipknot member Corey Taylor added that he was the one person with whom he'd least like to be stuck in a lift.

Realising the magnitude of his faux pas, Fred panicked; he'd officially lost his cool. Now ashamed to be associated with a bubblegum pop act, least of all one that had so badly tarnished his macho rap-rock image, he searched desperately for an excuse that might restore his credibility. That excuse was – to paraphrase one of his own songs – "I did it all for the nookie".

As the duet was labelled the worst moment in music that year – a horrifying slight indeed, considering its context in an era when S Club 7 and the Vengaboys were still musically active – Fred was explaining it all away with insinuations that the favour was a ruse to have sex with one of pop's most desirable women. "I did it for the nookie," he would repeat robotically any time that the subject arose. "Why else would I do that?" He asserted, "I want the girl and that's that... I don't want to make music like her. I can't stand that kind of music. People were like, 'What'd you do that for?' What do you *think* I did that for? It's obvious, isn't it?"

He'd later add to *Playboy*, "Who *wouldn't* [have a crush on her]? All I have to say to my fans who said, 'Fred's a fucking punk going out with

Christina' is this: 'If she came up to you in a fucking mall and said 'hey', you'd be all about it!'"

Unsurprisingly, Christina – sick of being objectified – had a different story. "To me, he was always saying, 'Christina, you're so talented', feeding me all this stuff," she recalled, "but he couldn't tell his fans that so he took the little man's route. I'm not the kind of girl who's gonna say 'Tee-hee' and laugh it off. Hell no, you didn't get no nookie! Screw you! He made such an ass out of himself and looks like a scumbag to everyone. End of story."

Indeed, not only was Fred despised by rap metal puritans – his own fans – but he'd exposed himself as a "jerk" to the general public as well. Moreover, he seemed oblivious to the fact that his rants were demeaning Christina and extinguishing any chances he might have had of dating her. However, as the ire of a pop-allergic fanbase descended on him, perhaps he did indeed feel trapped into taking the "little man's" way out – if nothing else, to save his flagging dignity.

It seemed more than a little disingenuous of Fred, who'd once claimed the way Christina sang "drives me crazy" – and in a good way – to now insist that he hated her music. She would subsequently allege that she'd received so many unsolicited phone calls from the rapper post-VMAs that she'd had to stop answering her phone – another indication that, no matter what he might say, he remained fond of her. Yet in public, his expletive-laden reprisals only continued.

"MTV wasn't going to let that bitch play because they didn't have a slot for her," Fred ranted to *Playboy* of their ill-fated duet. "They told Christina, 'If you do a song with Fred Durst, we'll let you play.' So she calls me and goes, 'Fred, MTV won't let me play the Video Music Awards. Will you do a song with me? Will you rap in the middle of my song? I was like, 'Hell, no. I've got an idea though. How about you do your song and I'll come up afterward and do my own thing, a little piece off my own record. I ain't doing no fucking skit with you. I'll come up, size you up and get the hell out. I'll do it as a favour for you because you're so worried that Britney is going to perform and you're not.' Her managers thought I was going to sabotage her but I did it as a serious fucking favour because she is so competitive with Britney."

As improbable as the story sounded to most, Fred had an axe to grind. He perceived he'd been diminished by the fiasco – although perhaps not for the reasons he'd thought – and he hadn't even won the girl he wanted out of it. Perhaps by his reasons, insulting her to anyone who would listen was a means of saving face, a type of damage limitation.

Sneering that she'd cried hysterically on the night of the awards, he continued, "She's fixing her hair. So I storm into her room going, 'What the fuck are you doing…, I ain't fucking doing this damn song.' So she starts crying hysterically, freaking out. I go, 'OK, I'll fucking do it.' I did her a fucking favour and all I got was a bunch of shit from my fans [who] were like, 'What the fuck did you do that for?'"

Therein, of course, lay the root of Fred's fury. He would rant that she was "ungrateful", "spoilt rotten" and "in the wrong world" before concluding, "She doesn't see what's in front of her because she's so young and dumb and it makes me think, 'What the fuck was I thinking?' But I did it and I know I have good karma coming. Fuck her man, I don't respect her."

He'd later turn his attention to Britney instead, telling the world in no uncertain terms that he'd had sex with her and even going as far as describing her breasts in graphic detail on national radio. Following her inevitable denial, he ranted that she was lying in a bid to make him look stupid. One suspected, however, that that wasn't an area where he needed much help.

For her part, Britney painted him as an obsessed fantasist who'd stalked her with love letters after a brief friendship they'd forged purely for work. In the years to come, a sex tape was released featuring Fred, proving, at least, that he'd genuinely had sex with somebody.

However, his brags were no longer Christina's concern. By September 12, she was celebrating the release of her first ever Spanish language album, *Mi Reflejo* (*My Reflection*). The CD's title promised a glimpse of the secret self that Christina saw in the mirror – that of a young half-Latino girl who, in her face to the outside world, had compromised her origins to blend in with American culture. After all, this was a woman who'd once been asked to change her surname so as not to alienate mainstream audiences. However, as *Mi Reflejo* would state, the girl in the mirror still held her Ecuadorian roots in fierce regard.

The album, produced by Cuban-American Rudy Pérez, featured Latin versions of hits such as 'Genie In A Bottle' ('Genio Atrapado'), 'What A Girl Wants' ('Una Mujer'), 'I Turn To You' ('Por Siempre Tú') and 'Come On Over' ('Ven Conmigo'), as well as, of course, the title track, 'Reflection' ('Mi Reflejo').

Meanwhile brand new tracks included the uptempo 'Falsas Esperanzas' ('False Hopes'), which critics would compare to Ricky Martin's chart-topping 'Livin' La Vida Loca'; 'Pero Me Acuerdo De Ti' ('But I Remember You'), a remake of Lourdes Robles' 1991 version; and 'Si No Te Hubiera Conocido' ('If I Hadn't Known You'), a duet with young Puerto Rican crooner Luis Fonsi. Another standout was a cover of the highly emotive Spanish song 'Contigo En La Distancia' ('With You In The Future'). "We had all of BMG Latin America come in for a listening party," Steve Kurtz would comment of the track, "and they were crying while they were listening to it."

The album's fusion of salsa, flamenco and tender traditional ballads was what made it sound so authentically Spanish and, as Kurtz would vocalise, "there's no element of jumping on the bandwagon – you can hear the sincerity in Christina's voice."

Yet although this was indisputably her chance to show her Spanish-speaking grandparents that she still identified with them and their culture and hadn't become lost in a sea of generic all-American girls, not everyone bought into the project. To some sceptics, the album was an act of rampant commercialism, a cynical ploy to play on her Latin roots to draw in a broader audience. This way, they surmised, she straddled the best of both worlds. Not only was she the archetypal American beauty teenage dreams are made of – slim, busty, blonde-haired and blue-eyed, she was a veritable Barbie doll in living flesh – she also had a hint of exotic appeal. With large, round eyes, a very slight Latino lilt in her inflection and a caramel-toned complexion that didn't need topping up with a tan, she fitted the mould of the American ideal but was just unusual enough to stand out from the beauty queen crowd. Not only that, but now teenage girls with two different mother tongues could relate to her and look up to her as their idol. To emphasise the rarity of this combination, the following year Christina would become the first American artist to win a Latin Grammy.

Yet she found herself struggling to assert her authenticity as the public accused her of being a white girl trying to play an unconvincing Latino role. It was an allegation that Christina had spent her whole career fighting against. Back in January, before there'd been even a whisper of a Spanish album, she'd had to defend to MTV, "A lot of people wanna perceive me as a little white girl, trying to sound however. I'm just singing what feels natural to me... and I'm not completely white. I am half-Hispanic, half American-Irish... I'm proud of my Latin roots. I'd like to get the Spanish community involved as well, being that my last name is Aguilera, and record a Spanish album one day and release it."

Finally that day had arrived – and it was overshadowed by public doubt. It didn't help, of course, that while Christina insisted she was well-versed in Spanish from growing up around the language for several years at home, her manager had insisted she couldn't speak a word prior to recording. Yet she would later concede that memorising her vocals wasn't as easy as she'd thought. "I thought it would be easy – Ecuadorian, remember?" she'd chuckled to *Dot Music*, "but geez, [my tutor] had to write everything out for me phonetically! I'm a hard worker, though – and I sure showed him that no matter how many foreign words I had to learn, I can still hit tons of unnecessary high notes!"

Hours of diction lessons clearly paid off, as Coca Cola deemed her accent authentic enough to use 'Ven Conmigo' in one of its adverts.

"Latin people are so hot-blooded and passionate about what they do," Christina announced triumphantly to *Daily News*, "[and] this is something to make the grandparents proud and my father proud!"

Of course, the album's acclaim didn't stop with her family. It would earn platinum status in Mexico, Chile, Argentina, Spain, Puerto Rico, Panama, Venezuela, Costa Rica, Peru and Columbia, too. With the help of its number one position on the Latin *Billboard* charts – which it retained for 20 weeks – it would also sell well over two million copies which, for a Spanish language album, was near unparalleled success.

The day after the CD's release, on September 13, Christina would perform 'Genie Atrapado' at the Latin Grammys, watched by fellow Hispanic stars such as Marc Anthony and Jennifer Lopez. The event, held at LA's Staples Center, was the very first Latin Grammys in music history. Regardless of what the critics might say, she was playing her part in the expansion of a genre.

Her performance that night would see her honour her culture with traditional clothing – a crimson bra top with long flared sleeves, together with glittered jewels displayed around her navel. 'Genie Atrapado' was nominated for Best Female Pop Vocal Performance and, although on that occasion she lost out to Shakira, she would compensate the following year when she'd be awarded with Best Female Pop Vocal Album.

Yet she didn't have to wait that long to reap the rewards of achieving a lifelong dream – a month after the album's release, *Mi Reflejo* would top the Latino album chart simultaneously with the single of the same name on the respective singles chart. Plus, just to prove she was still a hit with mainstream America, she also had a number one single on the *Billboard* chart, giving her a triple chart success. Fred who? She was on top of the world.

She'd also been putting the finishing touches on her festive album, *My Kind Of Christmas*, which was due for release on October 24. Tracks included a Spanglish version of 'Silent Night', where she'd alternate between both languages during the verses, a Thunderpuss remix of the classic 'The Christmas Song (Chestnuts Roasting On An Open Fire)', 'Have Yourself A Merry Little Christmas', featuring an enormous 70-piece orchestra, and 'Climb Every Mountain', the nostalgic track from Christina's favourite film, *The Sound Of Music*.

The latter was a defiant victory for Christina as the song – chronicling Maria's escape from an oppressive convent environment to pursue love, freedom and other dreams – symbolised her own escape. The music had helped her to zone out and leave childhood issues behind – and now that she'd committed her own version to CD, perhaps it could be a similar stabiliser to other troubled children. In addition, she was working on launching a shelter via her newly founded Christina

Aguilera Foundation, which would provide refuge for abused or homeless women and children back in Pittsburgh.

However, from a personal growth point of view, one of the most significant achievements of that year had been the release of the fourth and final single from her debut album, 'Come On Over Baby (All I Want Is You)'. In a number of ways, this song would symbolise Christina's transformation from a demure, obedient and passive pop princess – someone satiated simply by being given a break in music – to a raunchier and more confident businesswoman who didn't shy away from expressing herself and her opinions and demanded a little more autonomy.

The first indication that Christina was coming into her own was a change in the musical material. The original album version of the song – simply titled 'Come On Over' – was relegated to the scrapheap in favour of a more adult version that would prove sexy enough for the Disney channel to ban its former protégé's single altogether. A team known as Celebrity Status reshaped the song, adding a bridge and a rap from Christina as well as transforming it into a more upbeat track to replace the former piano-heavy feel. The rap replaced an interlude which sampled the Cheryl Lynn disco song 'Got To Be Real' – something that had made an appearance in live shows – due to the song's original writers refusing them clearance to use the lyrics. A section was also added in the second verse, featuring more sexually explicit lyrics. In spite of the tight rein of control her management held over her, Christina was already proving controversial – and perhaps it was inevitable, in view of the fiery Latin blood that the world now knew coursed unapologetically through her veins.

Changing public perceptions of her sound and persona would be a risk, but Ron Fair was on board as a producer – and surely that worked in their favour. He'd previously been an A&R professional who'd launched the careers of female powerhouses such as Fergie and the Pussycat Dolls, while he would later produce or co-produce plenty of lucrative singles, subsequently going on to engineer Lady Gaga's 'Speechless'. Dollar signs were associated with the mere mention of his name alone. However, Christina, too, was involved with rewriting the single – and she helped transform it from an arguably lacklustre piano ballad, which shared its name with the 1997 Shania Twain album *Come On Over* (hardly a way to gain teenage-level street cred), to an uptempo pop track that everyone was talking about.

The single would also mark a transitional phase for her image. Meeting Paul Hunter, the director of the official promo video, had given her the courage to experiment with her look. She had longed to change her hair, but blonde was beautiful – a safe way of guaranteeing an enraptured male audience – so her management had, for so long, firmly denied her request.

"I'd love to be able to dye my hair black one day, or put some crazy hot pink streaks in it, or whatever – but the record label wants me to stay very much mainstream," she had admitted to MTV forlornly. But, rebelling against the label for the new video, the impetus to put blue and red highlights in her hair had been all hers.

"Christina had been endlessly wheedling her management for a new look ever since her career started," an anonymous insider revealed to the author. "She was getting frustrated by how much they played it safe. She'd ask for something crazy, like new colours in her hair, and it was always a 'no'. This time, she got them."

It was the first time Christina had been given any say in how she was portrayed to the public – and, as far as she was concerned, this moment was long overdue. Reacting against continual comparisons to Britney Spears, she would sigh, "It was people being lazy and seeing a navel and some blonde hair and [saying] 'Oh, it's the same thing', without really researching." There was no chance of that now – not only had plain blonde tresses been replaced with multi-coloured ones, but the video had an *Alice In Wonderland* level of eccentricity, with neon colours and blue and white chequered trousers. To Christina, her management's influence had earned her little more than a place on Top 10 Worst Dressed lists, so a chance to express herself – however eccentrically – couldn't have come a moment too soon. As if to punctuate that opinion, 'Come On Over Baby (All I Want Is You)' made it to the number one spot in the States.

Christina's growing discontent with her manager led to her filing a lawsuit at LA Supreme Court on October 13.

Kurtz responded to the case by pointing out that under his guidance, "each of her singles and albums achieved the number one position on the *Billboard* charts, she sold over 10 million records and had a successful headlining tour".

Her attorney for the case against Kurtz, Daniel Petrocelli, had been the leading lawyer in the high-profile multimillion dollar wrongful death suit taken out by Fred Goldman against O.J. Simpson – if anyone was equipped to void the agreement she'd made with her manager, it was surely him.

But Kurtz wasn't about to take the allegations lying down. "This litigation appears to be nothing other than a transparent and misguided attempt by Christina to avoid her financial and contractual obligations to me," he responded. "What is most disturbing is that, after having spent more than three years together and having achieved incredible artistic and financial success, rather than seeking to amicably and gracefully end our working relationship, Christina has asserted false, defamatory allegations against me and others who have steadfastly protected her best interests." Somewhat patronisingly, he urged her to "use her intelligence and independent mind" and asked her to drop the litigation which he described as "baseless".

By now, the to-ing and fro-ing of the legal process was starting to resemble a soap opera and detracting from Christina's music in the process. By October 27, gaudy media headlines reported that Kurtz had filed a countersuit, in which he accused Christina of prematurely terminating his contract, thus violating the terms of their agreement.

For Christina, however, this wasn't a fanciful drama enacted for entertainment – it was her life. By now the stress of litigation had become too much and, just a couple of months after suffering laryngitis, she was diagnosed with a tonsillitis-related virus as well.

In the end the litigation between the parties was settled out of court.

As dancer friend Nick Aragon would explain, "I've worked with Prince and Ricky Martin, but Christina is the hardest-working person I've ever met. She gets this look on her face, almost like a glare, and I know not to go near her because she's focused."

In her working life, she had adopted a persona of steely strength and maturity which predominated to the extent that, until she let down her guard for a rare display of vulnerability – such as an onstage cry of "Where's my mommy?" – it was easy to forget that she was just 19 years old. "I feel like a 35-year-old businesswoman in a 19-year-old body," she would later vent to the press. "It's easy to lose yourself. You give all day to the press or the fans or the record label and then all of a sudden, it's like, 'Wow, I've got no time for me.'"

Let alone time for herself, Christina now barely had any time at all. Her mother, Shelly, confirmed, "She just never stops and she is always so afraid to disappoint her fans. I've seen her sick literally from exhaustion on more than one occasion even when I, and others, have asked her to cancel so she can rest – but she always says the people might be disappointed." Tellingly, she then added that she was proud of her daughter's "work ethic". Presumably Christina wouldn't have wanted to disappoint her mother any more than her fans. Her body had done the talking and she was finally taking a well-earned rest.

The break gave her time to contemplate and question just how she might have been perceived by those who managed her. Christina's exhaustion was far from just physical. It stemmed from the emotional trauma of feeling she was regarded merely as a necessary evil in the quest to create profit.

Increasingly, she was also beginning to feel like a sex object, a victim of sexist societal norms. One book in particular, *Reviving Ophelia: Saving The Selves Of Adolescent Girls*, had urged her to take a stand. A survival guide to the teenage years that doubled as a platform for debate on feminist issues and empowerment, it was – along with the comforting presence of her priest – what kept her sane. The author, psychotherapist Dr Mary Pipher, argued that, in spite of a rising wave of feminism, which demanded gender equality on the more conspicuous issues such as equal pay, little was being done to protect growing girls from the more subtle forms of discrimination. They were being poisoned by a culture that encouraged intense media scrutiny of women's bodies and, when it came to the fairer sex, seemed to transparently value looks over achievement – one that bred not self-confidence and healthy self-esteem, but self-hatred and inertia. In Pipher's eyes, the continuing – and unacceptably high – levels of anorexia, bulimia, self-harm and even suicide spoke for themselves. Her book's goal was to "illustrate the struggles required of adolescent girls to maintain a sense of themselves among the mixed messages they receive from society" – and Christina was hooked.

"I think society has created its own image of what is the perfect girl, like there's a certain body that's the right thing for girls to look like," she told the website Dr. Drew. "Somehow young girls are brought up to believe that. [The author] wrote all these facts down, about how from a young age, girls are really open about their ideas and opinions, then once they reach adolescence, suddenly it changes."

This notion struck a deep chord with Christina. She'd felt 'Genie In A Bottle' wasn't challenging enough for someone with her range, didn't showcase her voice – but she'd been persuaded to put her name to it anyway. Statistics and spreadsheets on the music industry's financial trends had dictated who she was and what she ought to look and sound like – not Christina herself. Now, however, she was rebelling – why should it be a disadvantage? Why not own her thoughts and not be afraid to speak on them? She had already found fame, so what was holding her back?

The book title had taken its name from the fictional Ophelia in the Shakespeare play *Hamlet*. She'd lost her identity after falling in love, living only for her partner's approval. Lacking any sense of inner direction, she was geared purely towards pleasing Hamlet and meeting his demands. Yet while Ophelia had lived in another era and was neither enlightened nor educated enough to take a stand, or even dare to imagine that life could be different, the same lack of insight did not apply to Christina. And while Ophelia's eventual fate was death by drowning, the aim of *Reviving Ophelia* was to make sure the same destruction didn't take place symbolically for a generation of teen readers, overwhelmed by a myriad of adult obstacles that they were not yet mature enough to overcome themselves.

The biggest challenge Christina would face, of course, was the inadvertently sexist culture that seemed to have saturated American society. Radio DJs, instead of discussing her voice, had unleashed a series of smutty jokes about her sex life and had debated over whether her breasts were real. On one show, she was described as "an unattractive girl hidden under four pounds of make-up" – an accusation that her fans would surely dismiss as both untrue and irrelevant. Yet somehow, so much of a female singer's package was deemed to be her looks.

What was more, once she'd displayed her assets, she'd be judged for doing so. "I think there are double standards," she would complain. "If Justin from 'N Sync were to appear on the cover of some magazine nude or in the least way suggestive, people would say, 'Oh my gosh, that guy's so hot', whereas they would look at Britney and say, 'Oh my gosh, look, she's being a little, um, well, slutty.'" Meanwhile male artists such as Fred Durst and Eminem had sexually objectified her for entertainment, delivering the unspoken image that her sole purpose in the music business was to provide visual pleasure.

"Unfortunately, pop is often about eye candy," Christina would lament on BBC Radio 1, adding that she'd been ordered to wear her hair straight even though she preferred it curly. "It can be hard to be [this age] and to be in this business – your album is huge and these people 20 years your senior are seeing you as a product. That can be scary. I just wanted to make music and all of a sudden it was all about this package – what your look is going to be. All of these decisions are being made for you."

Unsurprisingly, Christina's Barbie doll image – paradoxically both highly sexualised and virginal at the same time – was enormously popular. Yet in her eyes, an entire nation had been socialised to think it was acceptable to view a musical entertainer as a metaphorical blow-up doll – an inert sex symbol without opinions, feelings or a personality of her own. At times, a frustrated Christina saw comparisons between herself and Marilyn Monroe. "Everyone expected her to be this sex object 24 hours a day and there was a part of her that wanted to be just plain Norma Jeane," she had told *Cosmo Girl*, adding that she obsessively collected Marilyn memorabilia. "I can sort of relate to feeling like that. It's so easy to lose your true self in this business."

The problem seemed to be society's complex reaction to the sight of a good-looking woman who also happened to have a talent. Christina was fair haired and beautiful, meaning that some automatically typecast her as "stupid". In their eyes, she was the archetypal "blonde bimbo". Those women who were low in self-esteem might internalise this pitiful self-image, consequently making them prone to exploiting their looks to get ahead in the business. This, of course, was ammunition to perpetuate the stereotype that such girls' looks were all they had to offer and that they were the real life "whores" of rap artists' baseless fantasies.

While feminists might have stood together in sisterhood, the stereotype of a shameless opportunistic slut selling her body increased resentment between women while simultaneously giving male misogynists all the evidence they needed to ridicule people like Christina. This was a recipe for attractive women to be despised by their peers of both genders and, most of all, by themselves.

Meanwhile the Fred Dursts of the entertainment world might well have felt threatened by the double-edged sword of both talent and beauty and perhaps it would be easier to patronisingly dismiss such women as mere pretty faces. It was a complex psychological dynamic, but it was currently weighted in the favour of Fred Durst types, those who thought nothing of categorising her as a "dumb bitch" – especially when they didn't get their own way. "My pet peeve," Christina would sigh, "is dumb blonde jokes". She was resisting falling prey to a lifetime of mindless sex kitten clichés and she was determined that her good looks shouldn't dent her chances of being taken seriously. However, how was she going to succeed in her quest of standing out as a serious artist when, as she regarded it, she had been marketed as the exact opposite?

Time magazine seemed to guess her predicament when it wrote, insightfully, "Teen pop in one way or another is here to stay, [but] most teen pop stars are not. They can perhaps resurface later in life as second leads in Broadway productions, or radio hosts in mid-size markets. In the end, their posters leave more of a mark on our walls than their music does on our lives." Christina, on the other hand, the magazine calculated, was "shooting for something that outlasts trends". She'd realised she didn't want to be a flash-in-the-pan, a short-term prospect to be cashed in on momentarily by calculating and cold-blooded music moguls, before being kicked to the kerb when a slightly younger model came in. She was loathe to surrender herself to becoming another victim of a notoriously ageist – not to mention intensely competitive – industry.

Her concern was that she would be seen as a shallow, superficial fantasy image. Inevitably such a career would be a transitory one as looks faded with age – and besides, she felt she had far more to offer than mere surface appeal. "I'm in it for the longevity," she would tell *Launch* earnestly. "I have a vision. It's not a one or two album or single thing. I wanna be seen as a real vocalist because that's where my heart's at – doing those ballads… requires a little more depth than a catchy pop melody or hook, because it just means a lot more to me."

She wanted to convey a deeper meaning to her audience, too. She'd already endured the agony of feeling like an afterthought in her own career when she'd been overlooked for a suitable credit on 'Genie'. Yet in passing over Christina, perhaps those concerned hadn't realised that, in the long term, they'd been doing her a favour. The experience had made her tougher, smarter and more resilient – it had removed the naivety and the soft edges and compelled her to start looking out for her own interests. Now she anticipated "rip-off merchants" before they'd even encroached. She had learned that, in a world like hers, trust could easily and frequently be misplaced – and it was easier not to give it out in the first instance.

Britney had come to the world's attention under the slightly demeaning guise of a paedophile's version of soft porn when she'd posed in her school uniform for '…Baby One More Time'. Christina, on the other hand, was adamant that she didn't want to play that game. Although she'd had to play along while others commandeered her career initially, the difference between then and now was that – several million albums later – she finally had the public's attention. After biding her time benignly for so long, perhaps, with all eyes on her, now was the right moment to unleash the real Christina. "There's a time and a place for everything," she'd grinned knowingly in an interview with *Entertainment Weekly*. "I understand that. You've gotta grow into it. I'm just gonna push the growth a little faster."

This was no pop puppet. As one anonymous industry insider told the author, "Some people don't mind being moulded – look at Rihanna. Girls like her are happy to milk the success, the fun and the parties and have no desire to take control of their sound or how they come across when someone else can do it all for them. But from the beginning, Christina was no one's puppet. From day one, she was waiting for her moment to break free."

Perhaps parting ways with her manager was a symbolic message that this moment had arrived. To Christina, everything that bridged the gap between a short-term star and a timeless icon was at her fingertips. She felt with intense conviction that every trait she possessed that distinguished her from "pop tart" gave her the edge over the competition and the potential, unlike many of her peers, to stand the test of time.

To do so, however, she'd need to uncover a side of her that had previously been suppressed – one that was uniquely her own. If that meant saying goodbye to Kurtz and resolutely regaining control of her own voice and image, then so be it. Her time was now.

CHAPTER 5

Drinking Champagne With Diamonds In The Glass

People magazine sarcastically introduced *My Kind Of Christmas* with the words, "In a time when musical careers often flame out within a year or two, it's best to be prolific." The magazine presented this as the reason for her release of three albums in a little over a year – and an exhausted Christina was inclined to agree. Certainly, the album – craftily released in the height of her popularity – would quickly be certified platinum and make the inevitable number one spot on the Holiday Albums chart, but, as she had reiterated countless times, she was looking for more than a short-term career as a prelude to disappear into the "faded pop star" abyss.

The voices that warned her of that were shouting louder than ever now and she accepted the Best Female Artist trophy at the December 6, 2000 *Billboard* Awards with a tribute to her new manager. "Irving Azoff, thank you for showing me what true management is," she announced. "I have such an incredible team of people behind me now."

The last imprint of Kurtz's influence on her life would come in the form of the *ABC Christmas Special*, a TV show he'd booked for her to promote songs from an album she hadn't wanted to record. Reviewers labelled it "cheesy" and perhaps with good reason – at one point she donned a festive elf outfit, while duets included a rendition of 'So Emotional' with the pint-sized 13-year-old rapper Lil' Bow Wow. That experience ranked as one of the most "unsupportive" acts of her former manager, along with forcing her to take part in "stupid Beanie Baby contests".

Under Azoff's wing, she'd be taking things slower, with an emphasis on quality rather than quantity. Before long though, she was back in the studio following an offer she couldn't refuse – a duet with Ricky Martin.

Ricky's story was an unusual one – unleashed on the English-speaking public, he'd gone from virtual obscurity to enormous success almost overnight. His self-titled album, which arrived in 1999, sold almost 700,000 copies within a week of its release, while its first single, 'Livin' La Vida Loca', eventually sold eight million copies, making it one of the best-selling singles of all time. For most Americans, he was now a household name. In fact, his fame had arguably surpassed even Christina's. While 'Livin' La Vida Loca' would tie with 'Genie In A Bottle' in the record books for the longest reign at number one on the *Billboard* charts – dwarfing all of the pair's fellow performers that year – overall, Ricky's singles had outsold Christina's. Plus while American audiences' first glimpse of him had been via that fiery single, in the Hispanic community, he was an old hand – he already had four Spanish language albums under his belt.

His warm welcome by the American public had taught the music industry some uncomfortable home truths, not just about their former failure to embrace something different from the standard formula, but about the senselessness of institutional racism. Prior to Ricky's unexpected breakout success, having a Hispanic heritage had been seen as a near impenetrable barrier to mainstream appeal – hence why Christina had originally been asked to change her surname. The controversial question remained: if her dual nationality hadn't endowed her with classically American facial features, would her path to success have been quite so smooth?

Either way, Ricky's arrival would inspire change, facilitating the breakthrough of subsequent Latin artists such as Shakira and Jennifer Lopez. The fusion of their own distinct rhythms and sounds with traditional American flavours would – for a nation tiring of its long-standing diet of generic pop and evolving to cater to an ever-increasing Latino population – prove an irresistible combination. In her status as the first American artist to clinch a Latin Grammy, Christina might just have played a role in the crossover effort, too.

As arguably the hottest male and female on the music scene at that time, a duet between the two would have been explosive – or so their respective record labels thought. In reality, insiders would claim the pair had virtually zero chemistry. Perhaps explaining some of their awkwardness away, Ricky – like another in-the-closet Puerto Rican in Christina's life – was gay. It would be years before he found the courage to admit it, however. He'd had the misfortune of being raised in a country and culture that abhorred homosexuality and ostracised anyone who practised it. Depending on his audience for his fame to survive, he'd fiercely denied his inclinations for years. When he eventually came out, he recalled "living in fear" and "hating myself" because he "grew up listening to a very crooked concept – 'You're gay, you belong in Hell.'"

Rewind several years, however, and there he and Christina were in Miami, desperately attempting to feign a sexual attraction in the name of professionalism, on the set of the video shoot for the ironically titled 'Nobody Wants To Be Lonely'. While Ricky would – somewhat ambiguously – describe its meaning as "going from darkness to light, from being lonely to finding someone", it could just as easily have referred to the crippling loneliness of painting on an artificially constructed image to please a fanbase, the irony of being adored by so many but hated by oneself and of battling internal conflicts so strong, despite having millions of fans.

Of course, such a dark meaning wouldn't endear the track to mainstream audiences, so its outward image projected the usual – two archetypal beauties singing to each other and falling in love. A heterosexual couple of course – that way it was easier for the public to swallow. That was another way in which pop music videos diverged from reality; they put celebrities on a pedestal instead of showing the grim reality of their humanity.

Christina would deal with her own loneliness later that year, but for very different reasons. Her life, versus the ideal that many believed it to be, was virtually unrecognisable. In the USA, the song lacked a commercial release (although it charted highly in other parts of the world) and fans who owned a copy of Ricky's new album, *Sound Loaded*, needed to download the track from the internet using a product key. Nonetheless it was popular, not least with the Latin community.

Christina would achieve one for the team the following month, on February 21, 2001, when she performed at the Grammy Awards in Spanish, again victoriously bringing Latin rhythms to the mainstream with her album tracks 'Falsas Esperanzas' and 'Pero Me Acuerdo De Ti'.

While a collaboration with Ricky had been the obvious choice for someone playing up to their Latino roots, Christina was also primed to do something her fanbase would least expect – a track produced by hip hop/rap star Missy Elliott and creative partner Rockwilder.

Missy had a straight-talking, street, rough 'n' ready urban image, while – for those who judged her purely on her looks, Christina was still a picture of innocence, the angelic princess of pop. So far, her sex appeal had been focused around her wide-eyed, innocent brand of beauty, while Missy, with her explicit lyrics, was crude on Snoop Dogg's level. To the untrained eye, they just didn't match.

Moreover, image aside, their musical styles up to that point couldn't have been more different – but Christina was determined. Dismissing the industry's concerns as one-dimensional and unimaginative, she shot back, "So many executives were like, 'She can't do this. It's too Rockwilder and Missy. It's too urban' and I was like, 'I'm doing it!' Whether you like me or hate me, that's me."

Christina would be lending her vocals to the soundtrack of forthcoming film *Moulin Rouge*. The star of the movie was a high-class courtesan with shamelessly expensive tastes who just so happened to double as a cabaret dancer in one of Paris's most legendary burlesque clubs, the Moulin Rouge. The film was set in the avant-garde Montmartre district, home to the real-life Moulin Rouge, made distinctive by the iconic red windmill atop its roof. Since 1889, it had been delivering a variety of striptease aimed at the thinking man – dance that was as much about skill and creativity as it was about sex appeal, paired with exquisite bejewelled costumes that drew in female audiences alongside the men. Meanwhile the hilltop district in which it was set, with its sex shops, edgy nightclubs and art boutiques, appealed to libertines and creative types.

While linking burlesque with prostitution was a lazy and at times tenuous assumption, the leading lady of the film was a courtesan, so the accompanying soundtrack was loaded with references to selling sex. Madonna's 'Like A Virgin' would be followed by 'Material Girl', while a rendition of 'Roxanne' by the Police urged a lady of the night not to turn her red light on.

While some of the songs used were established classics, the producers were keen to revive a track from the past by drafting in new performers. That track was 1975's 'Lady Marmalade', originally performed by LaBelle – and Christina was much in demand as the lead singer. She was joined by Lil' Kim, a fierce 4' 11" rapper whose diminutive stature belied immense strength on the interior; Pink, a tomboy pop singer who'd recently replaced the bright pink hairdo she was named after with a blonde alternative; and finally, R&B/pop singer Mya. To add to this eclectic mix, Missy Elliott would momentarily step out of her production role to appear on the track herself.

Christina was caught up in the excitement – as she would later comment, this was her one and only opportunity to experience life as part of a girl group. However, not everyone was quite so welcoming. Admitting an instant flat-out dislike to Christina, Pink sneered caustically, "I'm not a 'yes' person and I don't think she liked that." Christina had secured the most dramatic singing role in the song and Missy Elliott would assert that this was down to possessing "the strongest voice".

"We knew that whoever sung the highest would sing first and Mya has the lightest voice," Missy added. "So Mya would sing first and then we would gradually build because Christina has the strongest voice, so Pink would go second and we would put Kim in the middle, with the little rhyming part, and then we would let Christina take it out along with everybody else."

Pink, a self-styled "competitive type", would endure yet more disappointment when the song's original lead performer, Patti LaBelle, singled out Christina individually to praise her voice. She marvelled that she'd "sung her ass off", but neglected to give a specific mention to any of the other girls. As far as her voice was concerned, she was regarded as the standout performer.

Moreover, Christina was running the show — it was her personal stylist who would dress all four girls and her choreographer, Tina Landon — who'd won an MTV award for her work on 'Come On Over Baby (All I Want Is You)' as well as a Best Dance Video accolade for Ricky Martin's 'Livin' La Vida Loca' — who would direct the dance moves. Then there was Christina's string of number one singles — 'Lady Marmalade' would be her fourth, but for Pink and the other three women, it was just their first. Perhaps it was wishful thinking to hope that a group of direct rivals could ever become friends.

However, while there wasn't a sisterhood, there was a cohesive theme. With a French language chorus that translated to "Will you sleep with me tonight?", the meaning of the dance was undeniable and, vamping up the sex appeal, Christina's stylist Trish Summerville transformed the girls. Her participation was a risk — while Tina's choreography was award-winning, the same could hardly be said for Trish's clothing choices, which had earned Christina the dubious accolade of a prominent place on more than one national Worst Dressed list. However, everyone was happy with her efforts for 'Lady Marmalade', a collection of vintage-style outfits that screamed the peak of the Parisian burlesque era, yet with modern twists throughout. That wasn't to say modelling them would be easy. "The clothes were not comfortable," Christina had grimaced. "The tight corsets, high lace-up boots and big bustle — I couldn't even sit down — were awkward at times. I waited until the last possible minute to get dressed."

That said, she adored the look — although her enthusiasm wasn't always matched. Some critics would cynically describe the video as "whorehouse chic", while the Singapore *Straits Times* would judgementally chastise that Christina's hair extensions "probably weighed more than the basques she wore" – but in reality, the look was more of an artistic interpretation of the vintage burlesque scene. Such women were dancers, not prostitutes, but as the film centred around a performer who doubled as a courtesan, bringing both lifestyles together, perhaps it was easier for critics to assume that the entire era had been about women selling their bodies.

The video itself certainly played up to the prostitution connotations. It had chosen to emphasise the glamour of being an actress, deceiving men about their affections under the false pretence that hips didn't lie and being paid handsomely for the privilege. Meanwhile it omitted the gritty reality of selling sex, with all the accompanying health risks and emotional agonies. It depicted hard-hearted, materialistic women who cared little for romance and viewed love purely as a business transaction, evidenced by Lil' Kim when she casually and contemptuously hurled a gift of a bouquet of roses over her shoulder.

Meanwhile Christina played up the diva role while being fussed over by two maids-slash-make-up artists in her boudoir, springing to her feet suddenly to spill the entire contents of her dressing table on the floor. As a giant cloud of talcum powder rose, she was off, leaving a trail of chaos in her wake – later scenes would see her performing a partial striptease with the help of red velvet elbow-length gloves.

The make-up had been equally dramatic, inspired by the mercenary, materialistic vibe of the video. Christina had demanded real diamonds as eyelash jewellery. She'd got them, too. "It was all about being over the top," she would recall. "Big hair, big lashes, flashy nails, rhinestones galore – on the face and hair. I wanted really strong hair. I wanted really strong make-up. I had pink and black shadows, rhinestone sideburns and real diamonds on the end of my lashes."

This video, one of her first under new management and certainly the first in which she'd showcased a daring look, was symbolic of the new Christina. It divided fans, stunned by her transition, between those who saw the look as trashy and those who regarded it as merely another string to her pleasingly overcrowded artistic bow. She would be the subject of derision when she stepped out soon afterwards in outfits such as a crimson velvet dress featuring only tassels from the thigh downwards, paired with a concoction of blood red lips in a shade so dark it was almost purple, dark blue shadow smeared generously both above and below her eyes and – most attention-grabbing of all – a curly blonde afro. She was widely criticised for her look, but, in honour of 'Lady Marmalade', Christina was merely channelling the disco era of the sixties and seventies, when no self-respecting diva would have taken to the stage without a burlesque or carnival-inspired head-dress, a wonderfully wild afro or simply big hair in some shape or form. LaBelle themselves, the Supremes – who would later take on former LaBelle member Cindy Birdsong – and Gloria Gaynor were all leaders in their department and Christina had been keen to bring back some Seventies flavour to her song. It was a bold decision that would attract disapproving glances, but she was defiant; she was raising a middle finger in the face of the elitist world of fashion snobbery.

Members of Destiny's Child, too, would try to get in on the act. The following year, Kelly Rowland would record a song formerly performed by Patti LaBelle, 'Dilemma' – the diva would also appear in the accompanying music video as her mother, albeit without the afro. Then Beyoncé would don a huge afro-inspired hairdo for her video 'Work It Out' as well as for her Foxxy Cleopatra film role in *Austin Powers In Goldmember*.

Yet Beyoncé escaped unscathed for her stylistic choice – which would later come back into fashion after designer Marc Jacobs reinvented it – while Christina attracted nothing but taunts for her own attempts. Perhaps the public were unaccustomed to seeing an afro hairstyle on a white face. Regardless, she was nonplussed. For her it was about experimenting, pushing boundaries and taking risks and, above all, having fun in the process, rather than taking the crown for Most Fashionable. She'd rather let the music win the awards.

In fact, 'Lady Marmalade' did just that, gaining two trophies at the MTV Europe Music Awards the following month. "I guess the big hair paid off!" a beaming Christina would joke from behind the microphone as part of her acceptance speech. While the song made it to a triumphant number one position in the charts, it wasn't to everyone's taste, and it was now that she began losing some members of her loyal fanbase, to be replaced with more adult listeners.

Meanwhile, mischievous media sources began a rumour – reported as fact – that Christina's grandmother Delcie Fidler had been horrified to see her blood relative "shaming" the family by "dressing like a whore". The reports insisted she hadn't understood that they were acting up to a film role. In reality, her grandmother was furious, but for very different reasons – according to Shelly, the story simply wasn't true.

Rather, it seemed it was the public who couldn't distinguish between role play and reality when Christina's reputation began to precede her in real life, too. More and more fellow celebrities had been coming forward to depict her as the diva she had posed as in the video. In their view, she embodied arrogance.

One of the first complaints came from Irish pop giants Westlife, who objected to what they saw as a self-important attitude. According to the group, she had giggled triumphantly, "loving every minute of it" as she instructed a nightclub bouncer to remove them from a table so she could take their place. The lead vocalist, Kian Egan, did not elaborate on whether she had reserved the table, but, either way, their minds were made up – she was the "nastiest", "ugliest" person they'd ever met. An incredulous Kian seized the moral high ground, adding, "Westlife would *never* behave like that."

H from Steps was also on the war path, declaring her "without a doubt the biggest pop bitch I've ever met". He elaborated, "The first time we met she came up and said 'hello' but that was before she'd released a single. Afterwards, with all the fame and attention, she went nutty. What a nasty piece of work she is – really diva-like and unfriendly."

Fellow pop starlet Jessica Simpson independently agreed, "She definitely knows she has sold eight million records and I don't really like that... people lose their heads in this business. They lose who they are as people. I knew Christina before her stuff came out and she's a great girl, but BOOM! She hit so fast and some people just can't handle it. She is one of them."

The message was clear – in these singers' eyes, fame had substantially changed Miss Aguilera. Yet amid rumours that stardom had overinflated her ego, was it really that simple? In just a couple of years, she'd been bullied relentlessly by male contemporaries, pressured into a chaotic, exhausting day-and-night work schedule, while everything from her image to her sound and even her opinions was controlled and, even worse, objectified by seemingly anyone and everyone with a penis. Perhaps she felt she'd had to toughen up as a survival strategy, even if it meant losing some of her charm. She'd already learned to assert herself more forcefully, simply to avoid being walked over in an industry that required rhinoceros-scale thick skin.

Meanwhile her mother, Shelly, remained adamant that she'd instilled humility in her daughter. "I just tried to ground her in religion," she would later reveal, "in the sense that [her talent] is a gift and it can be taken away and all this attention is really for God. I didn't want her to think, 'How great I am'. I always told her, 'Your singing is nice, but what makes me proud of you is the kind of person you are.'"

Yet everyone – even those who'd never met Christina – seemed to have their own opinions on exactly what kind of person that was. After watching her MTV diary, the notoriously outspoken rock singer Shirley Manson of Garbage posted a vitriolic rant on her band's website – one that arguably said more about her own character than that of the singer she was attempting to verbally assassinate. "There's a particularly nauseating scene," she announced of the video diary, "where we lucky viewers get to witness something really intimate and sacred. We get to see a cheap rehash of a scene pulled straight out of *In Bed With Madonna*, where we get to witness tiny Christina backstage at a show surrounded by her wonderfully sincere circle of true lifelong 'friends'."

Mocking Christina's pre-show ritual of holding hands with her dancers in a circle and praying for a prosperous concert before taking to the stage, she added, "I know this may come as a ghastly surprise, but I'm pretty sure that the Lord God Almighty just might have some rather more pressing matters to attend to than to ensure you and your 'friends' have a good show... why not struggle to be a nicer person, Christina? Perhaps that would bring you closer to God because rumour has it... that you're an absolute cunt."

Of course, Christina was all too familiar with the rumours. Following one interviewer's questioning on an unrelated issue, she'd sighed, "There have been gossips and lies told, but the most important thing is to know that everything you see me do or say is from the heart."

No matter what she did – whether it was something as provocative as ousting a pop group from their seats or as innocuous and innocent as engaging in group prayer – there'd always be someone who found fault with it. With that in mind, why keep listening? The trick was surely to distinguish constructive criticism from baseless accusation, ignore the snipes of her enemies and simply stay true to herself.

By April 16, the wheel of fortune had spun back up again – she'd triumph in two categories at the *Billboard* Latin Music Awards, with *Mi Reflejo* winning her both New Artist and Female Pop Album of the Year. The following week, she'd continue the theme at the World Music Awards, when she was declared the world's bestselling Latin female artist.

In May, world domination continued with the nationwide airing of an advert for Coca Cola, part of her lucrative sponsorship deal with the brand. At the time news of the deal became public, her hometown newspaper, the *Pittsburgh Post Gazette*, had commented, "Christina Aguilera has a rival. No, not Britney Spears. That cute girl from the Pepsi commercials. Wexford's most famous pop star has signed a deal to appear in print and TV ads for Coca Cola."

The true irony of this statement was unveiled when the girl from the Pepsi commercials *became* Britney Spears. Sensing the commercial potential of a brand rivalry involving two of the most famous women in pop, Pepsi signed a similar deal with Britney, then pipped Christina to the post by airing its own advert on May 13, just a day before her rival's was due to appear.

These provocative timings were no accident – after all, two blondes in bra tops pitted against each other created a sense of drama that enhanced the image of both brands. To the record companies, likewise, it meant greater exposure for their artists. As for the male public, they were free to fantasise about the fictitious and sordid naked wrestling sessions between a pair of sex symbols at war.

It was only Christina, it seemed, who was unhappy. Britney was almost a sister to her, symbolising treasured memories of the *Mickey Mouse Club* days when they'd both broken into pop stardom at the same time. Between these makeshift siblings, there was no rivalry.

Nonetheless, the media was hellbent on inventing a feud — and Christina was reduced to tears after reading a newspaper article which cruelly compared everything about the pair from album sales and internet hits to sex appeal, wardrobe and, ludicrously, the number of online hate campaigns devoted to each. According to the tabloid, Britney was the clear leader in that department, with 182 websites to Christina's five. "It just ripped Britney to shreds," an enraged Christina recalled. "It said, 'One Grammy for her and none for her. This for her, that for her. This is her strong point. This is her weak point.' It is sad to pit two young girls against each other over and over. I just broke down and started crying one night about that article because of how mean it was, just to talk about, 'Oh, Britney's Madonna without the brain'... it's like, shut up already!"

As much as Christina loved her alleged rival, there might also have been a twinge of irritation that reviewers couldn't tell them apart. As a bilingual performer, someone whose aspirations both visually and in the studio travelled beyond the realm of the cookie-cutter model of mainstream pop, why was she still blighted by comparisons? She sang onstage, Britney infamously mimed. She aspired to write and produce, while Britney preferred to be the voice of others' songs. Plus, while Britney's salacious onstage routines involved pole dancing and dressing in school uniform, when it came to her own reputation as an artist, Christina didn't want her sex appeal to be part of the picture. Even if it had been, her dress sense was eclectic, daring and alternative, whereas Britney's was more traditionally sexy.

There were also enormous differences in the type of women that each lyrically portrayed: 'What A Girl Wants', for example, seemed to be Britney's 'Born To Make You Happy' in reverse. In the former, the emphasis was on the male partner in a giving role and Christina would sing appreciatively of how *her* happiness set *him* free. In stark contrast, Britney's insistence that she existed purely for her boyfriend's pleasure and that, in satisfying him, she'd found her life's true purpose, seemed to be the antithesis of even moderate feminism, depicting the girl Christina's copy of *Reviving Ophelia* had warned her against becoming. Instead, Christina had taken on an agony aunt role to her younger peers in interviews, warning them not to give their partners "all the power" in a relationship and to make sure they got back just as much as they gave. Her manifesto was one of female empowerment while Britney's seemed to perpetuate the treatment of girls as mere objects, avatars of carnal desire.

Some comments and comparisons along these lines were extremely sexually degrading, such as an outrageous claim made by gangsta rapper Snoop Dogg that Britney would make a better prostitute than Christina because she was "thicker" – American slang for more voluptuous – and would attract clients all day long. Doubtless, Snoop had deliberately been trying to shock in an attempt to court publicity for his latest projects, including promo videos that paired his music with pornography – but it was a reminder of how prone both women were to sexist stereotypes. And as much as Christina was keen to distance herself from the image that Britney portrayed, for myriad reasons, she was protective of the woman she fondly – if a little patronisingly – remembered as "little Brit Brit" – and wouldn't want to see her slighted any more than herself.

Unfortunately that was wishful thinking, and Christina would soon receive another snub, this time at the hands of the Moulin Rouge club. A spokesperson for the burlesque nightspot publicly disassociated the brand from her, defending, "['Lady Marmalade'] is not a good advert for us. Our club is not a sex club – we are trying to draw attention away from the whole topless image that people know about. Anyone who comes hoping to see dancers like those in the video will be disappointed."

While Christina – who had never appeared topless – seemed to be the victim of snobbery, the club did begrudgingly acknowledge that business had boomed since the video's release.

Meanwhile the rumours of a feud with Britney were put to bed when the pair fronted an annual rights campaign together, both joining PETA in a bid to abolish the consumption of cat and dog meat in South Korea.

In June, days after 'Lady Marmalade' had hit the top of the charts and outraged the Moulin Rouge, Christina found herself locked in an acrimonious court battle with some unwelcome faces from her past. *Just Be Free*, a collection of amateur demons from her early teenage years, had resurfaced to haunt her.

Producers Bob Alleca and Michael Brown had given Christina her first studio experience at the age of 14 and she'd been delirious with excitement. They'd recorded 11 tracks. A much younger Christina, then totally anonymous and desperate for her first break, hadn't put much thought into protecting her legal rights in the event that she became a star. Success had seemed a faraway prospect in those days and she'd leapt at the chance to record. This spontaneous decision had turned out to be a bad one and Christina's naïve mother, who, by her own admission, had been "clueless" about the industry at that stage in her daughter's career, had made no move to stop it. Regardless, she wouldn't have had much negotiating power at that fledgling time. As a result, she was facing the release of demos that, according to insiders, were low quality and "quite frankly embarrassing".

A doctor's skill with patients would never have been put to the test on the first day of a gruelling seven-year medical degree, but Christina was now facing the equivalent of that in her singing career – and it was humiliating. The temptation hovering over little-known, scarcely successful producers to capitalise on their former client's popularity – especially when there was no legal agreement in place to prevent it – had been too much to resist. They'd also sent artwork to Amazon ahead of the release, featuring a 14-year-old Christina with a strawberry blonde bob that had a hint of ginger – and she was beside herself.

But all that paled in comparison with her embarrassment over the material. Lyrically, the demos were clichéd, uninspired and on occasion, in context of her age, a little sexually provocative and inappropriate. Three of the tracks were almost identical lyrically, telling of the pleasures of moving to a good rhythm at a party. Meanwhile the other major theme in the ballad-heavy collection was eternal, unconditional love, of the "I'm-so-in-love, we'll-always-be-together-and-I'll-never-leave" variety. It was either extremely sentimental or nauseatingly cheesy, depending on the listener's predilection – but either way, neither was something Christina wanted to portray.

'Believe Me' was the only track that had the slightest trace of her true persona as an individual, touching upon her feelings of exclusion and isolation at the hands of cruel peers. Yet going on to thank those among her circle who are true friends for contributing to her success might have seemed premature when at that stage she had barely achieved any. Quite simply, the tracks did not represent Christina as an adult woman and she was very reluctant to be associated with them.

The company ready to release the tracks was Warlock Records and, sensing that it was sitting on a potential goldmine, it remained defiant. "The truth is," label boss Adam Levy stated, "we went to court first. We wanted to seek a declaration as to who owned the rights before releasing it, because we take that stuff very seriously."

Far from the long months of bitter acrimony and stubborn disagreement that characterise the average court battle, the matter was resolved surprisingly quickly when a settlement was made in Warlock's favour. Unfortunately, the only clarity that existed was the fact that the producers held legal ownership of the tracks, and with nothing in writing to state otherwise, it was likely Christina knew that trying to prevent the release altogether would be a losing battle. The only condition she had made to secure her agreement was that a personal letter from her to her fans should be included within each copy of the release, publicly distancing herself from the project.

Her lawyer, Carla Christofferson, seemed to emphasise her overall powerlessness when she stated, "They were going to put it out one way or another and this way Christina got to make a statement on the album and she's happy about that."

For Levy's part, he claimed, "Christina knows that these guys did work on the record and it was recorded, so they do have rights to it... she might have preferred for the record never to come out, but at the same time she's involved and it is what it is."

Christina was momentarily distracted from her legal fiasco when she was invited, at the personal request of Whitney Houston, to honour her with a cover song at that year's inaugural BET (Black Entertainment

Television) Awards. The channel was kicking off its first year in business by presenting a Lifetime Achievement Award to Whitney and she'd chosen Christina to perform her legendary single 'Run To You'.

Upon subsequently accepting the award, her idol of a lifetime praised, "I would like to thank Ms Christina… you're one that I truly enjoy in today's music. You've done the best rendition of 'Run To You', besides myself. I thank you very very much!"

Such praise, considering its source, was an award within itself and perhaps it soothed the exasperation of the August 16 release of the dreaded demos. Reviews were both scarce and almost universally negative when they did appear. One from *Jam Music* dismissed the CD as a collection of "terrible, dated club tracks overwhelmed by poor effects and mundane beats". While it praised Christina's "obvious ability" as a vocalist, it noted that the work was diminished by the lack of professional guidance in the studio that might have been offered by more well-established singers. According to the reviews, that could have made all the difference between polished vocals and ones that were merely promising. All in all, it was widely seen as a poor showcase for her then shyly emerging talents and, in her accompanying letter, Christina said as much herself.

The lengthy disclaimer read: "*Just Be Free* was recorded when I was only 14 or 15 years old. At that young age, I made the recordings as a possible stepping stone to a career in music, which is my ultimate passion. They were made just so that I could get my foot in the door of the music business. I did not intend that the recordings would be widely released, especially after [I signed with a major record label]. I had not updated or finished the versions recorded in my childhood and they are being released 'as is', although I have tried to prevent the release for several years. The recordings do not in any way reflect my current musical taste and where I am as an artist. The growth and vocal development I experienced as I matured in young adulthood is not reflected in the recordings. The album of new recordings that I intend to release this fall will be the album that truly reflects my artistry, my vision and my passion. The *Just Be Free* recordings will hopefully be a footnote in a musical career that I dream will last for many years to come."

Perhaps Christina's explicit disapproval of the CD had an impact on its poor sales, with the release failing to scrape even 150,000 copies. While some die-hard fans were compelled to satisfy a burning curiosity about her early work, many merely accepted Christina's advice that they would be disappointed if they did.

The remainder of the summer was relatively event-free, with her hectic promotional schedule winding down in preparation for the studio sessions that would give birth to the second album. Yet there was a sense of electric anticipation in the air when it was announced that Christina would again fly the flag for Latin America by hosting the Latin Grammy Awards. Regrettably, it was ill-fated from the start. First, the location had to be hastily changed from Miami to Los Angeles. Only sea separated Florida from its neighbour, Cuba, and the large community of exiled Cuban Americans in residence there were planning a protest against artists from their country of origin who struggled under Fidel Castro's Communist regime.

Cuba was poverty-stricken in comparison to wealthy America – doctors in Havana barely earned $10 a month and were forced to supplement their income selling bric-a-brac on the city streets. Natives often lived in crumbling, dilapidated houses and still made use of ration books. What was more, innovation and self-employment had once been illegal – it had since been allowed within a narrow range of categories, one of which was "gang leader". With an embargo on the importation of any item originating from America for political reasons, the contrasts between Cubans living in America and the deprived citizens of their motherland was a patent one. Members of this protest group were coming together to deliver a resounding message: Communism hadn't worked.

Nervous at the prospect of being caught up in a political scandal, the organisers of the Grammys had decided relocating was the best decision all round. The event, at which Christina had been nominated for two awards, was scheduled for September 11. However, when that day came, the city was virtually on lockdown, on its knees in the wake of the now infamous terrorist attack on New York's Twin Towers and Washington D.C.'s Pentagon building.

Then, the very same day, another thing that Christina held dear would crumble, lost to her forever – a secret relationship. For while the media circus fabricated fantasy affairs for the amusement of the American public – with reality an optional extra – Christina had quietly been enjoying a committed relationship for well over a year.

Of course, her rampant crushes on fellow celebrities might have suggested otherwise – on one occasion, she had licked her lips lasciviously over an illustrated interview with rapper DMX and gone on to make a public service announcement, courtesy of *Rolling Stone*, that she'd like to date him. The magazine would wryly comment that she seemed to regard interviews as "dating services" rather than mere promotional opportunities.

Perhaps, however, these comments also provided a way to divert attention from her private life. Cunningly throwing interviewers off the scent, she'd talk breathily of her desire to date a "roughneck" New York boy – little did the magazine editors know of the irony that she already had a New Yorker of her own, in the form of on-tour dancer Jorge Santos.

The seductive Latino, originally of Puerto Rican descent, had captured Christina's heart after auditioning for a part in her live show. By the start of 2000, the pair were perpetually on the road together and it wasn't long before romance blossomed.

Yet in the early part of their relationship, a flighty Christina had been spotted passionately kissing Enrique Iglesias, flirting with Fred Durst, holding hands with Carson Daly and, by her own admission, "having fun" with several other eligible men. She was certainly painting a plausible illusion that she was single. However, the reality was that she was terrified of commitment – as her parents' marriage had taught her, tying herself down emotionally meant losing self-control.

For those without a history of family breakdowns, loving wholeheartedly and losing all power of reasoning as a result could be liberating, but for Christina it simply meant laying herself bare to get hurt, and after seeing the agony of her mother's marriage, it was the one thing she'd promised herself she'd never do. "It's a little bit scary," she'd admitted. "I'm used to being this independent chick, not really thinking about boys and all of a sudden, whoa – like, this guy takes over everything! It makes me vulnerable and I don't like to be that way. Why? Seeing my mom go through a really hard divorce – or marriage, rather. The divorce was the good thing. But just watching her vulnerability in staying in that relationship, I promised myself I would never put myself in a position where I'd be that vulnerable."

Possessing maturity and wisdom beyond her junior years, it had been hard for Christina to fathom why her mother was so inextricably tied to her father. It was as though invisible handcuffs restrained her. The thought would burn through her brain: "Why doesn't she just leave?" Christina grew to realise that her mother's passion had rendered her powerless and that, for an unlucky few, this was what being in love meant. "I thought, 'I'm never going to let a man do that to me,'" she continued. "I thought of being in a relationship as being weak."

Her past highlighted exactly why it was so difficult for her to fearlessly fall in love. Keeping her liaisons light and commitment-free had felt safe to Christina, but in reality she'd been running away from her feelings – and it wasn't long before nature prevailed. "I fell in love for the first time [and] it was the most beautiful feeling in the whole world," she enthused. "I had butterflies in my stomach and a permanent smile on my face… for a while, it was perfect."

The news had come as a disappointment to those who'd harboured fantasies of her settling down with the more classically handsome Enrique Iglesias – in fact, no one more so than Grandmother Aguilera. "She's so funny," Christina would chuckle. "She says, 'Why didn't you stick with the Enrique guy?' I was like, 'Grandma, I'm not in love with him – I fell in love with somebody else.'"

Yet there was more to her change of heart than met the eye – Jorge appealed to Christina's need to remain in control. While Enrique was famous, empowered and successful, Jorge was a comparatively poorly paid back-up dancer – and in her relationship with the latter, she was the one that called the shots. Knowing that made her bolder and it wasn't long before she was subtly announcing her devotion – a spontaneous new piece of hand-holding choreography here, an onstage mention of a Puerto Rican boyfriend there.

Yet the same power imbalance which endowed Christina with security was proving ever more difficult for Jorge to handle. He wanted more than mere fame by association – he was seeking success on his own terms – and, by his own admission, he was becoming increasingly frustrated with the notion of being tied to his lover's apron strings.

It didn't help that a besotted Christina had already begun to talk of marriage. "For me I was 18 and definitely not ready," Jorge would later confirm. "I was ready to keep dancing and I think she wanted me to just be there for her, on her path. I wanted to do more than just be Christina's boyfriend." Fiercely proud, and as independent as Christina herself had once been, he felt he'd lost his own identity and had been reduced to a wealthy woman's plaything.

"We come from two different places," she would bluntly explain. "He's a dancer and I'm a star... it can be hard for a guy's ego." Plus, imbued with the type of machismo characteristic of someone with traditional Latin roots, Jorge saw his role as that of the provider. "He felt he had nothing to give me," Christina continued, "and I was like, 'But I said I don't need anything from you except you and your time.' But I guess it's hard for a man to date someone like me because I can take care of myself materialistically."

Both had debilitating insecurities resulting from their conditioning in early childhood. Christina had struggled with her "vulnerability issues" and a reluctance to love wholeheartedly, until her affection for Jorge had melted her and she'd discovered that "it's really a beautiful thing to give your all to someone". However once she'd bypassed her own emotional roadblocks, it was Jorge's that were standing in the way.

To make matters all the more complicated, he was openly bisexual. "I was involved with someone who had a gay past," Christina would later comment to *The Advocate*. "I was in the relationship knowing that... it was a paranoia at times – like when you walk into a room with a guy that you know has feelings for other men, you're like, 'Is he looking at the guy or the girl over there?'"

While his sexuality in itself was a non-issue for Christina, what would prove more problematic was his inability to commit solely to her. He'd got up, close and personal with her in the video for 'Come

On Over Baby (All I Want Is You)', but within weeks, he'd been gyrating on the dance floor of Manhattan gay clubs in his home town of New York.

A friend of the pair elaborated on the ill-fated love affair, telling the author, "She found out because she found a gay magazine in his luggage with pictures from a party – and it just so happened that he was in one of them, kissing a porn star! He couldn't exactly deny it. She was incensed and instantly threw him out."

It seemed that all of her worst fears about the perils of vulnerability had come true. This was underscored by her willingness to forgive – within weeks, he'd won her heart again; performing suggestive dance routines together onstage made the chemistry that still existed between them very difficult to ignore.

Jorge's friend said: "They broke up, got back together, broke up, got back together. It was never-ending. Things finally ended when he left her to be with another man. I know she was heartbroken, but it seemed like the kindest thing to do – his desire for men wasn't going to go away."

Thus Christina was back on the roller coaster – and in some ways, her love life was now more complicated than ever. "The attention I get is flattering," she would fret, "but it's kind of superficial. I have this obsession with Marilyn Monroe and she said in her biography that she felt she could never be herself because everyone expected her to be the person they saw onscreen. So when people give me flowers, make comments or even want to date me, I'm thinking, 'Are you doing this for the girl in the video, the character I'm playing, or for me?'"

This type of comment highlighted Christina's insecurity and flagging self-esteem. Wounded and maybe even a little scarred by her break-up, she wasn't sure if the real her could live up to the image of painted-over perfection that adorned magazine covers and TV screens. Despite being a regular on 'World's Hottest Women' lists, she would later comment incredulously that her pictures had been digitally altered to the extent that she often barely recognised herself. In reality, the media images accentuated the features of already beautiful women rather than creating them, but, nonetheless, she had become afraid of what others – including prospective partners – would now expect her to live up to.

The Christina the public knew was both beautiful and carefree and, increasingly, the real woman feared she couldn't match her stage self in either regard. How would she bridge the gap?

CHAPTER 6

Stripped: Behind Blue Eyes

It was time to let the songs do the talking – and her sophomore album would show the world what Christina, behind the guise of innocent blue eyes, was really like. She'd been hiding for far too long.

There was no chameleon-like transformation; rather, she was peeling back the layers of externally defined perfection to reveal a woman that not even her die-hard fans knew existed – the true Christina.

Her 21st birthday, a shamelessly decadent affair, set the tone for the transition. If her account was to be believed, the party would put subsequent video 'Dirrty' to shame. The scene of the crime was Hollywood nightclub Deep which, in the words of owner Ivan Kane, was the number one venue to "push the envelope in terms of sexuality, decadence and voyeurism".

Christina paid tribute to the theme by making her grand entrance on a jet black Harley Davidson, dressed in an eye-popping ensemble of a barely-there dress made of feathers, indecently transparent pink panties and a black leather bra. "Me and my girls rolled up on the backs of motorcycles," she boasted. "There were crazy dancers in cages, a ménage a trois going on – it was pretty dope."

That was an understatement – and her appetite for private parties would soon secure her a place on the blacklist of several eminent LA hotels. Her favourite nightspot was the Standard and, when guests in adjoining suites complained about the noise, she'd simply rent out the entire top floor. Meanwhile, those in charge of the clean-up operation were left wishing she'd kept the genie safely tucked away in the bottle.

A party hosted by Christina typically cost a six-figure sum and, as long-suffering hotel staff would sarcastically snipe, the subsequent costs were almost as high. Champagne that cost hundreds of dollars per bottle was purchased in abundance and, much to the wrath of the chambermaids, spilt in equal measure. There'd be cigarette burns on plush pillows, quilts of the finest Egyptian cotton stained with vomit, torn wallpaper and heavy metal tunes blared out at deafening volume. The walls would vibrate, with paintings rocking precariously at the mercy of Christina's musical earthquake, before shattering and falling to the ground. Her parties embodied every single rock 'n' roll cliché – with the exception, perhaps, of hurling TV sets from windows – but the final straw came when she took to smashing empty bottles at night to unwind.

During this era, Christina was romantically linked with Robbie Williams, Justin Timberlake, actor Tobey Maguire and Dave Grohl of the Foo Fighters. Most rumours, however, were unfounded. When questioned, a visibly embarrassed Grohl would squirm sheepishly in his seat before retorting that not only did he live with his girlfriend but, "I'm like 33 and [Christina's] a kid!" A romance with Robbie looked equally unlikely after he sarcastically quipped, "She needs a wash" and Justin was merely a good friend from the *Mickey Mouse* era. "I wanted to disappear from the public eye for a minute," she said. "I wanted to live life."

And live life she did. During a year of dodging the cameras, Christina would resurface from her secret den for just a few main public appearances. October 2001 would see the promotion of a celebrity cover version of Marvin Gaye's 1971 hit 'What's Going On?', with the proceeds divided between two charities: the Global AIDS Alliance and the United Way's September 11th Fund. Co-produced by artists including Bono from U2, the track guest-starred Usher, Alicia Keys, Destiny's Child, Britney Spears, Fred Durst, Nelly Furtado, 'N Sync, Gwen Stefani and, of course, Christina, to name just a few. Christina was one of those to be photographed with her face obliterated by a blindfold – a symbol representative of people's inability to see the perils of racism, sexism, homophobia and AIDS.

Then in February, she found time for a striptease at the 2002 Grammys, performing 'Lady Marmalade' with her fellow divas before accepting an award for the song under the category of Best Pop Vocal Collaboration. The style stakes were high – her rival Pink stepped out in a pale pink feather boa tossed around her shoulders with a matching glittery gown – a statement of glamorous femininity that stood out in striking contrast to her butch, tomboyish, cropped blonde haircut. Yet with her white hot pants, minuscule black bralet, crimson Playboy-style bow-tie, thigh-high leather boots and a Marilyn Monroe-inspired mass of tight blonde curls, Christina managed to upstage her.

She continued the burlesque theme by becoming an honorary member of the Pussycat Dolls for the night at LA's Roxy Theatre, just as Gwen Stefani and *Baywatch* actress and glamour model Carmen Electra had done before her. She would ooze sexual energy on tracks such as 'Fever' and 'Big Spender', dressed in fishnet stockings, black PVC lingerie and red knee-high boots.

She'd clearly taken the theme to heart as subsequent nights out regularly featured Christina wearing little more than her underwear – on one occasion arriving at a club brandishing a sexually suggestive riding crop. Yet – arguably unlike the Pussycat Dolls – the biggest impact Christina made was with her voice.

In fact one insider told the author that it was Christina's appearance that had influenced Ron Fair, Robin Antin et al to take the Pussycats from a show that was most famous for its burlesque routines to a serious singing group. "They kept the sex appeal and the high octane trashy glamour," the insider elaborated, "but they made it all about the songs too. Later they recruited Nicole Scherzinger and become world famous with 'Don't 'Cha'. Seeing Christina on their stage made them dare to believe in a new vision for the group where they were noted for their music too. If it hadn't been for Christina, the Pussycats might never have released an album and we might never have seen Nicole on our screens."

The same month, Christina debuted new song 'Infatuation' at the Olympics Closing Ceremony to a TV audience comprising almost an eighth of the US population. She had to fight back tears of both rage and nostalgia in her dressing room – the memories were bittersweet because she'd written the track about her Puerto Rican lover from the past, Jorge Santos. Telling the story of her irresistible urge, despite her better judgement, to fall in love, it was a high impact song, but, as Christina was extremely keen to point out, not her comeback. "I'm really mad that a lot of people thought that was my comeback performance," she ranted. "It wasn't. My comeback will be explosive!"

For the most part of Christina's break, she was contentedly incognito, until the summer, when the dramatic comeback she'd vowed to deliver hit America with full force. In just four short minutes, 'Dirrty' was the embodiment of every conservative mother's worst nightmare. The new single, on constant rotation on every music channel over the summer, lived and breathed wanton, unapologetic sexuality.

But while the words were provocative, it was the video that had everyone talking. It began with a leather-clad Christina stepping off a motorbike to declare with great gusto that she was "dirty", "filthy" and "nasty" – sentiments echoed by hip hop collaborator Redman. Not one to let mere words do the talking – especially if her hips could do it better – she then rode the bike through throngs of clubbers before being lowered into a boxing ring, restrained behind the bars of a metal cage. While the cage might have seemed like a sexual kink in keeping with the video's theme, it was actually a metaphor relating how trapped she'd felt. In her own words, she'd felt "caged in", "stifled" and "locked up".

It was when she was released, both in the video and in real life, that the real fun began. Surrounded by scantily clad partygoers of both genders, who rubbed salaciously up against her, Christina began writhing in time with the sexually charged club beat. It was reminiscent of the shower scene in rapper Nelly's 'Hot In Herre' video, but – by Christina's strict instructions – "edgier".

She was first seen in lingerie and leather chaps, occasionally swerving round to reveal a tell-tale 'X' on the back of her panties in celebration of her new stage name, X-tina. In other scenes, she sported a minuscule pinstripe denim skirt with chains attached to it – a cue for horrified mothers to question why she was wearing just a belt – and a red fishnet top, which was quickly peeled off, Moulin Rouge style, as part of her dance routine.

Yet overall the video couldn't have been more different from the subtle striptease of Paris's favourite burlesque nightspot – it also doubled as an informal A to Z of fetishes. There were implied "water sports" when Christina and her troupe crouched near urinals, being splashed with water; S&M, depicted lightly by spanking and more strongly with so-called "foxy boxing" and the use of rubber bondage masks; close-ups of Christina spitting in a bucket; hints of lesbian sex; multi-gender orgies and much more. In fact back in those days – when Rihanna was still a child back in Barbados and 'Rude Boy' nothing more than an unrealised figment of someone's imagination – the video was one of the most overtly sexual of its era.

It had all begun when Christina approached Rockwilder, the producer with whom she'd worked on 'Lady Marmalade', looking for something similar but "down and dirty" and more provocative. Her muse had been a track he'd worked on for rapper Redman the previous year called 'Let's Get Dirty (I Can't Get In Da Club)'. It was a ghetto rap track with the words "niggas", "bitches" and "motherfuckers" in regular supply. The video featured packed-out crowds of clubbers who'd already started the party in the queue outside, many dancing in red lingerie. After failing to push his way to the front, with bouncers shaking their heads in disapproval, Redman concocted a plan to overpower security and storm in, despite illicitly carrying weed in his pocket. Inside was a boxing ring where women caked in mud wrestled with each other.

Since turning 21, Christina's age had no longer been a barrier to clubbing and 'Let's Get Dirty' had appealed to her new-found love of the nightlife. If the vision for her comeback single was to showcase the real her, she had to include those experiences. "Turning 21, I wanted my single to have that sort of hip hop clubbing feel," she recounted, "so I called Rockwilder."

Hip hop was his trademark – one of his biggest clients being Jay-Z –

and he had his finger on the pulse of the street-style sound she craved. As a vocalist, Christina would turn out to be one of his surprise favourites – he would recall admiringly, "You don't think her little body can hold all those octaves!"

At her request, they would work together on a remake of 'Let's Get Dirty', featuring a rap from the original performer, Redman himself. Her unusual decision to collaborate with Redman was made all the more controversial in the knowledge that he'd previously teamed up with Eminem on 'Off The Wall', where the latter spoke of grabbing her by her hair and dragging her across the Sahara. Of course it wasn't the only time Eminem had made a lyrical attack against her, but in the interest of diplomacy, neither she nor Redman made mention of it.

To direct the video, she chose David LaChapelle, whose credentials were impressive – few other photographers could claim to have been discovered by Andy Warhol. Not only that, but he'd also shot Madonna, Christina's "ultimate role model" when it came to being "different, rebellious and provocative". The crowd scenes and wrestling scenes had been directly influenced by 'Let's Get Dirty', but Christina also added her own personal touch, for example, some aspects of the video were modelled on her legendary 21st birthday bash, including the dramatic arrival on a motorbike, while the boxing scenes reflected her passion for the sport in real life. In fact, matches with her personal trainer had become so frequent that she'd even looked into getting a boxing ring installed in her house.

That this was the real Christina was evident from a mere glance at her gleeful enthusiasm. As incongruent as an aggressive role might seem played out by someone so petite and feminine, the video was all about challenging preconceptions of who she should be.

What's more, it had succeeded – in some people's opinions, a little too forcefully. Rumour had it that the single had hit the airwaves later than anticipated because Christina's label was terrified by the implications of her dramatic makeover and had been trying to buy time as it begged her to tone it down. Even Redman felt she'd taken things to extremes, chuckling, "She got her driver's licence and [straight away] she crashed her car down the block!"

Then there was producer Linda Perry, who'd worked with Christina on album tracks such as 'Beautiful'. She believed that, in a world where women were blighted by judgmental and sexist stereotypes, artistic credibility could only be achieved by toning down the image and making the main focus music. Tellingly, her own career highlight had been a leading role in eighties group 4 Non Blondes – and that moniker spoke for itself. She had deliberately and defiantly rejected mainstream ideals of beauty and, courtesy of her group's sullen gothic image, had refused to play up to sexy visuals. In her eyes, the only fans this trick would win them were superficial ones.

Her fear for Christina was that viewers, distracted by all the skin, would forget this was not a masturbation aid but a music video. That was the difference between the two of them – while she dodged sexist attitudes, Christina fought them head on. "Are you high?" Linda had gasped incredulously on first seeing 'Dirrty'. "This is *annoying*. Why are you doing this?!" She'd add with a touch of exasperation, "Christina's so talented, I don't know why she's hiding it behind all this sex stuff, but that's just who she is. She dresses like that in the studio... that girl just doesn't like clothes!"

Regardless of the warnings, Christina's mind was made up. "[The video] may have a couple of indecent scenes," she would argue, "but it is exactly how I wanted it to be. I'm not interested in moralists. I am happy and the video is certainly not pornographic. I feel good in sexy outfits. I'm only 21 and under no circumstances do I want to dress like a square! I hate conservative people!"

Yet those conservative types weren't going anywhere – and it was when 'Dirrty' was released to the public that the backlash truly began.

The fallout was extreme, and it had made Middle America sicker than a nuclear explosion. One former fan publicly exclaimed, "At the start of her latest orgy-esque video, she mouths 'Dirty, Filthy, Nasty'. She seems proud of the adjectives I'd use to insult this piece of trash!"

While Shakira and Avril Lavigne – perhaps hypocritically – also spoke disapprovingly of 'Dirrty', a petition was released by members of the public asking the regulators to deny it airplay altogether: "We, the normal civilised people that we are should ban Christina's latest slut-fest video!" it raged. "This should not be aired to kids on MTV!"

She was also to endure snide remarks about her heavily made-up look, with *Time* magazine commenting that "she appeared to have arrived on the set direct from an intergalactic hooker convention". Other media sources would sneer that she was "repulsive", resembling "a drag queen" and "an alien".

However, Christina was unconcerned about whether she was seen as a beauty queen and was determined – now more than ever – that it wouldn't interfere with her artistic freedom. "Before I was pretty much a manufactured bubblegum pop tart," she revealed. "As I've grown into a woman, I could see I was changing and that sweet, blonde, good girl just wasn't me. Pretty? Fuck that, I hate pretty!"

"Even down to my hair," she would exclaim. "I couldn't stand the white blonde, straight hair. I had to do something more street. Street means real to me. I felt unreal being so beauty-pageant looking all the time."

It was an image that Christina had almost grown to resent. She didn't want to be the pretty bird whose presumed dainty fragility had condemned it to a life locked away in a cage to be kept on display. She would later recall, "I was like, 'If I do music my heart isn't into one more time, I'm gonna have to wear a straitjacket because I'll go insane.' I could do the 'Genie In A Bottle' image when I was so hungry [for success] but it was hard to smile and just go with it."

As one psychologist would explain, "When you try to repress someone's identity, their true self will eventually come spilling out – but 10 times as strong." If the record label was fearful that it had spawned a monster, perhaps it only had itself to blame. For better or worse, 'Dirrty' was Christina's opportunity to rebel.

"I wanted to play off of all the different forms of [the word 'Dirrty']," she would reveal. "Also in the video I didn't wanna be too girly or pretty so I wanted to not be afraid to box, or get dirty as far as scraping my knees or my elbows – sweating a bit, dancing hard... just being 21!"

The trouble was that much of America, accustomed to the censored, family-friendly version, thought it was the new Christina that was a pretence. She was quick to insist otherwise. "It's shocking for people coming off an image which, at the height of the teen pop phenomenon, was so cookie cutter and clean-cut," she would reason, "[but] it was an image that really wasn't me. If anything, I'm looking at it like 'What was I doing *back then*?' I got caught up in that whole hype of playing up to a certain image and the press making me out to be a certain way that I wasn't. It was really, really hard. You get the reactions from certain people, 'She's done a whole 180. This isn't her at all', when I've been saying the whole time, 'That [old image] wasn't me at all!'"

Frustrated with being misunderstood, she became bold in her efforts to set the record straight. With unprecedented candour, Christina admitted for the first time that she'd played up to her former image – with reluctance – "just to get my foot in the door". She would add, "I was never great at trying to fake my way through being Miss American Virginal Sweetheart – I just have to be me."

The message couldn't have been clearer – but even so, many critics still refused to take her words at face value. One blogger quipped sarcastically, "She is reclaiming her individuality by demanding she no longer be considered a pre-packaged corporate controlled innocent faux-virginal sex object with minimal integrity and instead be thought of as an artificially self-controlled ass-flaunting faux-nasty sex object, with even less integrity." To critics like these, her new image was just as manufactured as its predecessor, with a carefully calculated shock element to court yet more press attention.

This opinion was publicly parodied by *Buffy And The Vampire Slayer* actress Sarah Michelle Gellar, who joked on *Saturday Night Live*, "When people see this video, they're gonna stop thinking of me as some blonde-haired, bubblegum music industry hoe – and start thinking of me as an actual hoe!"

Christina was not amused. Dismissing it as puerile and "boring", she claimed, "I could have written a much better script myself." Taking the opportunity to slip her boxing gloves on, she added, "I didn't think it was funny at all... but soon I'm a guest at *Saturday Night Live*. Let's see what I'll do there. Maybe 'the little vampire slut'..."

Of those that did believe Christina's transformation was genuine, many – emotionally tied to her Disney origins – were left wishing she'd kept the real her under wraps. One reviewer from *Lumberjack Online* reminisced, "I still remember her on the *Mickey Mouse Club* singing cute songs and performing choreographed hip hop dances. If what we see now is the real Aguilera, then I think I respected the fake Aguilera more... if she revealed any more to us, she might as well pose for *Playboy*." He added that she had "compromised all her integrity" and that Walt Disney would have "rolled in his grave".

Yet it seemed that for every squeaky clean fan waiting to erupt into an episode of self-righteous histrionics and overactive morals, there was another who appreciated the change. The song debuted at number one in liberal Britain and, while it narrowly missed the mainstream market in America by peaking at a modest number 48 – perhaps due to the overtly sexual content – it remained in the top 100 for 40 weeks, certifying it the longest charting single in the history of Christina's career.

One place where it wouldn't be welcomed, however, was Thailand. Beady-eyed natives quickly realised that Thai-language posters pictured on the video were emblazoned with seedy phrases advertising "Thailand's Sex Tourism" and, alarmingly, "Young Underage Girls". Perhaps someone had been playing a practical joke, but, needless to say, neither Christina nor David LaChapelle had been aware of it. The latter was forced to issue a public and grovelling apology denying all knowledge of the posters' true meaning and reassuring the Thais of his utmost respect for their nation.

However, the damage was already done – Christina's Thai record label was compelled to ban the video from local TV stations, while the debate even reached the authorities, with the government ominously threatening to "take action" if the video had a negative impact on tourism. When Christina had sung mischievously that, at her party, someone would have to "call the cops", underage sex charges wasn't quite what she'd had in mind – and the faux pas was a humiliating mistake sorely felt on both sides.

Back home, there was the lesser issue of allegedly demoralising teenage girls with which to contend. "Promiscuity isn't a sign of maturity," raged one columnist. "It's a sign of self-loathing... the era of radical feminist sexual liberation has produced a generation of shameless skanks."

Of course, Christina was at the forefront of the argument, packaged as "a sad symptom of this cultural zeitgeist". Yet – adding fuel to the fire of middle America's incandescent fury – there was the controversial question, as much as straight-laced critics might hate to admit it, of whether 'Dirrty' Christina might actually be a *better* role model than her virginal twin.

To Christina, the video's message was one of empowerment and she would insist, "I'm very much in control of the situation. It's not like I'm being degraded." Later she would elaborate, "OK, I may have been the naked-ass girl in the video, but if you look at it carefully, I'm also at the forefront. I'm not just some lame chick in a rap video, I'm in the power position, in complete command of everything and everybody around me. To be totally balls-out like that is, for me, the measure of a true artist."

Meanwhile it could be argued that 'Genie In A Bottle', in stark contrast, depicted the lifeless woman *Reviving Ophelia* had warned every teenage girl against becoming, someone who'd wait passively for a man to awaken her sexuality and soul and who'd then take the reins over her life forever after in the process. The lyrics of 'Genie' even referenced the fairy-tale imagery of *Sleeping Beauty*, where a fragile, virginal girl – instead of being in control of her own destiny – is imprisoned for 100 years, or, in the words of the song, a "century of lonely nights". Without someone to awaken her, she is regarded as impotent as a human being, whereas the scandalous girl depicted in 'Dirrty' was anything but. Indeed, Christina's manifesto was the exact opposite of the genie – she'd taken control and awakened herself.

As she tried to make sense of the copious criticism that had come her way, Christina would comment that although she wanted to be free to "play and experiment" and to be "as tame or outlandish as I happen to feel", there was a risk that "when you are bold and open artistically... a whole bunch of people automatically feel threatened by you". Perhaps that really was at the heart of people's dislike for her. The demeanour of power and confidence she exuded flew in the face of stereotypical female imagery, blowing apart some men's world views in the process. She wasn't displaying the reassuring age-old role of passivity that many traditionalists felt comfortable with seeing in a woman; rather, she was intimidating, untouchable, free, and she ostensibly owned her own sexuality.

This one video had extended beyond the nightclubs and music channels and infiltrated into real life, shaking the very structure of society. It provoked fierce debate on what it meant to be a feminist and, equally, what it meant to be a whore. Clearly Christina wasn't the demure, giggling woman that the average man might feel confident enough to approach in a bar – might those who felt uneasy about that respond by lashing out against her?

Meanwhile women less sexually driven than Christina might feel equally intimidated and obligated, perhaps, to live up to her highly sexualised attitude and imagery in their own lives. One reviewer seemed to prove that theory when she observed, "What she's depicting is subcultures within sexuality and to say that this is a normal young woman's sexuality is just not fair – even Madonna never did that to girls."

Perhaps then, some negative attitudes were fuelled by insecurity, a concern on the part of the average woman that they couldn't match Christina's zeal or live up to the drama of what she portrayed. On a related note, Christina's undeniably gorgeous physicality had unlocked the green-eyed monster in many a woman – even those of the seemingly immune celebrity world.

Provoking jealousy even from the A-list, it was scarcely surprising, perhaps, that the general public might have felt insecure, although Christina was determined to be a woman's woman and stand up for the rights of female kind. She was an entertainer and, as such, her videos might deliberately be extravagant or larger than life, but in any case, her intention was not to alienate other women – by her account, she was trying to free them. "Go to any college sorority," she would insist. "They're not sitting around looking at each other. They're flirting and having fun and being 21. I think whatever size or shape body you have, it's important to embrace it and get down! The female body is something that's so beautiful. I wish women would be proud of their bodies and not diss other women for being proud of theirs!" Revealing that her mother had "loved" the video and been fully supportive, she added, "I think the female body is something to be proud of, not to be ashamed of."

Realistically, it was inevitable that a video with such strong imagery would provoke so many different reactions, from triumphant liberation to fearful intimidation. Yet Christina's attitude remained upbeat. "If I come out and sell two damn records to people who can appreciate my music or what I have to say," she vowed, "that's cool with me."

In the midst of the 'Dirrty' furore was another public scandal waiting to erupt – Christina's first encounter with Eminem since the fallout from 'The Real Slim Shady'. Christina's last word on the matter had been far from flattering: she'd accused him of insulting her "to make sure he had a hit record, even if it was at the expense of using other people's names or dissing them". She would continue caustically, "If that's what he has to do to make hit records, that's pretty sad. It seems pointless to say anything more about a guy who is basically retarded."

At the VMAs on September 7, organisers – all too aware of the tension – had mischievously scheduled Christina to present her "retarded" rival with an award, and reviewers would later joke that she'd looked as though she'd "rather have dropped it on his foot". A confrontation seemed well overdue and, backstage afterwards, an enraged Christina made sure she got it. "He thought I'd just roll over, smile and forget about all that shit he spouted in his songs about me," she later recalled. "Men are so like that… I took Eminem to one side and confronted him and told him he was wrong. He was like a puppy!" She'd told him that she'd never singled him out for scrutiny, but that her background had sensitised her to talk of domestic issues and it had been vital to her to speak out. Eminem had allegedly replied meekly, "Well, we all have our backgrounds," before adding, "You know what? Come here" and pulling her into a reconciliatory embrace.

It wasn't quite the boxing match for which the media might have hoped – Eminem had even delivered a half-hearted apology for the slight, admitting that he'd made the insults against her purely to disassociate himself from the bubblegum pop scene he despised and ensure that he wouldn't be mis-categorised by the press and public. Yet behind the scenes, as he would later confess, he flew into a rage. "When I hugged her, I thought I was being as mature as I could be," he reflected, "but when I got behind closed doors in the green room, I threw a fit. There was a cooler with drinks in it, and I asked if anybody wanted to grab a water or something. Nobody did. So I picked up the cooler and threw it against the wall and kind of fucked up the whole room, basically... This is the kind of shit that happens that makes me think to myself, 'Maybe you need to go back to anger management class,' because, obviously, I haven't learned... this is one reason why I never go out."

Ironically, little had he known at the time that Christina had felt exactly the same way as he did about the pop music scene. Her sophomore album, *Stripped,* however, released on October 26, would leave no uncertainty as to where she stood.

While its title might conjure up images of top-shelf posing, it actually represented Christina's desire to peel off the layers of deception and reveal her true self. "I named the album *Stripped* because it is about being emotionally stripped down," she would clarify, "and pretty bare to open my soul and heart." She achieved that by focusing less on virtuoso singing and more on expressing emotion, no longer telling generic stories but instead ones that were personal to her, even getting involved in the writing and production of the songs – something the average pop artist couldn't dream of doing.

Christina would agonise that, starting out, she'd had "no credibility as a writer" and had struggled to be taken seriously, but it was evidently a battle easily won as she ended up co-writing all but two of the 20 tracks on the album.

"Record labels take a risk with new artists, so they tend to be controlling at the outset, when the artist doesn't have clout," hypothesised psychologist Lilli Friedland. "But once you get the Grammy, you can say, 'It's my time, I get to do what I want.'"

One of the first things Christina wanted was to capture every stage of her ill-fated relationship with Jorge Santos on CD. She did so across four songs with the help of co-writers Scott Storch and Matt Morris.

Matt was an old friend from the *Mickey Mouse Club* days; Christina had taken a chance on him as the studio sessions with her would comprise his first ever songwriting credits.

Scott hadn't been an obvious candidate for Christina to collaborate with, either – until then, he'd been almost exclusively a hip hop producer, writing for the likes of Snoop Dogg, Busta Rhymes and Dr. Dre. Yet it was his work with the latter that first attracted her. "I originally wanted to work with Dre," she would confess, "and then I started to work with Scott regularly and I just fell in love with his style."

One of the first tracks the three wrote together was 'Loving Me For Me', a silky ballad that depicted falling in love. As a perpetual performer, Christina had finally found someone with whom she didn't need to put on a show. Someone she felt loved her without make-up, hair extensions and expensive stage costumes, and who was equally infatuated with what was underneath the showbiz mirage. Of course, it was an enormous confidence boost to know that her stripped-down self – in contrast to the exaggerated stage self she portrayed – was adored. She'd found something real, an asset all too rare in an industry as superficial as hers. The song was an honest reflection of how she'd regarded her lover at the time. For example, she'd sing approvingly of how the money she made and her star status was irrelevant. While the flamenco-inspired 'Infatuation', which Christina had debuted at the Winter Olympics earlier that year, was equally romantic, Jorge's underdog status had been a large aspect of why they'd parted ways.

'Underappreciated' spoke of another deficit in the relationship – Jorge's lack of attentiveness. "It's about a girl who has been in a relationship [where] the newness has worn off," Christina related, "and he can't turn his head away from the TV and you don't lay awake any more talking about dreams and things. I think I felt a little underappreciated sometimes, because I gave a lot, especially trying to make him feel good."

Finally, 'Walk Away' was the last nail in the coffin for her and Jorge. The song described the addictive quality of a failing, toxic relationship and the senseless temptation to keep going back to the source of bittersweet pleasure and pain. Christina turns for comfort to the same person that caused her to feel pain in the first place. Each time she crawls back to get her fix, she sacrifices a little more control and dignity until her worst fears come true – she has become the vulnerable, tormented and powerless-in-love woman she promised herself she'd never be.

In the same vein, 'Impossible' captures the frustration and futility of loving a man who never makes it easy, in a bluesy package produced, written and arranged solely by Alicia Keys. Christina had been a big fan ever since hearing 'Fallin'', which she confessed enviously that she wished she'd written herself. Working with Alicia, a competent composer in her own right, was bound to boost Christina's credentials – particularly as it was hard to imagine her duetting with performers like Westlife or Britney.

'Get Mine, Get Yours', on the other hand, was the polar opposite of the album's string of tortured love songs. "It's about casual sex," she would clarify. "I'm in it to get mine and you get yours – I want your body, not your heart." She'd originally agonised over whether or not to use it over concerns that it lacked any "depth of meaning" but, like 'Dirrty', it had the type of beat that would instantly get listeners on the dance floor.

Meanwhile tracks such as 'The Voice Within' and 'Keep On Singin' My Song' had an uplifting theme. For Christina, with growing maturity came the gradual empowering realisation that it was impossible to please everyone all of the time and that sometimes it was better simply to follow one's own individuality, instincts and dreams and please oneself. Liberated from the fear of going her own way, she decides to follow the voice within.

Then there was 'Soar', in which Christina queries whether if she compromises her artistic integrity to become a sellout she will be able to look back without regret and love herself. While the 'Dirrty' critics felt she'd already lost her integrity in the mere act of stripping off, her argument was that she'd lose far more by hiding behind a fake persona to fit the mould. The most arresting imagery of the song is that of Christina looking into a mirror to find that, after all the years of pretending, she no longer recognises her own reflection.

One reviewer from the *Oregon Daily Emerald* felt that songs like these exposed Christina as a hypocrite. "She claims and flaunts her individuality," he argued, "but neglects to realize or address the fact that she is only able to do so because she meets the acceptable standards for what society deems 'physically attractive'. The question raises itself: how successful would she be if she were considered 'ugly' by the majority of her listeners?"

Yet years later, the presence of bestselling artists such as Susan Boyle would answer that question by itself – talent *could* transcend an artist's surface value, especially if that artist represented something with which ordinary people could identify. The theme of 'Soar', advising against changing for someone else's benefit, while challenging listeners to step out of a pre-ascribed mould, was relevant to modern audiences and could be applied just as readily to the life of a teenager suffering peer pressure as to that of showbiz stars.

Meanwhile, Christina had promised to keep it real, but 'I'm OK', one of the darkest tracks on the album, was disconcertingly so. The song opens with the sound of her sobbing. Behind the scenes, she had been lying on the floor of the studio, propped up on her elbows with genuine tears of distress streaming down her cheeks. For this was the moment that she'd confront the demons which kept her awake at night – the memories of her childhood. Flying in the face of critics who mocked her "generic lyrics" and accused her of lying about writing them herself, Christina maintains the song related to her mother's experiences.

Even worse, there was little chance of delivering the track to Fausto in person. Since they'd reunited in New York back in 2000, the relationship had petered out – and not of Christina's volition. She'd revealed to a German magazine that he'd broken off contact because, in her words, "He didn't care for me any more."

Yet while any chances of reconciliation seemed to lie in tatters, she was adamant that the track wasn't a bid for vengeance or a wish to publicly humiliate someone who'd troubled her. "I'm not trying to punish him," she would insist. "If anything, I'm speaking out for my own benefit and the benefit of others that might be going through it.

Hopefully he will understand where I'm coming from and what he put us through and be a better man for it. I mean, I can't help what he did – I just hope he respects the fact that this is part of the healing process for me."

The song would concurrently provide a supportive voice for the domestic violence victims who had poured their hearts out to her in emails. They'd be read by her mother, as the manager of her fan club, and when she shared them with Christina, they'd cry together. 'I'm OK' was, above all, a tribute in their names.

This dark side of her past might come as a surprise to the part-time fan. After all, in public appearances, there was no hint of vulnerability – a smile was permanently etched across her face and she exuded a strength and a seemingly unbreakable spirit; in fact, maybe even more so than most. However, she would explain, "Bruises fade, but the pain still remains – even though you can't see it on the outside, it's got some long-term effects... no matter what, you have to have faith that you will come through this."

Subsequent songs like 'Fighter' would tell the story of how her background had given her a steely determination not to become a victim, but, in itself, 'I'm OK' would highlight one of the many reasons why Christina just couldn't play up to the role of a vacuous, superficially sweet pop star. A couple of years earlier, she might have come across as an unreachably glamorous, cooler-than-thou celebrity, with whom the public couldn't identify – but now she was offering up a taste of her gritty reality. She'd given her fans powers of X-ray vision, a glimpse into her soul, and shown that stripping was about far more than just shedding clothes. This posed a serious challenge to theories that her repertoire consisted purely of soulless stripteases, carried out with no deeper meaning than a bid for attention – and, consequently, commercial gain. 'I'm OK' humanised Christina – and it also conquered the hold her father had over her emotions. She'd been frightened to open up and display her vulnerable side, but now she'd done it to millions of people. She would comment later, "I was half-crying [through the song] trying to hold back my tears. It was the hardest thing I've ever had to sing" – but she had done it. This was the moment that Christina removed the invisible handcuffs digging into her soul and reclaimed her real, undamaged self.

She would compose her "twisted lullaby" with just one other writer – Linda Perry. The pair had met after Linda had approached her in a nightclub and, with a mixture of intuition and sheer audaciousness, told her she could see she was in the depths of depression. She claimed she could see her heart wasn't in writing vanilla love songs and that she should tap into her melancholia for creative inspiration. "Everyone knows you can sing, but it's not convincing emotionally," were her exact words. "I think you're depressed. You should get in touch with it, use it in your songs." An indignant Christina turned on her heel, initially furious with Linda's nerve – but not before she'd had the chance to press a business card into her hand.

Once back home, Christina had reflected on the opportunity. On Pink's 2001 album *Missundaztood*, all of her favourite songs had been co-written by the same person – Linda, including the title track, 'Let's Get This Party Started', and tracks that could inspire on an emotional level such as 'My Vietnam'. This told her Linda could strike a balance between meaningful, hard-hitting songs and those that were commercially successful on a chart-topping scale – and she was hooked.

That said, recording 'I'm OK' had been far from easy – and on one occasion, a sobbing Christina had begged for the session to be abandoned. "It sounds ghoulish, and she didn't think she could do it, but... I *made* her do it in tears," Linda would later confess. "You've got to be feeling something before you can create. Some people will reveal nothing and just grind the stuff out. That's factory work."

The pair would end up working together on three other tracks, too. Linda's penchant for rock vocals excited Christina – as someone who'd defined pop as her "least favourite" genre of music because it "lacked depth" and who, in spite of her fracas with Fred Durst, could often be found vibing to the Limp Bizkit CD in her Discman, she was looking to expand her vocal territory.

Again, Linda declared she knew Christina still had dark sides to her that deserved to be coaxed out and, by prescribing musical therapy, she found it. The problem was convincing others of those inclinations. "I have a lot of aggression in me that needs to come in a not very precise or articulate way," Christina would reflect. "Like, there's this one track where I'm screaming at the top of my lungs, kind of like Courtney Love! It's crazy!"

However, she failed to persuade Courtney herself. The ex-Hole star and widow of grunge rocker Kurt Cobain had regularly written with Linda, so Christina, desperate to secure a collaboration with the woman she regarded as a rock goddess, had been near hysterical with excitement when studio scheduling gave her an opportunity to meet her face to face. Concentrating hard to contain herself, she sidled over with as much nonchalance as she could muster and enquired of Linda, "What are you doing? Writing rock for your friend Courtney?"

Before Linda could respond, Courtney turned round and witheringly remarked, "Christina, do you even know what rock is?"

Not content with the use of a one-liner to humiliate her, she later turned to the internet to do so, telling her fans gleefully, "I almost had a fist-fight with Christina." She continued, "I got an email from her. Know what she wrote? 'Na, na, was up?' You know what I wrote back? 'I'm in bed watching an Eleanor of Aquitaine documentary – do you know who Eleanor of Aquitaine was?' I am not gonna sit there and go 'Wass up?' That fucking Disney tutor should be shot! And Christina doesn't understand why I don't want to sing back-up on her record!"

Incidentally, while Courtney had mocked Christina's intellectual prowess, she herself usually wrote without any punctuation and with numerous spelling mistakes when she appeared, using her official account, on the forum of her own website. It seemed that Courtney subscribed to the popular trend of writing Christina off as a puerile blonde bimbo who, on account of her looks, was a fake who lacked musical or intellectual talent.

While it was an unfair stereotype with which to immediately tar her, at least Linda's enthusiasm remained intact. She and Christina wrote 'Cruz' together, a fitting continuation to 'I'm OK'. In soft-core Guns N' Roses style, it spoke of the liberation of leaving her past behind and embracing the tantalising possibilities of the open road.

Then there was 'Make Over', which bypassed the victim route – not for the last time, she'd emerged a fighter. She claimed she was ready to go to war with those attempting to make her over to ensure everyone knew she wouldn't be moulded to their vision.

At the end of the recordings, she even received an unusual accolade – a begrudging acceptance from Courtney. "Aguilera owes Linda more than money," she wrote sarcastically via her website. "These songs of hers for Christina are fucking unbelievable. I don't really like Christina's initial impression, but when I've heard the voice controlled and produced by Linda – not doing those silly scales, which Linda forced her not to do – you may actually be blown away!"

Her words of muted praise even extended to Christina's second single, 'Beautiful'. However, ironically, it was perhaps one of the reasons for hostility between the two – Courtney had originally asked Linda for the song and been refused. "In my entire life," she raged to MTV, "I've never wanted a song fully rendered, that someone else has written, ever... It was 11 years old at the time... and she ended up giving it to Christina Aguilera, but I begged her for it. She said to me at the time, 'You're not ready for Top 40 – you will be. You'll hate this song because you didn't write it', which is totally true... and then we got into a fierce fight about whether she should give it to Britney or Christina."

Written solely by Linda, the track broke down the barrier between superstar and fan, offering an uplifting and unifying concept that could apply to both. "I was trying to write a song that affected everybody," she would recall. "This almost desperate cry that 'I am beautiful, no matter what you say'." Christina would concur, "It's all about being proud of who you are... it's an amazing thing to say 'I'm beautiful' without feeling cocky."

Courtney wasn't the only artist who'd had to fight for the track – Christina, too, almost missed the chance to record it. It had been so close to Linda's heart that she'd guarded it possessively for her own album. Yet one evening at the studio, she had been caught off-guard and had given in to Christina's pleas to hear it. Sitting at the piano, she began to sing – and Christina began to beg for the track almost instantly. Yet as someone who had been wryly rolling her eyes at the 'Dirrty' persona, Linda was surprised. "I never in a million years expected her to gravitate towards that," she would recall, "and when she did, it was hard for me to let go of the song, because it's really special for me. So the deal was, 'I need to hear you sing it.'"

Christina passed the audition, but Courtney had been right on one thing – Linda really had been forced to reign in her over-zealous vocals. Part of the reason she over-sang was her desperation to "prove myself and prove that I have talent" – but Linda encouraged her to believe that was never in doubt. "When she sang it, I tried to keep it straight," she'd explained. "I told her to get rid of the finger waves. Every time she'd start going into hoo-ha, I'd stop the tape. I'm like, 'You're doing it again!'"

In the end, Christina came round to her way of thinking, later commenting, "I did the vocal gymnastics thing because it was fun. That's why I like blues too, because you can experiment more with that side of your voice – but I thought the lyrics on this record are so personal, deep and good that I wanted to make them stand out more than what I could do with my voice technically."

It seemed that Linda – not merely her co-writer and producer, but also a loyal confidante, regular ping pong partner and firm friend – was responsible for giving her the confidence to see things that way. Christina would subsequently add, "It's so not a diva kind of record." Take that, Mariah Carey!

In the end, writing on the premise that the emotion in her voice was more important than the delivery, her "raw" first take would be used on the finished song. "Linda taught me that imperfections are good and should be kept because it comes from the heart," Christina elaborated. "It makes things more believable and it's good to share them with the rest of the world."

That was the theme of the video, too – celebrating imperfections. Christina's casting call raised a few eyebrows when she requested, among other things, a woman who "must be extraordinarily skinny and must look anorexic". She had also requested "lesbian women, 40s, all ethnicities. Should appear instantly feminist... I know not all feminists are lesbian, truly I do... but do you get what we're going for here?"

She also recruited from her personal contacts: Jordan Shannon, an actor friend she'd met at her 21st birthday party would play one half of a gay male couple in the video.

The new single, released on November 16, was a chance for Christina to display her diversity – not only was she capable of a risqué club track where she experimented with clothing boundaries, but she could also deliver a heart-rending ballad, looking and sounding the opposite of what anyone might have expected. Yet if the song was hard-hitting and intended to blow apart stereotypes, the video was even more so. Dressed down in a pair of baggy black trousers and a T-shirt, a barefooted Christina softly whispers, "Don't look at me!" before the music starts. Her words, a portrayal of painful shyness, precede sequences of people haunted by their failure to conform to society's standards of beauty.

One emaciated boy, grimacing despairingly, lifts weights as he looks at walls plastered with posters of muscular body-builders. These photos are more a source of pain than motivation, as their imposing physiques are about as far away from his own as it is possible to get. Meanwhile a frustrated girl resorts to burning the magazine images of glossy perfection that so haunt her. Then the isolation of a goth whose piercings and alternative lifestyle alienate him from his peers is depicted when he sits down on a bus only to find that those surrounding him instantly move away.

The video also has an emphasis on alternative sexualities. A transgender man is seen applying a wig and make-up and becoming the woman he's always dreamed of and a gay couple kiss on a bench, oblivious to – and uninterested in – the reaction of those around them. This was a gesture of defiance, about having the courage to embrace one's own looks from within, instead of turning to society for approval on matters of how to look and act and who to love.

In this way, although 'Beautiful' was Linda's creation, it echoed the similar sentiments of 'Soar', in which Christina *had* taken a writing role. "This song is definitely a universal message that everyone can relate to," she would later affirm. "Anyone that's been discriminated against or unaccepted, unappreciated or disrespected just because of who you are."

Near identical images of the gay kiss would later appear on Katy Perry's video 'Firework', suggesting that she may have been influenced by the track. Additionally, faux lesbian duo Tatu would also explore the theme – although arguably demeaningly, given that neither girl was authentically gay. Their video seemed to exploit lesbianism for press attention, seeking titillation rather than genuine emotion and failing to reach the feelings of those who belonged to that lifestyle in reality.

Regardless, Christina had done it first and, in April of the following year, she would even receive a Special Recognition Award from the Gay and Lesbian Alliance Against Defamation, noting the video's role in raising morale among those of alternative sexuality. Joan Garry, the charity's executive director, would praise, "At a time when many in the music industry avoid lesbian and gay themes altogether or, even worse, use defamatory images to appear 'edgy', Christina's decision to feature gay and transgender people in her video is a strong statement of inclusion, affirmation and acceptance."

Christina would respond with equal fervor, replying, "I cannot express in words how much the LGBT community means to me. On my darkest day their support lifts me up. I feel honoured that some of my songs have become anthems to them as well."

However the song would later be subverted by Pink's twisted sense of humour when she performed 'Lady Marmalade' on her own tour, with blow-up dolls portraying Christina and the other girls. After performing aggressive sexual acts on them, she would single out the Christina doll and imply that she was ugly, sarcastically improvising the words, "You are beautiful, no matter what I say."

The same month as the single release, Christina found herself head-to-head with Eminem in a chart battle. His album, *8 Mile*, which benefitted from one of the most aggressive promotional campaigns in rap history and was released to coincide with his starring role in the film of the same name, instantly topped the charts, selling over 700,000 copies in its first week. Both at the box office and within the music world, he had succeeded in transferring the rap genre to the mainstream.

Plus, while rap culture was typically associated with misogynistic posturing, violence and criminality – and was usually banned from most kids' Christmas lists for that very reason – Eminem had made scandalous, aggressive lyrics au fait with the wider public. Coupled with his status as America's first major white rapper, he'd become quite a record breaker.

Meanwhile, *Stripped* would debut at number two, selling almost half as many copies in that critical first week. This result put the two artists in direct competition. Yet just when the media world was poised for World War II to break out between the pair, Christina surprised everyone by attending his movie premiere. Onlookers were open-mouthed, but most astonishing of all was her choice of clothing – a plain white shirt, trousers and trainers – and no chaps in sight. "People were like, 'Oh my God! Christina's wearing some clothes for a change!'" she chuckled at the event. "I get a kick out of watching that kind of reaction."

The transformation was about as counter-intuitive as Lady Gaga wearing flats, but, of course, it was a one-off – she'd normally make headlines for her outrageous outfits. For example, on one occasion, she posed by New York's Brooklyn Bridge donning chaps in a shade of yellow so fluorescent that it resembled a railway worker's glow-in-the-dark uniform. Needless to say, some would argue that she was an insult to public decency.

At times, the condemnation of the public would escalate into a witch hunt and Christina's appearance on *CD:UK*, a Saturday morning show aimed primarily at teenagers and children, was one such example. Her "suggestive" dance routines and leather chaps, which exposed pants emblazoned with the word 'Nasty', attracted dozens of complaints. Yet the inaugural episode of primetime TV show *Jamie's Kitchen*, which had opened with celebrity chef Jamie Oliver cursing, "Fucking bollocks! I've fucked it up!" after burning a sandwich, went largely unnoticed. Was this a matter of hypocrisy and double standards? Christina would certainly think so.

In any case, her primal, patented and pronounced brand of titillation felt threatening to conservative values – and the next time she appeared on *CD:UK* – for a rendition of 'Impossible' – she was under strict instructions to dress down or bow out. Taking extreme measures to censor her sexuality from modesty and decency zealots, she would compromise by donning black trousers with a shirt and tie and would even sit motionless on a stool to tame her restless hips.

Yet even when she was supposedly dressing down, she would often manage to cause a stir. She would greet one member of the media in a baseball cap, pyjama top and casual combat trousers. So far, so unremarkable – until it came to light that the trousers were unbuttoned and gaping open to reveal her underwear. She'd also customised the outfit with an armband featuring the number '69'. Tellingly, that innocuous looking pyjama top had the word 'Gotcha' on it and, by continually staying a step ahead of others' expectations, Christina knew that she had.

Even when she was trying to go incognito, Christina struggled to avoid standing out. "I don't wear long floral skirts down to my ankles," she would shrug when questioned. "This is just me, I guess." Judging by her skills of effortless provocation, perhaps controversy simply resided in that fiery Latin blood.

Her nonchalance was perhaps the secret behind her unique style. Christina's sartorial standards did not pander to the snobbish advice of glossy magazines such as *Vogue*, where wearing a print that was condemned as "sooo last season" would be regarded as a fate worse than leprosy. She had no interest in collecting cool credentials or fitting in with the fashion pack – or indeed, even the ego-massaging prospect of looking attractive. In fact, when choosing pictures for her single's cover sleeve, she was openly contemptuous of a photo her aides deemed to be pretty. "I look like an opera singer!" she spluttered incredulously before adding with a touch of boredom, "I don't like pretty. Fuck the pretty." She wasn't looking for sophistication, maturity or elegance – and, as her stylist had pointed out, why should she? She was just 21 years old. She paired over-accentuated make-up, which often reached drag-queen proportions, with an overall look that seemed to come straight from the cover of a pornographic movie. Although she'd be hard-pressed to find a photograph where she wasn't pretty, it wasn't about becoming the pageant queen that 'Tasteful Beauty Awards' coveted – rather, it was about making a statement.

She had no qualms about confessing that wrapping a scarf around her cleavage as a makeshift top, as she had done at the VMAs, could be construed as "hookerish", but it didn't matter to her. "If I was in a back alley at midnight and wearing a get-up like that, I could see, yes, that's a little bit hookerish," she conceded. "But I'm at a damn awards show! I'm an entertainer! I'm playing a part. I don't go out to clubs like that at all."

However this was the point where – to some – her argument would fall apart. Keen to make a distinction between herself and the larger than life impression her stage clothes suggested, she gave multiple interviews insisting that she dressed modestly away from the spotlight. "I don't sit at home with my chaps on and my knickers showing!" she'd insist. Yet in an interview with men's magazine *Maxim*, she would claim the opposite, confiding, "At home I walk around all the time in just panties!" Perhaps, ever the slick PR machine, Christina was simply modifying her answers to pander to what an exclusively male audience wanted to hear. Undoubtedly, it would boost her popularity, but hadn't she always vowed she'd never compromise herself like that?

She'd also promised she'd never do a naked *Playboy*-style photo shoot, primarily because she was "a musician, an artist and not a model". Adding that she didn't want to lose her credibility by being typecast as one, she continued, "I just want to be respected for my voice."

Not only did this make a striking contrast to the undeniably aesthetic aura for which she was known, but in a matter of weeks, she'd fly in the face of her own advice. In fact, a journalist at *Maxim* would quip that he'd had to cover her "hot" photos with a fire retardant to keep them from bursting into flames. In her cover shoot with the magazine, she'd disguised her naked breasts with her hands, while just a strategically placed 'Dirrty' slogan obscured the space between her legs. While the text made it impossible to say whether or not she was wearing a thong, her *Rolling Stone* cover shoot that December would leave no room for uncertainty. In that picture, just a guitar would preserve her modesty – and beneath it she was fully naked. A year earlier, she had insisted, "I don't believe I would go as far as stripping", although the evidence now spoke for itself.

Amid criticism about why she hadn't been consistent, things had nonetheless come full circle – Christina had peeled back the layers and become both physically and emotionally stripped. Adore or despise her, she'd revealed herself to the world in transparent Technicolor – few could argue with that.

CHAPTER 7

Unleashing The Genie

In 2003, Christina's intimate revelations showed little sign of slowing down. In a quote the media seized upon as a thinly disguised dig at Britney Spears and her virginity vows, she insisted, "I could not be up there saying I'm going to wait 'til marriage. I'm not conservative when it comes to that sex stuff." However, in some people's estimation, she'd taken her candour a step too far. While the likes of Britney and Mandy Moore had a PR team working overtime to preserve an innocent, good-girl image, every time Christina opened her mouth, she portrayed the exact opposite.

She spoke nonchalantly – though perhaps tongue-in-cheek – of her penchant for sexual violence: "I like to wrestle around and get really aggressive [and] I don't like [my partner] to let me win anything! That's why make-up artists hate me – because I'll turn up to shoots all bruised and whatnot. I like to play rough. Handcuffs are fun!" If her team could cover any bruises with an extra layer of concealer, there was little they could do to rein in her outspokenness. Before long she would also cause tongues to wag by suggesting she had an interest in being sexually submissive – an image which, to some critics, directly contradicted her feminist persona.

Yet surrendering control in the bedroom didn't have to mean being a doormat in real life. According to Susan Wright, president of America's National Coalition for Sexual Freedom, "There's a big difference between structural sexism and negotiating power with someone you trust in the bedroom... being submissive is very compatible with feminism because it is choosing your own form of sexual expression."

Plus while the stereotype of a submissive woman might be of a shy, quiet wallflower without her own opinions or ambitions, in reality the reverse could be true. A woman who regularly took control in her working life might want to liberate herself from being the boss and explore new aspects of her personality through her sexuality. Years later, Rihanna would confess to being sexually submissive for that very reason – she'd tired of a life where she continually called the shots.

Yet while this covered just one area of a woman's life – her sexual preferences – and didn't necessarily equate to passivity in everyday life, there was something of a more disturbing nature in Christina's revelations. For those who had heard her crying bitter tears on 'I'm OK', her preoccupation with sadomasochism might seem troubling.

While in many cases S&M could be a way to experience relationship-enhancing heights of intimacy and trust, a scenario that so closely resembled elements of her own non-consensual past hinted at a darker explanation.

Christina's penchant for piercings was not all that it seemed either. She would reveal to journalists that she had 11 in total, half of which were in secret places. Although tight tops boasting the outline of a nipple ring often betrayed where some of these private places were, she would also elaborate on those that were totally hidden. Of one such piercing, she would confide, "It just seemed erotic in a place that most people wouldn't have the guts to do it." She added, "You hear things like, 'Oh, it will help you reach sexual heights' – whatever – but I just think it looks pretty. I think it accents things quite well." That was just as well, because her diamond-adorned jewellery didn't come cheap – it was rumoured to have cost hundreds of thousands of dollars. "It's going in a special place," Christina would shrug by way of explanation.

Teasing that she'd had "a lot of compliments on it", she would screech with laughter when a blushing journalist raised his eyebrows.

"Don't take it that way!" she chuckled. "I mean from my gynaecologist and my waxer."

While Christina merely came across as adventurous, avant-garde and rebellious, her description of her piercings as "extra puncture wounds" was more revealing as to the real reasons she was collecting them. Some critics saw extreme piercings as self-mutilation, while others speculated on the possibility of severing a nerve and losing sexual sensitivity – but in reality, the biggest danger was that she'd become addicted to body modification as a means of asserting control. "It was a lack of being able to express myself in other ways," she would later reveal. "A way of letting aggression and anger out."

"What, like, 'I'm depressed. Let's get pierced'?!" asked the incredulous interviewer.

"Exactly," she would confirm. "If I was having a bad day or something was getting me down, I wanted to go out and get a new piercing. It was definitely a release for me, something that made me feel a little more strong or empowered because it had something to do with me and no one else."

This admission stripped away the image of a style-conscious woman experimenting with her own aesthetic trademark and instead pointed to someone desperately striving for control to cover up the reality of feeling powerless. This urge had surely stemmed from some deep-seated issues – and she would soon reveal what they were.

Lifting the lid on the repressed fury behind the scenes of her last tour, which had seen everyone from Westlife to Garbage label her a "bitch", she confessed, "I used to get so angry. I felt really caged for a while on tour because people were handling me in not a cool way like, right after the Video Music Awards, I was rushed in a helicopter to do this little show on the internet, but it wasn't on my schedule; no one told me about it. All of those things were going on behind my back."

Moody, ungracious, bratty, self-absorbed: all of these were accusations levelled at Christina when few knew that, behind the stage smile, her exhaustion and tensions were sending her to breaking point. "It was to the point that I was losing my voice," she would add, "and I thought I was going to have to be hospitalised if I kept working myself into the ground. I ended up getting really introverted. I wasn't happy… I need to eat, I need to sleep, and sometimes these things weren't considered. It was like, 'When do you think I'll have time to go to the bathroom?' That wasn't on the schedule."

Although months would sometimes pass without a single day off – or even so much as a moment of peaceful reflection to safeguard her sanity – she revealed she was worried about the loss of her recording contract if she didn't maintain her insanely busy schedule to a T. While she made a personal vow to do whatever she had to do to save her coveted career, before long she was questioning whether she even wanted a part in the industry any more. "When you get signed to a label," she would muse, "people decide what you're going to be, but you're so excited to be doing it, period. Then you realise, 'Man, I don't know if this is what I really want.'"

The adage "Be careful what you wish for" was by now playing out a bittersweet melody in Christina's ears and, by this time it was too little too late – she was heading for a nervous breakdown. Phoning her family in hysterics and threatening to self-harm, she induced her frightened mother to book the next flight to LA to be with her.

While Christina had been unusually coy about her desire to "hurt myself", it seemed that the psychology behind it might have been the same as for her piercings. According to psychologists, self-harm is driven by a yearning for control, kick-started when an external situation renders a person incapable of achieving it. "Anything set me off," she recalled. "I almost wanted to, you know, hurt myself – and it was the first time I'd ever had thoughts like that. I have a lot of pain and anger."

One of the many difficulties she faced was her feeling that some friends had let her down. Prior to that, they'd been a stabilising influence. While the industry might have been full of people with dubious intentions and, likewise, those outside of showbiz might have been hungry for VIP perks, material gain and fame by association, Christina knew those who had been a constant in her life even before she hit the big time were her real friends. They'd ground her if she became big-headed, love her regardless of her status and distract her from her troubles by talking about their comfortingly normal, everyday lives.

As she hadn't made friends easily in her schooldays, she cherished the few she did have all the more. The music business was a surreal world, but they were her reality – or, at least, that's what she'd thought.

The one thing that had kept her sane was pouring out her pain in a diary – and the poetry that resulted would provide the inspiration for 'Fighter'. The song would thank all of those who had betrayed her for giving her strength, resilience and a fighter instinct. For instance, the school bullies had been a blessing in disguise for Christina because their hostility had obliged her to focus on her career from an early age instead of superficial friendships. Meanwhile her parents' separation had encouraged her to fight back – not with her fists, but as an activist – and her craving for fame had been driven by the desire to speak about this experience. Even the dark cloud brought on by so-called friends' behaviour had a silver lining – her experiences had transformed her from a naïve, trusting child into someone determined to rise above her enemies to succeed.

That transformation was portrayed on screen with the help of video director Floria Sigismondi. The Italian creative was no stranger to noir subject matter – her speciality was rock and alternative music and she'd worked with goth rocker Marilyn Manson. The macabre, theatrical videos the pair had created included 'The Beautiful People', which incorporated close-ups of earthworms. Then there was 'Tourniquet', which included a lyric about flies laying eggs, a metaphor for a relationship becoming toxic and decayed over time. Floria symbolised this condition in the video by depicting an infestation of flesh-eating maggots gorging on a lifeless body before being spooned into someone's mouth.

Fortunately Christina's scenes wouldn't be quite so gory – according to Sigismondi, she'd be undergoing that transformation in reverse, going "from a very poisoned place to an empowerment, a place of strength".

Appearing as a brunette for the first time ever in the video, Christina donned long jet black hair extensions and white geisha-style make-up. Early scenes depicted her trying to break out from a suffocatingly small glass box, her black cape billowing up behind her like a parachute on an escape mission. Each time it would deflate again in failure, until, finally, the glass smashed and she was freed. She then crawled along the floor, dislodging the pins in her back that were weighing her down – perhaps the metaphor was that she had become a voodoo doll in which people who wished her ill will would stick pins to live out their frustration. She had become a type of storage vault for others' resentment and fury, which she exorcised when she removed the pins, simultaneously shedding the skin of her former, weaker self. As her former skin burst, a new Christina was revealed, wearing a white dress and white blonde hair.

Continuing the insect theme for which Sigismondi was now infamous, dozens of moths broke into flight, landing on and around Christina. Ironically, this scene would prove more squirm-inducing for the video director than the maggots and worms of her former videos. "I've always had a fear of moths," she would shudder on set, "and I subconsciously wrote this thing with moths in it, so I guess I have to deal with it. They're furry and they carry dust. I found out in old mythology they are supposed to represent the soul. I think that's very appropriate."

Yet while 'Tourniquet' showed only the disintegration of a relationship turned rotten, 'Fighter' showed the triumphant rebirth of a poisoned soul. If earlier scenes had depicted her changing from a larva into a pupa, then the best transformation of all was yet to come. Resembling a regal warrior princess in black velvet and then finally donning a spider dress, Christina had entered her final stage – that of a fighter.

"The whole purpose of the video is this whole metamorphosis of me turning from this weak kind of cocoon-like person into this strong, beautiful butterfly or moth," she would later reflect. "It's all about overcoming some sort of hard time with someone who does you wrong." Those who had hurt her had merely exposed the chinks in her armour and given her an opportunity to work on them – now she was unbreakable.

That she had chosen 'Fighter' to cast aside the innocent blonde look of her past was no coincidence – like 'Dirrty', it was yet another visual representation of how the Christina the world had known had gone forever. She might have lost innocence, but she'd gained wisdom, too.

Her cue would soon come to live up to her fighter image when she was dragged into a feud with professional brat Kelly Osbourne. Kelly's claim to fame was having a former rock star as a blood relative – her father, Ozzy, had been the vocalist in Black Sabbath. To most, the enduring memory of his career was not the music, but the fact that he'd bitten the head off a live bat on stage. Meanwhile his wife, Sharon, who'd first come to his attention as his manager's daughter, claimed she'd become his partner purely because she was the only woman willing to turn a blind eye to his infidelities and prolific drug binges. She'd later launch a career judging the abilities of would-be pop stars on shows such as *The X Factor*. She was the formal leader of the household, as Ozzy suffered permanently slurred speech and drug-related memory loss, often rendering him a little incapable. This dysfunctional family was comedy gold waiting to happen – and they made history by becoming the first celebrity household to agree to be filmed living their everyday lives for TV entertainment. Back in the days before the likes of *Big Brother* existed, they'd given birth to the reality TV craze with their own show, *The Osbournes*.

On one episode – the one that would ignite fury – Sharon boasted that she'd successfully goaded Kelly to spit on Christina's car. Sharon had previously admitted mailing her own faeces to those who displeased her, so by Osbourne standards, merely spitting on a car was classy. Kelly went on to mock Christina's voice on *My Kind Of Christmas*, saying, "I'm not kidding you, I wanted to fucking stab myself!"

While initially it all seemed too puerile and petty to dignify with a response, Kelly's vitriol continued, with her later telling interviewers, "Christina is one of the most disgusting human beings in the entire world... I've seen drag queens who look better."

Eventually, Christina was goaded into action and when she caught sight of Kelly at a Hollywood party, she dragged her into a headlock. According to onlookers, she "hissed with venom" at a terrified-looking Kelly, advising, "If you've got something to say, say it *now*!" Yet Kelly backed off sheepishly, insisting, "That's not me, that's my mother."

"She just talked herself out and said that it's all her mother's fault," an incredulous Christina would recall. "If people talk negatively about me behind my back, they should have the guts to tell me in person. But Kelly is just a little kid who needs attention."

Kelly's version of events, when questioned later, was somewhat different. Taunting her rival for speaking in "Ebonics" – her way of describing slang used by those from black backgrounds – she claimed, "She was like, 'Yo girl, artists for artists, yo, why you been talking shit?' I couldn't understand a word she was saying." While that was a claim one might more readily make of her father, Ozzy, who often struggled to string a sentence together, she continued, "She made out like she had started a fight with me to make herself look cool. She's like a fucking feather. I could pick her up and chuck her across the room. She's such a pussy." Delivering another backhanded insult, she added that the feud had begun solely because "we both like to be bitches".

Yet in Christina's eyes, not only did she "not have a problem with" Kelly but she hadn't provoked the dispute. "Personally I think she has a crush on me," she reasoned, "because she seems so obsessed with talking about me."

On the other hand, perhaps Kelly was jealous of Christina's career trajectory – she'd been discovered courtesy of a vocal talent and had risen because the public appreciated it, while Kelly had been born into a lifestyle of fame without earning it in her own right. Perhaps she felt threatened and mocking her was the only way of resolving the internal conflict.

Christina had the last word when, in conversation with a journalist, she made her fighting spirit all too clear. "There are girls that talk a lot of nonsense about me in the press, but when I get up in their faces they kind of back off," she observed, "which is a shame... I'd like to punch these girls! They're wannabes." Later, when the interviewer asked who in the world she would least like to see naked, she answered without hesitation: "Kelly Osbourne. I think I'd be a little frightened – wouldn't you?"

With that, the feud paled into insignificance and Christina's name soon became associated with 'Fighter' instead. Released on March 13, it became a number three hit in the UK and made the Top 20 on the US *Billboard* chart.

While the track was scaling the charts, Christina was already working on a follow-up release to show the world yet again that she wouldn't suffer fools gladly. This time she'd set her sights a little higher than Kelly Osbourne, focusing instead on all of mankind.

'Can't Hold Us Down', which hit music channels over the summer, aimed to expose double standards in society. "I don't think we would get such great artists as Madonna if they weren't brave enough to come out of what society wanted to see [but] everybody who does that gets bashed!" Christina stated. "I'm trying to set a new standard of thinking, open up people's minds of certain double standards... like how a guy can speak his mind and tell his crew what to do and he's praised for it. It's like, 'Oh, look, he's smart as a businessman. He's aggressive.' But if a girl is aggressive, she's called a bitch!"

She added, "Guys also get to be a lot more sexual in videos and nobody says anything, yet if a girl does it, she's labelled a slut. The best example of that is Ricky Martin's video where he's pouring hot wax down a naked girl and gyrating and the public says, 'It's sexy and he's hot.' In another video, he's basically having an orgy in a shower with guys and girls touching themselves and nobody says anything! But when a girl wears a short skirt, or if I'm in a video shaking my hips, it's jaw-dropping and 'Can you believe that?!'"

She blamed stereotypes depicting women as passive, gentle, eternal mother-figure types who ironed the shirts, doled out the cuddles and always turned the other cheek when angry. In her opinion, any woman that didn't adhere to that stereotype took people out of their comfort zone and saw them shift categories from "Madonna" to "whore".

In the song, Christina was joined by the ultimate straight-talker – Lil' Kim. When the pair teamed up, she had still been reaping the rewards of press attention for her 2000 album, *The Notorious K.I.M.* She too was categorised as a bitch, with her lyrics disapprovingly described as "gangsta porn rap".

Kim was a big hitter, having made the number one spot on *Billboard*'s R&B and Hip Hop chart, while the album's Top 5 position on its mainstream chart pointed to crossover appeal. In that sense, both artists were widening their audiences – while Kim was adding a pop hit to her collection, her rap verse gave Christina instant hip hop street cred. Kim was notoriously controversial and outspoken and her reputation added an edginess that was congruent with the song's theme.

Originally Eve had been pencilled in as the guest artist but, despite recording verses for the track, had been replaced at the last minute by Kim. An embarrassed Eve would later shrug it off, simply claiming that "people's visions change".

Indeed, Christina and Kim together would prove to be a dynamite combination. To add an extra later of frisson, David LaChapelle – the man behind 'Dirrty' – was directing. 'Beautiful' director Jonas Åkerlund would tell David that, as always, there'd be no need to play it safe where Christina was concerned. "Jonas said Christina is the new Johnny Lydon," David recounted, referring to the 'Anarchy In The U.K.' punk rocker of the Sex Pistols, "because she doesn't give a fuck. She does her own thing. There's not many people who don't have to ask their publicist if something's OK and it's fun working with people like that."

The video comprised a typical New York street scene, featuring Christina in a pale pink bustier and matching shorts and white knee-high socks, with her hair twisted into the tight black ringlets she'd rebelliously longed for since her career began. Onscreen, she angrily reacts to a man who objectifies her by squeezing her bottom and, as she confronts him, a crowd of supportive women join in, surrounding the offender. While he is chastised, he forms his own male army – until Lil' Kim arrives, ripping off her robe and launching into her rap verse. "It's a real female empowerment song, so the girls are getting theirs," David would comment. "Men objectify women all the time and it's no big deal, so this time the girl's doing it."

This was what separated Christina's brand of exhibitionism from that of the average boundary-breaking female pop singer. Both would attract derision from the public for allegedly lacking self-respect by bringing something as private as their scantily clad bodies into the public domain. Yet she was expressing a sexuality that already existed rather than wearing a fake one to gain fans and sell CDs. She was standing up for the rights of women to own their sexuality instead of stifling it or altering it to fall into line with repressive stereotypes. The song insisted that men and women should not have a different rule system.

The single was released on July 8, but – to Christina's horror – MTV heavily edited the video, censoring any scene that implied the objectification of men. To her, this seemed to prove her point about inequality. Her argument was that, in rap videos, the same attitudes prevailed all the time in reverse, but without anyone raising an eyebrow. Yet in spite of a fan-led petition calling for her rights of artistic expression to be upheld, MTV was resolute – the scenes would not be reinstated.

While the diluted video might have lacked the hard-hitting impact for which she'd hoped, there was a partial victory for Christina when she was invited to star in the MTV show *Fight For Your Rights: Busting The Double Standard*. A reaction to matters raised in 'Can't Hold Us Down', it would give women a voice about gender differences in sex and relationship issues.

The second half of the show gave men a platform for their side of the story, including why they might feel obliged to live up to the image of a perpetual player to gain credibility with the in crowd, but the first half – with Christina as the agony aunt – was all about the ladies.

Topics included virginity, teenage pregnancy, the Madonna–whore complex and, of course, overall sexism. "It's been taught to us from the beginning of time, with men trying to gain power by suppressing the woman and making her feel wrong about her sexuality and making up words that label women for being expressive of their sexuality," Christina argued. "You either take that and learn to live under that thumb, or you take that and learn to be on the same page as them and learn to change the game. One day I will do that – but this is the beginning."

She would also speak to survivors of domestic violence on the show – those whose partners had begged and pleaded with them to stay, promising to treat them better, only to revert to their old ways again soon afterwards. "I know how that goes," she would nod in recognition. "The abuser tells you they will change and then you feel bad for them so you stay."

That summer, Christina would also hit the road for a three month co-headlining tour with Britney Spears' ex, Justin Timberlake. It would promote both *Stripped* and Justin's debut solo album, *Justified*, across

America – and Britney would be seen in the audience in both Los Angeles and Justin's home town of Memphis. The decision to join forces would prove enormously successful and, combined with her solo tour, profits from Christina's 2003 performances would gross more than $115 million.

The LA concert would stand out for far more than Britney's presence – Dave Navarro would join Christina onstage during 'Fighter', while *Baywatch* babe Pamela Anderson would make an impromptu appearance as a stripper during 'Lady Marmalade', earning a kiss on the lips for her efforts from the star of the show.

As it turned out, this sapphic moment was just a dress rehearsal. Unless puckering up to Paris Hilton privately in the VIP section of a Hollywood nightclub counted, Christina's most high-profile lesbian kiss of all would be at the August 28 VMAs.

After originally threatening to take to the stage in a nun's habit, she opted to arrive at the ceremony in a less controversial bright pink Roberto Cavalli dress made from feathers. Within minutes, she'd changed into a white tutu for the most memorable moment of the show – a polygamous three-way marriage scene featuring Madonna as the groom and none other than Britney and Christina posing as her two wives. Dressed in a black suit and top hat, Madonna would emerge from a giant wedding cake to perform a medley of her hits 'Like A Virgin' and 'Hollywood', while her "wives" – wearing all-white outfits with matching patent knee-high boots – danced on either side of her. In an act that would have conservative Middle Americans shaking their fists in indignation, she then turned to each for an open-mouthed kiss.

The episode received nearly a quarter of a million viewer votes to become the official most outrageous moment in VMA history, even beating a kiss between Michael Jackson and Lisa Marie Presley in 1994 and, in 1992, an onstage act of self-harm by Nirvana's Kurt Cobain during 'Lithium', a song named after an antidepressant drug.

Needless to say, the kiss had got the public's attention, but had there been a reason, or was it mere meaningless titillation to massage the TV ratings figures? The concept was that Madonna, as the Queen of Pop, would pass her "mojo" on to the younger princesses who were next in line to the throne. Indeed, this was how she had explained her actions to her bemused daughter Lourdes, who'd agonised, "Mom, you know that people say you're gay?" "I'm the mommy pop star and she is the baby pop star," she would reply, "and I'm kissing her to pass on my energy onto her."

Of course, whether viewers found this prospect deeply erotic or about as appealing as a mother bird regurgitating food into the mouths of her young depended on who was watching. Either way, the theory might have seemed more plausible were it not for the fact that Madonna had openly expressed dislike for her young rivals just a few months earlier, claiming that both were bland and "homogenous". "I'm not saying these girls can't grow into something," she sniped condescendingly, "but I really don't know where we're going with the world."

From the beginning then, it had all the hallmarks of being staged purely for publicity. At that time, Britney's religious views were very much at odds with homosexuality – and, for that matter, even sex before marriage – while Madonna was a married woman with children. Even fellow celebrity JC Chasez was contemptuous, chuckling, "Everybody knows they're not lesbians, they're teasing the world. Girls are willing to do strange things to get our attention."

According to Christina, a reluctant Britney had to be prompted during rehearsals to even peck Madonna chastely on the lips. "She kept having to go, 'Britney, kiss me, kiss me!'" she recalled. She also insinuated that Britney was competitive and determined to overshadow her – despite insisting on a closed-mouth kiss for the show and maintaining that stance in rehearsals, Christina claimed that she unexpectedly switched to a more explicit, open-mouthed version for the actual performance.

Yet she needn't have worried – Christina's kiss went almost unnoticed by then, as the camera had switched to Justin Timberlake in the audience. Jaw clenched with tension, he managed a terse smile, but it was evident that, as a traditional man raised on Southern values in a Tennessee farming community, the sight of his ex-girlfriend's public display with another woman had unsettled him. Yet for Christina, it was an injustice that he'd even been televised at that time. "They didn't even screen my kiss properly," she'd raged. "How predictable – let's see

brightly coloured as a hi-visibility jacket, Christina poses by New York's Brooklyn Bridge in show-stopping neon yellow and
ck chaps, a look she first gave birth to in her video 'Dirrty'. REX FEATURES.

A raven-haired Christina poses with BMG Chairman Clive Davis at the 2002 Grammy after party.
GEORGE PIMENTEL/WIREIMAGE FOR SONY BMG MUSIC ENTERTAINMENT

Christina steps out for Halloween 2006 with her then husband Jordan Bratman. The pair—Christina posing as a pink-haired gothic bride and Jordan as an eyeliner smeared devil—partied at New York's Marquee nightclub. MAT SZWAJKOS/GETTY IMAGES

ristina lovingly cradles baby Max in the American flag, serenading him with a lullaby version of the anthem 'America The Beautiful'.
e ad campaign, for Rock The Vote, would encourage US citizens to lose their apathy and make a vote at election time.

Christina screams in triumph to celebrate her Best Female Pop Vocal Performance award at the 2004 Grammys for 'Beautiful'.
SGRANITZ/WIREIMAGE

Yet again a winner of the Best Female Pop Vocal Performance category—this time for 'Ain't No Other Man' in 2006.
CHRIS POLK/FILMMAGIC

Christina launches her tuberose-scented fragrance Inspire at New York's Macy's store in 2008. STEPHEN LOVEKIN/GETTY IMAGES

Showcasing a look that might have drawn suggestions she and Lady Gaga were separated at birth, Christina and her glam-rock era eyeliner step out at the 2008 MTV Video Music Awards in
KEVIN WINTER/GETTY IMAGES

istina strikes a pose live onstage during her 2007 Back To Basics tour in a sailor outfit. The theme matched a photo on her album ...e which saw her pose in the arms of a group of Swedish Navy sailors. KEVIN MAZUR/WIREIMAGE

Christina and Jordan Bratman enjoy a rare moment of relaxation, casually checking their phones from their courtside seats at the 201
NBA basketball finals, where the Boston Celtics would challenge the LA Lakers. RONALD MARTINEZ/GETTY IMAGES

Showing off a theatrical all-black outfit, Christina arrives at the
2010 MTV Movie Awards in Universal City California.
JON KOPALOFF/FILMMAGIC

A family moment: Christina poses delightedly with her mothe
half-brother at an induction ceremony to celebrate her own sta
the Hollywood Walk of Fame. STEVE GRANITZ/WIREIMAGE

ristina gets up, close and personal with a female dancer during a burlesque style routine onstage at the 2010 American Music Awards .A. CHRISTOPHER POLK/AMA2010/GETTY IMAGES FOR DCP

in a magenta halter-neck dress, Christina poses alongside fellow actresses Cam Gigandet, Kirstin Bell and Cher, plus director n Antin, as she attends the 2010 premiere of her debut film *Burlesque*. ODD ANDERSEN/AFP/GETTY IMAGES

Christina belts out the National Anthem live at the Bridgestone Superbowl Show in 2011. KEVIN MAZUR/WIREIMAGE

the ex-boyfriend's response. Pathetic! They just cut straight to Justin's reaction and it's like, 'God, there's a performance going on!' I mean, it's like, 'Hi, MTV – music television that doesn't even play videos!' It's not like Justin was going to give them [the satisfaction of] a reaction anyway. It's just bad that the one outlet we have to get a visual for our music has to become a tabloid."

To some, the lesbian routine in itself had reduced the performance to tabloid fodder – but, quick to counter such accusations, Christina insisted that it was a symbolic passing-of-the-torch gesture, and all in the name of art. She didn't, however, feel the same about Pink's subsequent kiss with actress Kristanna Loken – an act which she dismissed as jumping on the bandwagon. "I'm sure Pink and this girl did whatever they did on camera," she retorted, "and I'm sure that was the inspiration for it."

In stark contrast, Christina claimed she'd taken part in her own kiss in a bid to rebel against the media's efforts to split up the sisterhood and turn female pop stars against each other. Raising a middle finger to fabricated rivalries, she wanted to put on a defiant united front against the negativity – a sentiment which was apparently shared by Madonna. "She was like, 'The whole reason behind me trying to bring everyone together is that there's so much backstabbing and so many rivalry-driven rumours in the tabloids and it would be empowering to see all these females'," Christina recalled.

Unfortunately, it had the opposite effect – both she and Britney would fall into the trap and within weeks, they'd be involved in one of the year's biggest music industry feuds. One of the things Christina had been the most disillusioned about was that many of her fellow performers had lip-synched. "I'm trying to bring back the art in artist," she would rage. "It's sad because, with technology, art has become so easy to manufacture – you don't even have to sing any more. The VMAs were so, so vanilla. So safe, so predictable. No edge. Apart from Madonna, Mary J. Blige and myself, I cannot think of another female performer who had her mic switched on. That is very disappointing to me. I agreed to do it in the first place only because Madonna told me that it was mandatory to sing live."

As her frustration rose, Christina started naming names, directly implicating Britney. "Who knows what happened exactly? She was *supposed* to sing live," she revealed. "These people aren't artists, they're just performers – fake and superficial, like the entire event."

Christina – who'd won a brooch pinned to her dress at the VMAs after party, proclaiming "I fucked Britney Spears" – was also displeased that her former friend had refused to kiss her. The original programme had called for a mouth-to-mouth ménage a trois, but only one of them had been keen. "Actually I was up for kissing Britney," Christina would reflect, "but Britney wasn't. She seemed very distant, even during rehearsals. Every time I tried to start a conversation with her – well, let's just say she seemed nervous the whole time. I wanted to reach out to her, because I feel she needs somebody in her life right now to help guide her... we did used to be friends, after all. She seems to me like a lost little girl, someone who desperately needs guidance."

To Britney's fans, this would have seemed like a backhanded insult – a stab in the back shrouded in sisterly concern. The final part of Christina's rant, then, would confirm their suspicions. "Who knows, maybe I'm not the right person to give it," she continued. "We're different people, aren't we? In our world there are different types of entertainers. You have your artists and you have your regular performers. I'm an artist and, well... "

She didn't need to elaborate on where she placed Britney. To make matters worse, she had also been infuriated by a comment she'd made implying that kissing a woman was debauched. "I think I'm still clean living," Britney had simpered afterwards, when asked if her tryst with Madonna would tarnish her original image.

Christina responded in the Swedish newspaper *Aftonbladet* by calling her a hypocrite. "[These girls] like to show off their sexual side in videos, but when asked about it in interviews, all of a sudden they're all virgins! How can you do that and call yourself an artist?" she challenged.

Yet her most widely publicised war cry of all was in the American magazine *Blender*. "Look at people like Beyoncé or Britney," she would sneer. "They're desperate to come across as sweet, good little girls, but then you see them in photo-shoots that are extremely sexual – tight little booty shorts and not much else. So why do they try to be virginal in interviews? Like, 'Oh gosh, I haven't kissed a boy in I don't know how long!' Come on girls, stop contradicting yourselves! If you want to do those magazine covers and those videos then fine, more power to you, but don't revert to innocence afterwards. I will not hide behind anything, ever. I'm a sexually strong female and I'm proud to be one... if being a slag means being a strong woman, I'll gladly be that." Finally, she would add that "Britney's kiss was a publicity stunt. Mine definitely wasn't rehearsed that way."

This was the moment that the formerly fictitious feud between Britney and Christina erupted into a real one. Christina had challenged her rival's artistry and singing abilities, accused the devout Britney of being dishonest and, most inflammatory of all, had publicly demoted her to the status of a performing monkey. These were insults Britney would find it hard to ignore.

On learning that Christina regarded her as a "lost little girl" in need of guidance, her cool, calm and carefully controlled media front dissolved in an instant. "That's funny," she spat, "because I haven't seen her in two years and then she comes up to me in a club in front of all these people... I say, 'It's good to see you' and she goes, 'Well, you're not being real with me.' I was like, 'Well, Christina, what's your definition of being real?' Going up to girls and kissing them after you haven't seen them for two years?' A lost girl? I think it's probably the other way round." After a few seconds of contemplation, she added, "When somebody's been rude to you so many times, it's like, 'You know what, Christina? I'm really not about the fake shit any more. You're scary and I feel really dark when I get around you, so I need to be over here now."

While the feud was symbolic of everything Christina had tried to avoid, she stood by her original sentiments – she didn't approve of the person Britney had become. Behind the technological wizardry, the Auto-Tune, the disconnected microphones and the airbrushed imagery, could Britney really sing? Who was she behind the increasingly blurry media mirage?

As a reaction to recent events, Christina wanted her fifth and final single from *Stripped* to be one that would clearly and unmistakably set her apart from the likes of Britney. She'd initially been desperate to release 'Impossible' as she felt it would build a presence for her in the urban market, with Alicia Keys providing the credibility. Undoubtedly, it might have unlocked doors for her among urbanites and soul sisters who might previously have dismissed her as a mainstream pop artist without giving the album a second glance. It was a boundary-shattering, genre-defying chance to unleash her deep, velvety voiced Etta James impressions on an unsuspecting public – but ultimately it was not to be. After consultation with her label, Christina would opt for an October 26 release of 'The Voice Within', which would prove to be an apt choice. Both lyrically and visually, the single would be all about exposing her inner self and keeping it real.

She had all the ingredients to make it a success. Producer Glen Ballard was better known for his work with rock artists, having co-written and produced Alanis Morissette's multiple-Grammy Award winning album *Jagged Little Pill* and also worked with Van Halen, Aerosmith and even Katy Perry during her pre-fame rock phase. He also had diversity, as he'd been equally successful on Michael Jackson's albums *Bad* and *Thriller*.

All the song now required was a director to bring it to life – and the tried and tested David LaChapelle would fill those shoes. His aim was to reduce the final single from *Stripped* to a video of raw talent, without any outrageous outfits or controversial subtexts to distract the viewer.

While videos such as 'Dirrty' and 'Can't Hold Us Down' saw Christina take on every guise from porn star to feminist politician, 'The Voice Within' was about exclusively that – the voice. "I wanted to strip it down to one take," LaChapelle would explain. "Just her and this incredible voice and really not have anything that is going to overshadow that. She's trying to grow as an artist and along the way she's taking all kinds of risks and a lot of times people let those things overshadow her ability and her talent. I wanted to bring it all back."

By now, Christina had become so inextricably linked with the notorious image of 'Dirrty' that she was almost the word's dictionary definition. 'Dirrty' Mark Two would have been about as shocking as a grey sky on a Siberian winter's day, whereas, at this stage, a video *without* all the conspicuous sex appeal would likely be more shocking to the public than full frontal nudity. That was what LaChapelle and Christina's mutual vision embodied: erasing stereotypes. "Christina's explored a lot of parts of herself, her sexuality and this is a part of her too," LaChapelle would argue. "People say to me [about my photography], 'You're the colour guy'. Well, I spent six years only shooting black and white. People don't understand you can be an artist and do different types of things. Don't let other people's labels make you feel you're stuck in a box. It's not about living up to limitations people put on you."

Consequently, there was an unexpected simplicity to the video: shot in a deserted, bleak Los Angeles movie theatre, it portrayed just Christina – without the gimmicks, shock value, overwrought sexuality or technical trickery. LaChapelle had been inspired by scenes in Vittorio de Sica's film *Two Women*, which had featured actress Sophia Loren running barefoot across the country, so Christina wore nothing on her feet.

As Christina's tousled black hair and slightly smudged smoky eyes first come into view, the imagery is so intimate that the tiniest, subtlest imperfections in her skin are crystal clear. While LaChapelle had captured her beauty, it was nonetheless a variety so raw and intentionally natural that he felt few of her contemporaries could dare to embrace it, let alone pull it off. "It's not about showing a particular side of her face – she's not neurotic like that," he would explain. "She [just] wants interesting imagery… there's not a lot of artists who could do that sort of video."

In fact, surveying the barren, almost dilapidated movie theatre, he admitted to having some trepidation at first about whether he'd made a terrible mistake – until the cameras started rolling. The scenes portrayed a disarming vulnerability, while she acted out every extreme of emotion brought forth by the song. From furious anger and defiance to the blissful euphoria of liberation, she would throw her head back, tug her hair urgently in her hands and then break into grins so broad she seemed to be laughing. Her knee-length silk dress was positively demure in comparison with previous outfits, but there was also a tease about even that – was it daywear or silky lingerie? The video gave the impression of being a fly on the wall in Christina's bedroom pre-fame, while she enacts her dreams, with all the innocence, hope, electricity and exuberance of a young woman's first audition.

While Christina had previously celebrated the glamorous, fearless, avant-garde and at times taboo side of herself to deliberate excess, 'The Voice Within' stripped her bare beyond all possible doubt. Her self-revelation had come full circle – and it was a fitting end to the promotion of *Stripped*.

It wasn't, however, the end of her contractual obligations – for coming up was a hosting slot to present the Europe Music Awards on November 6. Former host Ronan Keating warned ominously that the stress of the show had given him an ulcer, which was hardly the best advertisement for the role – but Christina was nonplussed.

Living up to the promise she'd reneged upon at the VMAs, she opened the show dressed in a nun's habit. She'd then go on to honour the show's Edinburgh location that year by performing 'Beautiful' with the 40-strong National Youth Choir of Scotland. She also took the opportunity to acquaint the audience with her mischievous sense of humour, participating in a skit that saw her throwing darts at a board bearing Kelly Osbourne's picture.

Kelly's subsequent enraged reaction would see organisers threaten to ban her. "If Christina Aguilera has to resort to throwing darts at my head after everything she's achieved and everything she's done," she would challenge, "then she's a really sad, sorry person and I take it as a complete compliment."

While Kelly would face a stern talking to backstage, that was nothing compared to her offstage remarks during interview. "Everyone I know and have met hates Christina," she announced, more than a little dramatically. "It's fair to say she's been horrible her whole life. If Christina offered me a white flag, I'd kick her in the face. I couldn't even be in the same room as her."

Although it was safe to say there wouldn't be a reconciliation between Christina and Kelly anytime soon, Christina did feel differently about patching it up with Britney Spears. "I wrote to her saying, 'There's no need for this. We did have a friendship once. Let's not get caught up in the tabloids and have this craziness forced upon us,'" she later recalled.

"I went on to tell her that I have great admiration for her work and to hang in there."

After failing to receive a response, she would even make a public shout-out on national radio pleading her rival's forgiveness. Portraying them both as victims of overzealous media tactics, she claimed she could understand Britney's retaliation because the press had been deliberately "pitting us against each other".

"This business can make anybody a little… caught in a whirlwind and caught up in the wrong things. So just, you know, get back to basics, Britney," she continued, little knowing then that she was quoting one of her future album titles. "[My letter to her] was very personal and it was about the fact that, being two female artists in this industry, we've got to be there for each other… but I have yet to hear back from Miss Brit. So if you hear this, I'd like an answer!"

Although Britney would maintain an icy silence for the time being, she would have seen her former friend's presenting slot at the EMAs, which she also attended. She might also have found amusement as Christina's demand for a line-up of men in kilts to abandon their modesty and lift their outfits up, so that she could decide who would accompany her to the after-party. While it raised a laugh from the audience, the light-hearted banter disguised a deeper meaning – she had been parodying the objectification of women she'd challenged in 'Can't Hold Us Down' by doing the same in reverse. Plus, while MTV might have been disappointed by the edgier scenes in that music video, the piece of banter had slid easily past the censors.

Christina didn't win a trophy that night – but there was one award that she was even more disappointed not to have received. "I was actually disappointed that I didn't make this year's Worst Dressed List in *People* magazine," she claimed, "because those are the people that go out there and make a statement. It's so boring looking at the best-dressed people. Who can't put on an expensive gown and hire the right people to make them look presentable and safe?" In Christina's eyes, it took an edgier and altogether more devoted fashionista to risk public condemnation in order to be themselves. Instead of soaking up the praise courtesy of a conservative, classic choice made by a playing-it-safe stylist, she was willing to take risks and had grown to see the ridicule as a compliment.

While, to her displeasure, 'Worst Dressed' wasn't in her collection of accolades that year, 2003 did bring two Women of the Year awards courtesy of *Latina* and *Blender*, a Sexiest Woman of the Year award from *Maxim*, a Best Video Award for 'Dirrty' at the MOBOs, a Best Female trophy at the VMAs and Female Artist of the Year at the *Billboard* Awards. *Stripped* would also make the Top 10 of *Billboard*'s year-end album chart, while, overall, Christina was the top artist of 2003.

That was just the start for the album, which would go on to sell over 10 million copies worldwide. Yet instead of wallowing in self-indulgent triumph and popping open the Cristal champagne, Christina was spending the run-up to Christmas volunteering at a domestic violence shelter.

The Women's Center & Shelter of Greater Pittsburgh, of which her mother was a board member, had suffered crippling funding cuts that year and faced closure. By the time Christina stepped in with a big cash injection, 14 staff members had already been made redundant.

"Shelters are so important," she would reaffirm as she wrapped children's Christmas gifts in the shelter's modest playroom. "I've seen that in my life first hand and I always thought that if I was ever in a position to make a difference, I wanted to do something to help... for me, this is just the beginning."

Indeed, a link Christina added to her website would go on to receive an average of 194 referrals per month – from people who might never have sought help had it not been for her endorsement reminding them they had choices and that freedom wasn't as far away as they thought.

Her experiences at the shelter had been of women like herself but with one vital difference – they were desperately low in self-esteem. Their confidence and self-respect eroded by beatings, they hadn't felt they deserved a better life. Some had been chronically abused from the day they were born and had gone straight from a violent childhood home into a violent marital home. By then, submission was a deep-rooted learned behaviour and they saw no way to break the cycle. Yet maybe some sought escapism in Christina's albums just as she had found refuge in the *Sound Of Music* soundtrack. This was a woman they respected more than they respected themselves – and maybe it would take the intervention of an idolised public figure to rebuild their fractured self-worth. If there was the chance of rescuing even one child from the trauma of a broken home – let alone 200 a month – then, to Christina, the most important accolade of the year had already been won.

CHAPTER 8

Aguilera 3.0

Working with domestic violence victims had put fame into perspective for Christina. Whilst promoting *Stripped*, she had thrown herself wholeheartedly into a VIP lifestyle, with parties and paparazzi the central focus of her spare time, but as she grew up, she increasingly felt that unless she could use her position for social change, fame was ultimately shallow and meaningless. Now that the world was listening, she wanted to say something worthy.

Consequently by February 2004, she'd teamed up with cosmetics company MAC for another good cause – an AIDS awareness campaign. The diversity of the campaign – which featured Swedish supermodel Linda Evangelista, American actress Chloë Sevigny, homosexual British singer Boy George, black American rapper Missy Elliott and, of course, Christina – aimed to eliminate clichés and stereotypes about the typical AIDS sufferer and to illustrate that it could strike anyone – "all ages, all races and all sexes".

Indeed, the figures spoke for themselves: in 2003, five million new HIV infections were recorded, almost half of which were contracted by under-25s. It was a shockingly young age for so many to learn they were carriers of a life-changing – and ultimately lethal – condition.

Christina wanted to broadcast that, while the image she had created in her videos was one of defiant promiscuity, in reality she wasn't taking any chances when it came to her health. Saying so broke another important stereotype: that those who enjoyed casual sex were unclean. "There's nothing wrong with expressing your sexuality, being comfortable with your sexuality, or sex in general," she asserted. "It's just a matter of being sure you protect yourself... you have to respect yourself and your body. You have to take control over your own destiny [and] if you don't take action, the future you have planned will be at risk."

As part of the campaign, MAC had pledged to donate all of the proceeds from sales of its Viva Glam V lipstick to AIDS research and education. It was for this reason that Christina urged prospective purchasers to "never feel guilty about being beautiful".

The same month, on February 8, she won a Grammy – a Best Female Pop Vocal Performance Award to honour the release of 'Beautiful'. Yet Christina dressed down to receive the accolade. She rehearsed in jeans and a denim jacket, her hair swept casually back with a bandana, and, on the night of the show, she took to the stage in a suit jacket and black pinstripe trousers. The new image was miles away from that of the woman Linda Perry had claimed, even in the privacy of the recording studio, was opposed to clothes.

Within weeks, Christina's hair had followed suit, becoming a muted shade of caramel. This prompted headlines suggesting she'd toned down her image such as "From Dirty to Demure" and "From Crass to Class". On the contrary, some of the biggest moments in her style evolution were yet to come – but, as the publicity for *Stripped* died down, she was focusing on campaigning and, in an image-driven world, the look she'd adopted would help persuade others to take her more seriously.

On April 25, she would join the largest protest in US history – the March for Women's Lives. Over 1.15 million women in Washington, D.C. were taking a stand against a controversial 2003 law called the Partial Birth Abortion Ban Act, one which they argued would limit their reproductive freedom. The act prohibited anyone from partially delivering a foetus – for example, the head – before deliberately performing an act to end its life. According to Congress, the practice was "a gruesome and inhumane procedure that is never medically necessary", while medical evidence suggested that it could also actively endanger a woman's life.

Furthermore, some might argue that a woman finding herself pregnant but not ready to become a mother would have had ample opportunity to abort her baby more humanely in the early stages of her pregnancy. For instance, there is widespread medical consensus that foetuses cannot experience pain or awareness of their own consciousness until five to six months into pregnancy, whereas excruciating pain can be perceived thereafter.

While subsequent 2012 Republican candidate Mitt Romney's abortion ideals were far more stringent, advocating termination only in the case of incest, rape or risk to the mother's life, the comparatively moderate 2003 law merely prevented a woman from ending pregnancy during delivery — a dilemma that was unlikely to arise with a little forward planning.

What was more, the USA already boasted some of the world's most liberal abortion laws; less than a third of countries allow abortion purely because the mother requests it, while Britain forbids abortion after six months unless there are exceptional circumstances, allowing earlier termination only once two doctors have consented in writing. In Denmark, abortions must take place in the first three weeks while, for religious reasons, Ireland bans the practice altogether.

In contrast, many states in the USA routinely carry out late-term abortion by the injection of lethal drugs into the foetal heart. In adult humans, this type of punishment would be reserved for mass murderers and a select few hardened criminals — what had an unborn foetus done to deserve such a brutal fate?

Nonetheless, Christina — and the many other women involved in the march — rejected the Partial Birth Abortion Ban Act. To complicate matters, Christina had a Mormon background, and the religion's belief was that life begins at conception. Thus ending life at any time at all subsequent to the meeting of sperm and egg would, in the eyes of the church, constitute murder.

Yet pro-abortionists delivered an equally emotive argument at the march, believing that the laws reinforced gender inequality and female oppression. While a man could walk away from fatherhood and all its attendant responsibilities, women now lacked a legal right to control over their own bodies. To these protestors, their reproductive freedom was more important than the rights of an undeveloped foetus.

However, those carrying out partial birth abortions could face a two-year prison term, effectively withdrawing the liberties to which late-term abortion advocates were accustomed. The march was ultimately unsuccessful as the law was upheld but, in Christina's eyes, it was important to stay abreast of political developments and stand up to issues that were important to her.

In fact, she publicly condemned Jennifer Lopez for not doing so, criticising, "I just read this article where they asked her, 'So what are your views on the war?' and she said, 'Oh, I don't really think about that kind of stuff, I leave it up to him' – and she points to [her then fiancé Ben Affleck]. I understand if you say 'I'd rather keep my opinions to myself', but to admit you don't have any opinion about what's going on in your country or the world? I was just like, wow. So what, I'm just here to look pretty and entertain? It's just deeper than that for me."

Christina was on the warpath a second time in quick succession when she discovered a song she'd been involved in writing, 'Miss Independent' – which described how her relationship with Jorge Santos had transformed her from an intentionally hard-hearted ice queen hellbent on keeping her heart "protected" to a girl who'd dropped her guard and fallen hopelessly head over heels in love – was no longer hers.

American Idol winner Kelly Clarkson would later recall, "I had to argue with the record label to the point of literally crying to get 'Miss Independent' on my album." However, perhaps there was a reason for her label's reticence – the song had already been recorded by Christina.

According to her mother, "She wrote many songs and you can only fit so many on a CD. Some had to be chosen and others she decided to save for later. 'Miss Independent' was one of those to be saved." The producer who worked with her on the song subsequently offered it to Kelly who added some lyrics and made a success of it.

Christina was surprised that the song had been used but publicly congratulated Kelly for "doing the song justice". However one accusation that left her on the brink of legal action was speculation that arose that a summer tour she'd planned across America with R&B star Chingy had been cancelled due to poor ticket sales. Her official reason was vocal strain, but Britney Spears fanned the flames of uncertainty when she retorted cattily in one interview, "How exactly do you get vocal strain?"

Had Christina chosen to respond in kind, she might have informed her that it was an ailment caused by singing, rather than miming, and was therefore one she understandably knew little about.

The tension would build yet again between the pair when Christina took over Britney's role advertising Skechers footwear. The singer's three-year partnership with the company, which had seen her create her own Britney-branded line of roller-skates, had ended in acrimony when she'd filed a $1.5 million lawsuit for breach of contract. Claiming that the use of her image had increased sales by 50%, she argued that in return the company had reneged on certain contractual obligations, such as payment of bonuses, and had depicted her in adverts before her line was available, robbing her of potential royalties as fans inevitably flocked to the brand's other designs instead.

Skechers, on the other hand, claimed it had already warned Britney of its plans to sue, causing her to "jump the gun to try to deflect her liability". If this had been the case, her strategy had been a cunning one: she'd filed her suit over Christmas, when no one from Skechers was available for comment to the media.

The company eventually conceded that Britney's adverts had appeared ahead of her line of skates, but insisted that the responsibility lay with her for failing to approve the designs on time, potentially costing the company tens of millions of dollars in lost revenue. The dispute was settled out of court in May 2004 and within days, Christina had been formally recruited.

The timing gave rise to taunts that Christina was a poor man's Britney, the last resort for a firm that couldn't secure its first choice. She had battled with such comparisons since the beginning of her career, but now the statistics were rising in number. After Britney landed a deal with a soft drinks firm, its rival recruited Christina. Later in 2004, Nelly would offer her a part on his track 'Tilt Your Head Back' after an unsuccessful attempt to get Britney on board. Yet again, with Skechers, she appeared to be second best – an alternative to turn to when its negotiation with its number one choice had failed. Yet, undeterred, Christina would simply declare that her collaboration with the brand would be much "edgier" – and she was right.

The link between Skechers and Christina initially seemed a tenuous one, as she was more likely to be seen in six-inch stilettos than trainers, but she managed to put her own stamp on the brand nonetheless. She would take part in three role-play photo shoots, each of which portrayed both a "naughty" and a "nice" version of herself in the same picture.

The first was a slightly predictable schoolgirl cliché a la Britney in '...Baby One More Time', where she'd posed at her desk in a tartan uniform, deferring to her stern teacher alter ego, who menacingly brandished a board pointer that looked as though it might double as a spanking implement. Referring to the incongruent bright purple trainers she wore, on the board were the words "Skechers are not part of the uniform."

In a slightly racier image, Christina, dressed in a PVC police outfit, reprimanded her evil twin as she bent over a car waiting to be handcuffed and arrested.

However, it was the third photo shoot that attracted the most attention and controversy. It depicted Christina as a nurse, but not the kind one might find in one's local hospital – in her white knee-high boots, stockings, PVC nurse's uniform with a figure-accentuating belt at the waist and cap with a red cross, she wouldn't have looked out of place as part of a sex shop fantasy image.

Of course, this titillating imagery wasn't much appreciated by America's bona fide nursing community and those who saw her brandish a syringe at a cowering patient version of herself – clad of course, in pink Skechers trainers – complained in their thousands. Claiming that her syringe was suggestively disguised as a vibrator, they criticised her "mini dress that fails to conceal much of her breasts, her red heart-patterned white bra, her near fully visible garter belt which runs down to her white stockings and white dominatrix boots… not exactly what we had in mind to attract bright young students to nursing".

In addition to over 3,000 complaints, the American Family Association wrote a sternly worded formal letter blaming the adverts for perpetuating a global nursing shortage and insisting that they portrayed the profession as one "all about sexual servitude/pleasure/pain instead of education and hard work".

"Evidently someone has a reason to think that auto-erotic and/or sadomasochistic lesbian role-playing fantasies with a touch of petty rebellion sell consumer products," the organisation raged. "Perhaps you are not aware that we are in the midst of a global nursing shortage of previously unseen proportions… depicting North America's three million registered nurses as female sex objects suggests that nursing work consists primarily of satisfying the sexual needs of physicians and/or patients… This advert simultaneously exploits the 'naughty nurse' and the battleaxe/Nurse Ratched stereotypes, setting the nurse up as both an available sex object and a mock-malevolent authority figure rather than a competent professional. I urge you to end Skechers' use of the advert."

Of course the casual observer might argue that the long hours, arduous work and status as one of the country's most poorly paid professions all seemed more meaningful reasons for the nursing crisis than one over-sexualised role-play advert. Yet the letter held Christina indirectly responsible for staff shortages.

As ludicrous as the accusations might have seemed, however, Skechers instantly issued a grovelling apology, withdrew the advert and prepared for déjà vu. Yet the episode highlighted one clear difference between Britney and her livelier rival – wherever the latter went, controversy was sure to follow.

Meanwhile, as the drama unfolded, Christina was trying out new avenues of entertainment for size. Performing at the DSquared2 menswear show in Milan, clad in a leather mini-dress with fringing at the top and bottom, she developed a taste for fashion. "It's so much fun to be on this side of the spectrum and dabble my foot in the fashion world," she would enthuse. "It's such a live, fun energy, there's nothing like it."

Already an avid collector of vintage fetish wear from the twenties, thirties and forties, she was tempted by the experience to consider her own line of lingerie. Although she was, for the most part, resting her vocal cords and planning her next move while in hibernation from the entertainment world, her mind was still racing and her entrepreneurial spirit still alive. She had even been thinking of purchasing a restaurant in New York's SoHo district based on the traditional British food to which she'd been introduced on visits to the UK and branding the eatery Little London.

During her downtime, she also read a movie script for *Valley Of The Dolls*, a drama about a group of girls caught up in a showbiz world of high octane glamour and drug addiction. However, ultimately she wouldn't pursue the part. Her friend Donatella Versace, for whom she had modelled, had recently entered rehab for cocaine dependency, attracting a wealth of negative press. While many of Christina's acquaintances she'd in the industry had been users, she wasn't fond of it herself. Yet her mere friendship with Donatella, combined with the movie industry's reputation for being nose-candy heavy, had implicated Christina by association. If she took on the role of an addict on screen, would viewers be able to distinguish between fantasy and reality? Her first film role had to be as flattering as it was challenging – she didn't want, in the eyes of the public, to be demoted to just another drug-addled showbiz star.

For that reason, the closest she came to acting that year was starring in a Virgin Mobile advert. Mogul Richard Branson pulled out all the stops, inviting her to his private Caribbean island, Necker, to sign the contract. In the advert itself, Christina was virtually unrecognisable, boasting unusually muted make-up and sophisticated golden brown curls cascading above her shoulders.

Despite looking the picture of innocence, however, her "dirrty" background was still proving to be a tease. When two construction workers peep through an office window to catch a glimpse of Christina bouncing up and down, with only her face and upper body visible, they automatically assume they've caught her in a public sex session. After excitedly photographing the evidence, they call the media – on Virgin Mobile, of course – and the gossip spirals out of control. Journalists, paparazzi and curious passers-by form a crowd outside, ready to break the showbiz story of the century. Headlines scream "Christina Is Exposed!" but, all along, she has just been innocently bouncing on an adjustable office chair. As the screen switches back to the mischievous and undeniably smug construction workers cracking jokes, the advert concludes with the caption "The devil makes work for idle thumbs."

The advert would be the first public outing of Christina's new look. Yet at the MTV VMAs in Miami, held on August 29, the transformation was even more dramatic. Gone were the long blonde hair extensions that some classed as "trashy", while the borderline indecent, extra-minuscule mini-skirts were nowhere to be seen. Instead Christina was channelling Marilyn Monroe, even down to emulating a tiny, barely perceptible facial mole. Everything from her youthfully plump, cherubic cheeks and her pillar-box-red lipstick to her short, platinum blonde curls screamed Marilyn – in fact, the 'Christina' tattoo peeping through on the back of her neck was almost the only discernible difference between the two. A glittery silver chandelier dress completed the picture – she was a veritable china doll from a bygone era.

With her new look, she'd cracked a near impossible code: finding the key to being sexy but simultaneously elegant. The look was glamorous without needing to be overly revealing, tantalising but far from tawdry – and it portrayed the type of elegance that was arguably elusive to the average modern woman.

As Christina opened her segment, the sound of the piano filled Miami's ears – but the biggest surprise was yet to come when rapper/hip hopper Nelly took to the stage. Better known for his raps about double Ds, platinum credit cards and naked orgies, he was all about portraying the seductive and highly marketable image of a wealthy gangsta – and Christina was no one's moll. Yet, as audiences watched agape, the pair debuted their jazzy, horn-heavy duet, 'Tilt Your Head Back'.

Nelly was about the most unlikely musical partner Christina could ever have recruited – especially when she was in full-on Marilyn mode. Plus the song itself, which sampled Curtis Mayfield's 'Superfly', took both artists into unchartered territory. That the partnership was a counter-intuitive one was not lost on the public – and for some of Nelly's fans, accustomed to more of an urban flavour, it was a hybrid monster. The differences between the two were accentuated still further with the single's release on September 15.

The burlesque style party depicted in the accompanying video, resplendent with carnival style head-dresses and abundant vintage glamour, might have delighted Christina's female fans, but it wasn't the average rap devotee's typical scene. Rap fans often prided themselves on a resolutely macho image, at the centre of which was money, power and women, and the video for 'Tilt Your Head Back' was clearly in opposition to that. Of course, Christina added sex appeal, but rappers were more likely to feature scantily clad glamour model types in their videos, making borderline pornographic pelvic thrusts while leering at the camera, and Christina's current more refined image, as sexy as it was, might well have seemed tame in comparison. Then there was the undeniably effeminate fifties-style Hollywood glamour, complete with feather boas and top hats – it wouldn't be hard to imagine macho men shaking their heads in a mixture of puzzlement and horror.

Meanwhile, Nelly's gold teeth and modern urban image simply didn't translate easily into the overall scene – he seemed to be something of an anomaly. Ultimately the song's reception was a major disappointment for him – while his previous single, 'My Place', had been a number one hit in the UK and a Top Five hit in the USA, 'Tilt Your Head Back' had scraped a measly number 58 peak position Stateside and hadn't reached number one anywhere in the world. It also underperformed in comparison with Christina's previous single, 'The Voice Within'.

While the unusual pairing and risky change in musical direction was certainly a factor in the song's commercial failure, there was more to the picture than met the eye. Nelly's label had allegedly become concerned that Christina – who'd merely been performing a guest slot on his song – had overshadowed the star. Thanks to her makeover, it was Christina's name on everyone's lips, and while it was an official release from Nelly's album, *Sweat*, the public seemed more interested in knowing whether it would feature on Christina's next CD.

Reluctant to plunder valuable time and resources into promoting a song that was more about a rival artist, Nelly's label began to switch its attention to 'Over And Over', a duet for his *Suit* album, with Tim McGraw. While a collaboration with a country star was equally off-the-wall for Nelly, especially when his co-star was fervently religious, this was a track that the label felt could turn his bad fortune around. They were right; the subsequent airplay of 'Over And Over' would begin to detract attention from 'Tilt Your Head Back'.

However, by that time Christina was rocking the charts with yet another new single – on October 18, her collaboration with Missy Elliott, 'Car Wash', was released. The classic disco track had already been covered several times before, but on this occasion it would promote the children's blockbuster movie *Shark Tale*, a kitsch affair featuring the adventures of animated sea life. The simple video combined footage of Christina and Missy recording in the studio with scenes from the film that portrayed the pair as fish.

While 'Car Wash' would also fail to make its mark on the *Billboard* chart's Top 50, it was more successful than 'Tilt Your Head Back' overall – with more than 1.5 million copies sold worldwide, it would earn more than triple the profits of its predecessor.

Yet the real topic on everyone's lips was still Christina's style – not only had the Marilyn Monroe curls and bright red lips now become a permanent fixture of her look, but she had removed – with the exception of a solitary nipple ring – every single piercing. What had prompted such a titanic transformation?

All the signs pointed to her new relationship with music business manager Jordan Bratman. Although Christina had point-blank denied she was anything but single, there reached a point when she could no longer deny her relationship status. There'd been public displays of affection at an LA Lakers match, a romantic trip to India during the lead-up to Christmas and myriad public sightings in between.

Perhaps there was a good reason she had been able to keep the romance a secret for so long – she and Jordan were like chalk and cheese.

Shy, unassuming and a little socially awkward, he met the criteria for the archetypal nerd. He wasn't an obvious heart-throb either. Yet, as Christina would tell the media, she didn't go for looks. "I don't care about the six-pack," she would dismiss. "I don't care about a chiselled body. I like being able to have a damn good conversation. I'm into mind stimulation. I can stimulate myself in other ways."

The implication was clear – if superficial appearances were all that she needed, she could masturbate to a picture in a magazine. When it came to real life, she needed someone who had more to offer than his body to make a relationship worth pursuing. As she would witheringly remark, most celebrities she met were decidedly lacking in that department: "I just haven't met too many Hollywood pretty boys that I've been intellectually impressed with, or just impressed with, period," she confessed. "I find them to be very immature too, very stuck on themselves. I like a down-to-earth guy. That's why I usually go for a non-celebrity."

Jordan was that person – a former head of A&R for DARP Music in Atlanta and a soundtrack consultant for Universal Pictures, he'd first met Christina back in 2002 in his role as manager to multi-millionaire producer Dallas Austin. Dallas had made his fortune working with artists as diverse as Michael Jackson, Madonna, Pink and TLC, and he'd hired Jordan to take care of his diary and liaise with artists and record labels on his behalf. By definition, this was the down-to-earth, unassuming, ordinary man of her dreams. Yet at that time Christina had been younger, more reckless and less romantic, and was still wrestling with the contradictory nesting urges that crept up on her from time to time. Having written herself off as an independent woman and "not the marriage type", she'd enjoyed dating Dallas himself and several of her other friends. Someone who'd written a track called 'Miss Independent' didn't look as though she would change her tune anytime soon and so, although there was undeniably a spark between them, at the outset, they had little more than friendship.

Over time this evolved to a full-blown romance. "It completely took me by surprise," Christina would later confess, "because I wasn't looking for a relationship. I didn't say, 'Gee, I need to be happy, let me find a companion!' I've always been super-focused on my career. But when it happens, it happens, right? Jordy and I would hang out and he just had this positive energy. He would be my pick-me-up on down days. From the moment I met him, I gravitated towards his realness and sincerity. Over time I completely fell head over heels in love [and] I knew I didn't want to spend my life without him."

As their bond deepened, Christina – who would later reveal, in a blow to Jorge Santos, that she'd never had a "heartfelt" relationship with anyone before Jordan – became increasingly protective over it. In her experience, she felt that media involvement tended to sour romances, either by twisting stories out of all proportion or by being more attentive than the couple could cope with. She also felt it placed an unwelcome pressure on a couple to endure a continual running commentary in the early stages of a relationship, especially when she hadn't defined it fully in her own mind yet.

According to one friend, the constant reports in the press of "sightings" of herself and Jordan "made her feel like an animal". "The papers made it sound like a wildlife safari," Christina's friend explained to the author, "observing the mating habits of the lesser spotted whatever creature. She didn't want to be hunted down like an animal. She saw the relationship as like being pregnant. She was protecting and nurturing it in private until it was strong enough to survive on its own and was ready to come out and meet the world."

She'd also needed time to be absolutely certain that Jordan really was the one – not just another pretender in a long line of failed romances, doomed to fade out before they'd truly begun. She'd certainly had enough disappointments and setbacks in her love life to know it was possible to make mistakes.

Eventually, however, he would pass the test. "Before Jordy, I don't think I've ever encountered what a real man is," she would later explain. "Most men that I've known in my life – and growing up with an abusive father, trying to find a father figure in sketchy guys – tended to [be] just dogs. That's what I thought men were. He's the first guy that treated me like I feel a woman should be treated… he can get me out of my own box, my own depression. He's my angel. He saves me in so many ways."

That was the key, perhaps, to her sudden image overhaul. She'd been notoriously vague about her chameleon-like tendencies, merely saying, "As an artist, my look is forever changing." Yet she credited Jordan with lifting her out of the very depression of which her piercings were a central symptom. Each one had been symbolic of a dark moment in her life – when she'd turned to the sting of the needle for solace, claiming, "There's a comfort to me in pain." There'd been misogyny and bullying by fellow celebrities, disappointments with men, let-downs by supposedly loving long-term friends and scrutiny from the media, who'd held her every action under the microscope. There'd also been the trauma of reuniting with her father, only to lose him all over again within months. Her mother, Shelly, would recall, "He's writing me five page letters telling me that we are, and I quote, 'filled with evil hatred that God cannot love'… that we can't have the love of God in us because he says there is too much evil hatred. Well I, for one, don't hate. I'm scarred. I have post-traumatic stress disorder as a result, but I'm doing just fine."

Yet while both she and Christina would repeatedly insist they were "OK", in reality both were anything but. Christina's uncle Johann Aguilera would rub fresh salt in her wounds when he called the *National Enquirer* to deny every word she'd sung in 'I'm OK'. "Christina is a liar!" he would exclaim. "She's been brainwashed by her mother… it's lies, it's made up and it's getting worse the more she works on it. My brother could not do anything like that – who could?… It's a cruel, vicious fairy-tale!"

But meeting Jordan had closed the door on that period of her life. She was no longer the wounded, fragile, emotionally damaged and self-destructive young girl striking out in anger against anyone and anything – especially the nearest target, herself. Like Barbie-doll wallpaper in an adult's bedroom, the piercings were reminiscent of an era that was no longer relevant – in fact, one that she would rather forget. It was time to peel off the old wallpaper from her body and soul too, and start afresh.

Press reports suggested that she'd removed the piercings out of respect to Jordan, who thought they were trashy, but the idea of a woman as fiercely self sufficient as Christina changing herself to please a partner seemed preposterous. In fact, as she would later clarify, one of the reasons she'd been drawn to him was precisely because he embraced her image without disapproving or feeling intimidated – something she believed the majority of men would not have been secure enough to do. Historically she'd always been insistent on controlling her own universe and "not changing my world to appease anyone", even if her life in the spotlight left someone insecure. It was just as well then that, whether it was piercings, leather chaps or grinding with her team of predominantly heterosexual dancers, Jordan had no hang-ups and no jealousies. "He's so secure within himself that he would never, ever even be concerned with that," she explained. "He's right behind me, supporting every provocative outfit, every pelvic thrust. Sometimes he'll even say to me, 'Why are you covering up? You're sexy, show it off!'"

Thus Christina's new look was not the result of toning things down to please her boyfriend, but merely a symbol of an internal shift within herself. She was hasty to correct anyone who believed she might not be "still dirrty" – rather, she was now rebelling not against the world, but against her former self.

There was a serenity about Christina now that she could never have projected the year before, even if she'd been acting – and she was expressing on the outside exactly what she felt within. When she got engaged, she removed her very last remaining piercing.

It took place at Big Sur, California on February 11, 2005, where the couple had ensconced themselves in an ultra-private hotel suite for a Valentine's Day break. Jordan had allegedly been so excited about popping the question that he hadn't even been able to wait until February 14.

"It was unbelievable," an emotional Christina would recall of the proposal. "Every cute thing he did, I totally thought was just a Valentine's Day surprise – he got me! He sent me on a scavenger hunt. My mom used to do scavenger hunts for me when I was a kid, so it had sentimental value. Each clue was a poem – and in the final clue he proposed!"

From that moment, Christina was deliriously happy – it was as though nothing else mattered. However, there were a couple of hiccups around that time. For example, she had been invited to host the 2005 MTV Asia Awards in Bangkok the same month but had had to pull out. Following the tsunamis that had swept through the continent, it was being rebranded as a charity show, and the media implied without foundation that her withdrawal from the event was linked to the announcement that, as a benefit concert, it would be unpaid.

While Christina managed to keep a dignified silence about exactly why she hadn't been able to take part, the following month provided yet another embarrassment. Despite claiming the previous year that she'd like to found a lingerie brand, Christina allegedly told the *Daily Star* vociferously that she scorned any celebrity contemplating a clothing line. "I just think it's so tacky," she was reported to have said. "I have always thought that it's one of those things that makes people look like they don't know what to do any more."

Yet her comments elicited some gasps at UK company Basic Box, which claimed she had signed a contract for a seven-figure sum to launch a clothing line. "We had genuinely believed since coming to this licence arrangement with Christina at the end of last year that we were going to be able to put out an extremely successful range of clothing and accessories under her name," its official statement read. "We had understood that she was completely behind the project so, not surprisingly, her comments came as something of a shock. Basic Box has already invested considerable sums in the project and in the light of her comments, we had no choice but to terminate the agreement immediately."

The company then instructed lawyers to recover funds already invested in the now necessarily defunct project. Settlement was never disclosed, while Christina never made a public statement to clarify what had happened. To the general public, it might have seemed quite a comical crossing of wires, but unusually for her, Christina's mindset was focused on anything but work.

By April, she'd arranged a meeting in Santa Monica for both her and Jordan's respective families. At dinner, Jordan had even carried her over the threshold of the restaurant. As the wedding plans intensified, Christina withdrew more and more from the public eye, with just one track being released that year – 'A Song For You', which was a duet with the musician Herbie Hancock.

Herbie was well known as a jazz artist with a career dating back to the sixties, when he was part of Miles Davis' Second Great Quintet. The song, which would appear on his 2005 album *Possibilities*, referenced an enduring love affair. The subject matter was meaningful to Christina in her current situation and, according to Herbie, that made for a near faultless vocal. "Wow!" he would later recall. "I knew she could really sing, but I didn't know she could sing like *that*. She knocked me out. She did her first take and I said, 'Well, you nailed it' and she said, 'Oh no, no, no, that was just a scratch vocal.' I said, '*What*? That sounds like a keeper to me!' Her intonation was so perfect – I mean, not a flaw in it at all."

After that release, Christina withdrew completely to focus on planning her wedding day. On October 28, she and her fiancé had a joint bachelor-bachelorette party at the Las Vegas Hard Rock Hotel and Casino. Of course Christina wouldn't have been Christina if such a momentous event didn't have a trace of "dirrty" about it and, true to form, she arrived in a nurse's uniform, while Jordan dressed as a doctor. In fact, as Christina would later reveal tongue-in-cheek, those were the same fantasy outfits that they had previously donned in the bedroom. "I like to play doctor," she would explain. "I got Jordan a doctor's outfit with a doctor's bag full of sex toys. I wore the naughty nurse's costume, of course!"

The pair also prepared for the nuptials by getting tattoos for each other. Christina's, on her lower back, read "I am my beloved's and my beloved is mine", written in Hebrew in acknowledgement of Jordan's Jewish faith. Meanwhile Jordan's simply read "I love CA" and took pride of place on his arm.

The big day would come three weeks later, on November 19. Invitations in silk-lined boxes would go out to over 130 guests, including Justin Timberlake, Drew Barrymore, Cameron Diaz and Sharon Stone. Each emphasised a charitable mindset, asking guests to gift them with nothing more than a donation to a good cause. They read, "While we celebrate the richness of life and all the circumstances that have blessed us in career and love, we are mindful of those who are suffering greatly as a result of hurricanes Katrina and Rita. The best gift you could give us is a donation to any of the organisations helping the stricken citizens of New Orleans."

However, not everyone was feeling quite so charitable – in fact, one entrepreneurially minded guest had tried to sell her invitation to a member of the media. While Christina had been disgusted, to her, this type of exploitation had become an inevitable and inextricable part of fame. On the upside, it did weed out the fair-weather friends.

As a reaction, she and Jordan teamed up with a lawyer to write less-than-romantic three-page legal disclaimers to be signed by each guest – a necessity to protect their privacy in the face of unscrupulous ticket touts. Their apologetic opening line read, "We are sorry to have to ask you, our dear friends and honoured guests, to sign this agreement, but we feel it is the only way to ensure the security of our wedding."

The silver lining was her reinforced trust in Jordan, who she felt was interested in neither fame nor money. Yet one had to wonder what he might make of her slightly patronising public references to him that arguably depicted him as a faithful but rather simple family dog. "He's not trying to be on the cover of magazines," she would praise. "He's not trying to make a record. He's just good old Jordy."

Jordan's comparative lack of ambition had made him less competitive – an advantage in Christina's eyes, as it enabled him to devote more time and energy to being supportive of his wife. It was almost the role of the traditional forties housewife in reverse.

"Christina was totally in control of that relationship," clarified one friend of Jordan's from his days as a DARP employee. "She had him wrapped around her littler finger. He would follow her like a puppy, praising her, and she lapped it up. He almost saw her as a mother figure. Jordan comes from a Jewish family, where mothers are celebrated and often revered as the powerful figureheads of the household. Christina was that person to him in many ways – someone to look up to."

With all of this to commend him, Christina believed she'd found the perfect man – but it was a bittersweet wedding, tinged with sadness, because it reminded her with sickening force how much she lacked an opposite sex parental figure of her own. It was her father who should have walked her down the aisle, but his wedding invitation remained unsent. For the first time in her life, she realised that, instead of sharing this joyous occasion with the man who tradition dictated should give her away to her husband, she was totally alone. "When it came time to walk down the aisle, I was shaking," she recalled later, "and I realised how amazing it would've felt to have a man holding my arm to give me away to this next man in my life. That was the first time I felt or maybe even needed a father figure." However, she decided to resist her toxic cravings for paternal affection. "He never made an effort to be there," she reasoned, "so why now? I've gotten through life thus far."

It might have been difficult to break the ice, in any case, with a man whose last communication with her had been a letter declaring her "full of evil hatred". Perhaps that could have been overcome if they'd had a loving history together before, but his involvement in her life had been patchy at best. Her only consolation was the conviction that she'd found the right person to father her future daughter and that, when her big day came, she'd have no such dilemma to sour the event.

On the day of her wedding, set in California's scenic Napa Valley, a petrified Christina realised that no performance she'd ever put on would prepare her for the nerves associated with matrimony. A self-confessed perfectionist who'd condemned Britney's wedding the previous year – a low-key affair at a friend's LA house – as "pathetic" and "low rent", she was determined to get her own special day just right.

To Jordan's astonishment, she wore a long, flowing, exceptionally traditional white gown by Christian Lacroix – and the only thing that was unconventional about it was the price. Being accustomed to Christina's tendency for gleeful and deliberate fashion faux pas, he'd been expecting something outlandish.

Clearly ahead of her time, she paired the Spanish-style dress with Louboutin heels before the brand name had even become cool. Unlike Britney's self-bought wedding ring, which Christina had allegedly jeered resembled a cheap piece of junk from the QVC Shopping Channel, she wore a five-carat diamond ring custom-designed by Stephen Webster of London. Even the bridesmaids' dresses were designed specially by Stevie Wonder's wife, Kai Milla, boasting pink silk, chiffon and organza details.

Jordan's outfit was equally impressive – a crisp Christian Dior tuxedo – and a 14-piece orchestra from the San Francisco Symphony serenaded the party as he walked down the aisle. Then a choir broke into 'Morning Hymn' from *The Sound Of Music*, which had special significance to Christina as it symbolised the dual themes of rebellion and liberation. In the movie, Maria flees the convent where she is training to become a nun and surrenders to her desires to explore the tempting freedoms of the outside world. The performance of 'Morning Hymn' coincided with Maria's first escape and the song had a similar meaning for Christina, regaling her with memories of her own escapism; when things got tough at home, she had, of course, drowned out the shouting by turning up the soundtrack and losing herself in its melody. Maria's escape reminded her of her own life, marking her diversion from a standard prescribed path to follow her dreams. As she and Jordan exchanged vows, she would become that thrilled child surveying a new world, one of endlessly tall mountain peaks, and believing that the only limit to scaling them was her imagination.

Blinking back tears, Christina went on to share a bit of banter with her new family during her speech. "I have the most beautifully inappropriate father-in-law," she would chuckle. "We're on the same wavelength. I said, 'I want to thank Jordy's mom and dad for getting together' and he shouted, 'Donating sperm!' I was like, 'Well, I wasn't going to be that graphic.' For a wedding toast, it was very funny."

The proceedings ended with the traditional Jewish ceremonial gesture of "breaking the glass". The groom smashes a glass underfoot to honour the *Talmud*'s statement that "joining two people in marriage is as difficult as splitting the sea". Although it is an age-old tradition, accounts of the true meaning of the gesture vary. Some see it as a reminder of the fragility of a relationship, indicating how easily it can be crushed. It is also seen as an omen that life will bring its share of sadness as well as joy, a sentiment with which Christina was already well-acquainted.

With that, the guests headed to a nearby tent which wedding planners had transformed into a birch tree-filled winter wonderland. The food included a selection of mashed potatoes, macaroni and cheese, crispy chicken wings and onion rings.

After the guests tucked in, Christina and Jordan shared the first dance of the evening to the thirties jazz standard 'In A Sentimental Mood'. Originally written by legendary composer Duke Ellington and later covered by Ella Fitzgerald, it was one of Christina's favourites. The lyrics, thanking a lover for being the flame that lit the gloom, were almost personalised and symbolic of how Jordan had lifted her out of depression and become an uplifting light in her life. Rose petals are also referenced in the song, something which had surrounded the room the day that Jordan proposed. Aside from the obvious links, Ella Fitzgerald was also one of Christina's best-loved performers – known as "The First Lady of Song" and "The Queen of Jazz", she hailed from the same era as Etta James and was just as much an idol to Christina.

The occasion then called upon a reluctant Christina to perform herself. "Because I'm a music person, the thought of hiring a corny wedding band terrified me," she admitted, "so I asked a band that tours with me to play at my wedding. My producer, Linda Perry, got up and sang 'Beautiful' and I ran up on stage to give her a hug and my band immediately went into 'Lady Marmalade' and people starting cheering me on. I was like, 'OK…'"

A stunned Christina was forced to simply go with the flow – and before the end of the night, she took to the stage a second time to perform the Etta James classic 'At Last'. A jubilant refrain detailing the relief of having finally found the person she'd sought all her life, she dedicated it to her husband. "I was so not into the idea of singing at my own wedding," she would re-emphasise. "But when the energy's right, sometimes that's the best audience." She added, "Part of my tour set is doing 'At Last' and I thought, now is the most perfect time, now I have a substantial reason to sing it – so I dedicated it to Jordy!"

That ended the formalities, leaving the revellers free to retreat to an after-party in an underground wine cave. It honoured the Napa Valley region's reputation for beautiful vineyards and for being one of the USA's premier locations for wine production. With walls of plush red velvet, it had been transformed into a makeshift disco, where Mandy

Moore's partner, DJ AM, spun discs until 5.00a.m. That signalled a breakfast of waffles and, soon after, a retreat to the Auberge du Soleil resort for their first night as a married couple.

The following week they spent their honeymoon at Bali's Four Seasons Resort, Jimbaran Bay, in Indonesia, and she would enjoy a fleetingly short holiday before getting back to the grindstone.

★★★

In March 2006, Christina got back in touch with her Hispanic roots with the release of her track 'Somos Novios (It's Impossible)', a duet with Andrea Bocelli for his album *Amore*. A classical Italian tenor whose crossover appeal had netted him over 80 million album sales worldwide, he wanted to follow in the footsteps of artists such as Elvis Presley before him and record Armando Manzanero's 1970 Mexican bolero – this time, with a girl whose Latin roots meant the world to her, one who would authentically live and breathe the emotion of the song.

Christina now had two priorities: recording her third studio album and her commitment to keeping the romance alive with her new husband. Admittedly it was new territory for her; a couple of years earlier, anyone who'd suggested she'd soon be married would have been laughed out of town. "If you'd asked me on the last album if I thought I'd be married by the next album," she claimed, "I'd have been like, '*NO*! Are you kidding?!'"

Acknowledging that her dress was nothing like the outfits she wore onstage, she promised, "We want to renew our vows every five years, so next time I'll do it a little more rock 'n' roll. My husband was surprised at my dress, he thought I'd choose some crazy colour!"

Perversely, Christina had probably realised the best way to stand out and shock at her wedding was to break her usual mould by not standing out at all. Yet while her dress was staunchly traditional the first time around, she was determined that in married life, she wouldn't fall prey to the same clichés.

In *South Park*, during an episode where promise rings (rings worn as a vow of the wearer's chastity) are discussed, one of the bewildered young characters queries, "I thought that was called a wedding ring?" Yet Christina bypassed every stereotype about settling into a boring, sexless routine as a married couple. She and Jordan would read erotica together. "I love water eroticas," she would tell one interviewer with disarming candour. "Waterproof books full of erotic stories if you will. You can literally get the book wet."

She would also reveal that songs by Radiohead were her ultimate aphrodisiac and that every Sunday she had free was designated Naked Sunday. Even when cooking a roast, clothes were forbidden – a concept that was a little lost on Jordan's mother-in-law. "She's a New Yorker, very Jewish mom, and she's like, 'So do you really have these days where you just lie in bed cosy and you're naked?'" she chuckled. "Jordy's like, 'Yeah, sure, it's great' and she's like, 'Don't you get chilly?'"

Yet it was also their mental connection that Christina cherished. It wasn't lost on her that she seemed to have "broken the pattern" of marrying an abuser after witnessing abuse in her parents' home – and although she admitted balking slightly at the thought of having just one sexual partner for the rest of her life, she was in it for the long haul.

"It's an interesting concept to be dedicated to one person for the rest of your life," she'd mused. "I'm really intrigued by it. I mean, I could only do this with someone I wholeheartedly love and adore and respect and cherish. Not to sound clichéd, but I think there is something to be said for growing with someone. Younger, hotter boys? I can pass those up. I'm good. I've had my fun."

CHAPTER 9

Back In The Day

"I have no interest in working with the Neptunes!" declared Christina, dismissing in a single sentence one of the most ubiquitous production duos in musical history.

Comprising behind-the-scenes producer Chad Hugo and his more gregarious partner Pharrell Williams, who also rapped on his own tunes, the Neptunes were prolific chart-toppers, scoring hits for the likes of No Doubt, Gwen Stefani, Justin Timberlake, Jay-Z, Nelly, Britney and Beyoncé. Producers like these provided a safety net for record labels, as their distinctive beats almost guaranteed a hit. For example, when the duo turned their hands to 'I'm A Slave 4 U', it became the only one of Britney's singles that year to make the Top Five in the USA.

Having already taken risks by investing large sums in an artist's career, labels weren't about to take even more chances on the material; for most, tried and tested names were best. Yet to Christina, distinctive equalled predictable. After all, Pharrell's own song, 'Frontin'' – both written and produced by the Neptunes and featuring himself, together with Jay-Z, as singer and rapper – was very similar in sound to Kelis' 'Good Stuff' or Jay-Z's 'I Just Wanna Love You (Give It To Me)'. Meanwhile Gwen Stefani's 'Hollaback Girl' – an irritatingly catchy anthem that had recently made number one in the USA – was spreading through radio playlists like wildfire.

Everything the Neptunes worked on boasted an instantly recognisable trademark sound – and it was one that Christina was becoming increasingly tired of hearing. "A lot of what's on the radio sounds the same because everyone is using the same producers!" she criticised. "Music is suffering because nobody wants to step out on a limb and go for something different. Everyone wants to stay in their safety box!"

For her own comeback single, she was determined not to become a carbon copy of every other pop artist but instead to be a trendsetter and build her own iconic sound. To do so, she raided her vintage record collection for inspiration, nostalgically replaying everything from Marvin Gaye and Etta James to Aretha Franklin and Esther Williams. She hit upon a combination of a jazzy old-school sound paired with a modern, uptempo twist – and to achieve it, she turned to DJ Premier, a producer so obscure that even he was shocked to receive her call. "I was surprised because of our differences in the audiences we hit," he would recall later, "but I'm always up for challenges."

Premier had been working with predominantly rap artists, many of whom were unknown to the mainstream, since 1990, occasionally stepping outside his comfort zone to collaborate with soul singers such as Alicia Keys – but never anyone as high profile as Christina.

Her label bosses were petrified about the implications of his inexperience with pop artists, but Christina didn't care. She had been enthused by the sound of Gang Starr, a witty nineties hip hop duo comprising Guru and DJ Premier himself, and had set about exploring the rest of his back catalogue, too. "I figured out he used tiny snippets of 'I Put A Spell On You' to make Biggie's 'Kick In The Door'," she marvelled. "A lot of people wouldn't get that. It's genius... he searches through his vinyl, finds the obscure pieces and reinvents the old."

It was exactly that type of musical time travel that Christina had in mind and, within seconds of hearing the beat he'd devised for 'Ain't No Other Man', she was infatuated. He'd sampled two sixties tunes: a Latin soul number by Dave Cortez & the Moon People called 'Hippy, Skippy, Moon Strut (Opus #1)' and Soul Seven's 'The Cissy's Thang', before putting his own hip hop-style stamp on it. "I walked in and I was like, 'Oh my God, that's my first single!'" Christina recalled. "I hadn't written to it yet, but I was in love. It was high-energy and I could just imagine what dancers could do to it."

In fact, in the months to come, she would dance herself sore, later recalling that every muscle in her body ached from memorising the demanding choreography. At 130 beats per minute, it was much faster than the average pop track – and, for that matter, anything DJ Premier had ever worked on – but Christina was resolute that it would become a hit. "When we played it for the label," Premier recalled, "they didn't think that's the way she should start the project, but she was like, 'I don't care. This is the one.' That's why I love her, because she doesn't give a damn what anyone else thinks."

She was equally hands-on when it came to making the video, channelling a vintage singer about to perform at an archetypal smoky jazz-era bar in her home town. Her alter ego was Baby Jane, a pseudonym that appeared on her sheet music, her car licence plate and even her dressing room door. She claimed to feel an affinity with the character, whose nickname she carried in real life.

At first glance, there wasn't much evidence to link Christina with the film to which she was referring, *What Ever Happened To Baby Jane?* The 1962 movie was an ode to the twisted, destructive nature of celebrity, the sorely inevitable tendency for every shooting star to crash and burn. Bette Davis and Joan Crawford play Jane and Blanche Hudson respectively, sisters and stars of the vaudeville world. In their youth, Jane is the brightest star, even boasting a Baby Jane doll in her name. She becomes the archetypal daddy's girl, spoilt and doted on by her stage father, who treats her like a veritable princess. However, as the years pass, the tables turn and it is Blanche who becomes the stronger actress, fuelling an intense jealousy from the sister left behind. Then an accident, blurred by alcohol-related amnesia, results in the end of Blanche's career after she is left paralysed by a shattered spine. Flashing back to the incident, Jane fears that she caused her sister's injuries out of spite. Yet even when Blanche is helpless and handicapped, her resentment fails to recede and she slowly descends into psychosis, first killing her much-loved pet parakeet and serving it up for lunch and then following it up with a dead rat. She intercepts her mail, screens her phone calls and, little by little, isolates an increasingly lonely Blanche from contact with the outside world.

In desperation, Blanche flings a note from her bedroom window, begging for help, but it is found only by Jane, who mocks and ridicules her bid for escape. The twist in the tale comes when Blanche confesses that it was her who deliberately sought to injure or kill Jane, accidentally paralysing herself instead.

A cautionary tale about how stardom and sibling rivalry eroded the morals of the innocent sisters, turning them into seething and potentially murderous balls of jealousy, it made for unsettling viewing. Quite what Christina might have had in common with Jane remained a question mark, as, when probed by the media, she remained coy about the connection.

More transparent, however, was the plot of her own video. It depicted Christina reuniting with a man when she tours her hometown, but then automatically pushing him away. This was part of the chronology of her relationship with Jordan, too, and it corresponded with the lyrics about a lover who could talk her down from every ledge. Battling major trust issues, she'd been in a bad place when she'd first met him, enforcing isolation and loneliness on herself rather than risking vulnerability again. However, her lover had broken down every self-protective barrier and coaxed her down from her ivory tower.

As Christina was intent on personalising her songs and using each as a snapshot of that era in her life, it seemed fitting for her comeback single to serve as a tribute to the man who'd made her trust again. "I did just get married," she chuckled, "so ain't no other man but my husband!"

When the track was released on June 3, 2006, in spite of her label's misgivings, it became one of the biggest soundtracks of the summer. Worldwide, it would sell almost five million copies and one reviewer would review incredulously, "'Ain't No Other Man' is so urgently amped, it makes poor Beyoncé and Amerie seem like shy types who spend the hottest days of the year doing crosswords at the kitchen table." Mission accomplished!

Christina's comeback would soon see her switch allegiances by parting ways with Coca Cola and following in Britney's footsteps to sign a reported £2 million deal with Pepsi. The resulting ad was instant advertising, seeing her image beamed around the world – and, with the help of mobile phone technology, she virtually visited a few of those locations, too. She was depicted belly dancing in the Arabian desert, braving the cold in a Prague snow scene, channelling an Indian maharani in Delhi, dancing the samba as a carnival queen in Rio de Janeiro and finally indulging in her real-life "huge love" of Japan by dressing as a geisha girl. Most importantly, she was introducing the world to her new track, 'Here To Stay'.

A jazzier but no less feisty version of 'Fighter', Christina used the track to challenge those who criticised her look and attitude, asking whether they put her down to compensate for their own inadequacies. Like 'Still Dirrty', where she fiercely questioned whether her detractors reacted so strongly to her showing off skin because they simply weren't comfortable in their own, she vowed longevity no matter who objected.

Meanwhile, in honour of her rapidly emerging old–school sound, Christina got the chance to give voice to a longstanding obsession with Etta James. The pair met for a joint photo shoot with US fashion magazine *InStyle*. Christina's praise for Etta was clearly no token gesture to appease magazine bosses – 'At Last' had been a part of her live show for years. Plus, while Etta didn't realise it yet, she had been a direct influence for much of the new album. When Christina heard her admiration was reciprocated, it moved her to tears. "She has this fabulous little figure but a heavy, almost operatic voice," Etta had marvelled. "When I first saw her, I just couldn't believe that all that big sound, all that big voice was coming out of this little girl!" She added, "When I heard her say on TV, 'I grew up on Etta James', that made me feel so good. The last person who said that was Janis Joplin, but Christina can SING. Janis was good, but there's a difference in the quality of voice… tell me who you've seen that sings like [Christina] because there's nobody."

That was the praise the younger star had been looking for when she had sourced obscure samples and unconventional producers, yearning to stand out.

Turning to her directly, Etta would continue, "There's something about you that's like Dinah Washington, Billie Holiday, those kinds of chicks. I've never seen a girl sing as tough as you sing, as little as you are. It's like you're an old soul." With that, Christina would start sobbing, nuzzling her head into the shoulder her idol offered her.

Etta's affection was all the more prized because it was elusive – in fact, on the other notable occasion that a famous singer covered 'At Last', she would be belittled. Just three years later, Beyoncé would play Etta in the film *Cadillac Records* and would subsequently perform the track for US President Barack Obama to celebrate his inauguration, only to be ridiculed by the original performer. "I can't stand Beyoncé," she had spat. "She has no business up there, singing up there on a big ol' president day, singing my song that I've been singing forever." She added, in no uncertain terms, that if she had anything to do with it, Beyoncé would have her "ass whupped". She wasn't inclined to affect airs and graces and the fact that Beyoncé was a multi-platinum selling superstar meant nothing to her.

This might have made Etta seem like an intimidating, unapproachable diva – and Christina herself confessed that she was "a bundle of nerves" before meeting her. Yet that was a major part of why she loved Christina; she felt they both shared her unapologetically outspoken attitude. "Etta told me I was hot-headed," Christina swooned, "and you know what she said? 'Just like a girl after my own heart!'"

The top soul singers of Etta's era – typically black American women – all had strong personalities and, by their very demeanour, commanded respect. They hailed from a time when black women were downtrodden and mistreated in society and had perhaps developed their fearsome strength by necessity – as an over-compensatory survival instinct in a tough world. Yet in Etta's eyes, Christina had proved herself equally outspoken, with her crusades to wipe out double standards and her defiant promises to dress and act the way she wanted. This, in combination with her voice – something so comically incongruent with her slight stature – had allowed Christina to achieve the seemingly impossible and win Etta's favour. "I've always been a complainer too," Etta would elaborate. "She reminds me of myself when I was young."

And that was exactly who Christina aspired to be. "She's what I want to be someday," she would daydream, "sitting on a stool in some smoky jazz club, doing bluesy versions of my old hits like 'What A Girl Wants' with just a piano – I'll still be as raunchy as I wanna be and I'll have the memory of Etta James to back me up!"

She'd road-tested that tantalising image by premiering some new tracks to open-mouthed journalists at London's renowned jazz club Ronnie Scott's and following up for the public at a July 20 show at Camden's Club KOKO. Yet the biggest test of Christina's jazz credentials would of course be her new album, *Back To Basics*. Every showgirl or Marilyn Monroe-inspired hairdo sported since the wake of her 2004 duet with Nelly had been practice for that moment, when she would unveil herself as jazz-loving Baby Jane.

"[The past 18 months] was definitely a preparation for me," she would confess. "I wanted to really get into the mode and character of what those songs were conveying: the poppy, pin-up imagery... I wanted to put on my red lipstick and do up my blonde hair sometimes, just to get into that saucy mode or that old Hollywood glam kind of effect. I would surround myself also with old imagery of your Billie Holidays and your Pearl Baileys and people like that. I would have these tearsheets and pictures of even Louis Armstrong and Coltrane and Miles Davis and all these amazing jazz musicians. I just wanted to get into the heart and soul of the music, literally, and I guess the best way to describe it is what actors call method acting. It was kind of like my way of method singing in a way."

Yet there was one element of the music which Christina wouldn't need to act out – she already felt it. Far from being merely a catchy beat, jazz and blues was a language she understood. In fact, she was already fluent. Infused with pain and heartbreak voiced by the likes of drug-dependent Billie Holiday – who'd also been broken down by addiction to a violent, abusive partner – such drama gave music meaning and relatability. There was feeling in the voices of old soul legends that couldn't be faked and, having stored up years of her own emotional grief, it was something Christina ached to convey herself. Overall, her decision to move in a jazz direction hadn't been a difficult one. "I was like, 'What is it that really makes me want to sing? What is it that makes me want to dance? What makes me love and enjoy music?" she mused. "And it's really that old blues and soul and jazz music – music that really had heart. Not to say that music today doesn't have heart, but it's really few and far between, because technology has advanced itself so much that anybody can be a singer. Back in the day, you had to know how to sing."

It was a bold accusation to make, but she felt sure she could uphold it. *Back To Basics* was, in one sense, all about a rebellion against the manufactured machinery-driven faux perfection of modern music, in an era where Auto-Tune and deceptive special effects prevailed. However, in order to commit entirely to her convictions, Christina had to strip down the reverb and other effects she had formerly cherished. In spite of all that she'd said, that took some courage. However, who better to go to with that goal than Linda Perry? She had coaxed a reluctant Christina to find beauty in her imperfections and to believe that raw emotion was more meaningful than a polished virtuoso style, leading to her releasing 'Beautiful' with a first-attempt scratch vocal. She'd also coaxed out a part of her she hadn't known she was strong enough to share, when inner pain came spilling to the surface for 'I'm OK'. If anyone could bring out the best in her, it was Linda. "I would never be able to be as open with anyone else," she would explain. "It's recorded up close on the mic, with no ad libs, no nothing and that's so not like me," she added. "No effects, no reverb – and I'm a reverb queen. Every scratch, every little imperfection is there."

She also cut back on over-singing, focusing on the gentle emotion of 'Ain't No Other Man'. "I don't think I've ever been heard singing so quietly or so soft, but the emotion I wanted to convey was so vulnerable, honest and sincere," she reasoned. "It's the only song that's literally dedicated to my husband. It's thanking him for being the only person in my life that can really reach in there to take me out of whatever heavy space I might be in and let me realise all the beautiful and amazing things around me."

Every track she collaborated on with Linda was characterised by that stripped-down feel. "We just went from scratch," Christina enthused, "from ground up. There's no beat machines, no samples whatsoever. We just really went in there and recreated ourselves to get this old throwback sound. I'm most proud of things like 'I've Got Trouble', where we really used old vintage microphones and covered them up with old ratty cloths to get that muffled old crackly sound."

To authentically master that husky, bluesy drawl, as though Christina had smoked a few million cigarettes in her time, Linda also arranged for her to record the vocal when she had a bad cold. The track referenced vintage blues in the style of Bessie Smith and also gave a sly nod to classic tracks such as 'Kansas City', which, over time, was recorded by the likes of Little Richard and the Beatles.

Meanwhile 'Welcome' was a fitting introduction to Christina's work with Linda. With a touch of vaudeville, the track conjured up images of puppets, acrobats and dancehall stars. Its lyrics were infused with trickery, for example, were the references to painted faces and masks Christina's way of mocking the fake superficiality of the pop music industry, where nothing – from image to sound – was reliably real? Or, on the other hand, were her words merely a description of the vaudeville stage to which her track paid tribute?

Then there was the reference to being forced to smile when her heart wanted to frown; it could have been depicting the potentially self-destructive nature of showbiz. Yet on the other hand, was it simply a metaphor for the archetypal image in popular culture of the sad clown? The word "burlesque" originated from the Italian, meaning "to mock, joke or tease" – and it took on its true meaning here. It seemed Christina was using a circus theme to parody what she saw as a manic, chaotic, cut-throat showbiz world, where the aim was to get famous or die trying.

Meanwhile, to add to the song's diverse range of influences, its sound gave a nod and a wink to the Beatles' 'Magical Mystery Tour'. This was Linda's trademark – she'd previously spoken of her passion for the Beatles, drawing a comparison between 'Beautiful' and the work of the Fab Four.

'Enter The Circus' was another introduction to Linda and Christina's surrealist time-travel inspired world. The kitsch slice of fantasia began with the raucous trumpet of an elephant before a promise, delivered through a megaphone, that the viewer has walked into the most amazing show on earth. Visual evidence was barely necessary: the classic fairground vibe would inspire images of a carousel twirling in time to the music, while Christina danced decadently for the crowds.

The fantasy imagery would become even more apparent on 'Nasty Naughty Boy'. This track was an opportunity for Christina to live out her ultimate burlesque fantasies, evoking the atmosphere of an upmarket twenties striptease revue. Up until that moment, Britney had been considered America's premier entertainer, with stunts such as carrying a snake wrapped around her shoulders, while Christina had held the contrasting reputation of a serious singer. Yet this track – especially when subsequently performed live – would allow her to show the world she could wear both hats. The breathy voice and sexy showgirl lyrics had been inspired by the likes of Mae West and, when she brought her burlesque persona to life – even though she'd been alone in the studio – she'd vamped it up with an obligatory layer of heavy red lipstick.

The momentum would build further with the energetic, uptempo, jazzy circus performer sounds of 'Candyman'. "When we were recording, I was laughing!" Linda recalled. "It's swing music with a hip hop beat... people are going to go, 'What the fuck IS this? It's awesome." She added, "Christina's not a player, but she can really explain herself musically."

Of course, it wouldn't have been a session with Linda, the self-confessed queen of melancholy, who'd once argued that she enjoyed being sad, if it hadn't had a touch of darkness about it. When the trumpets faded and the pace slowed, it was time to step out from behind painted faces, strip off the glitter and reveal the murky underworld of Christina's tortured heart. In spite of a deceptively uplifting jazzy sound, the lyrics of 'Mercy On Me' spelled out the story of a women begging forgiveness for her sins and asking God to have mercy on her soul.

Then there was 'Hurt', which came about when Christina realised she had never written a song capturing the agony of losing someone close. The lyrics portrayed a bereaved woman's regret for walking away from someone and holding a grudge so long that it was now too late to repair. With its references to forgiving someone's mistakes and its apology for blaming the lost loved one, could the track depict Christina struggling to make sense of losing her father? While he hadn't physically died, his absence was a metaphorical death – and no less painful.

While 'Hurt' was ambiguous, however, 'The Right Man' was indisputably about Fausto. Her wedding day had given rise to thoughts she'd never had before. For example, years of tradition dictated that a girl's father should give her away to the next man in her life who was committed to loving and caring for her. Yet for Christina, marrying Jordan had been her moment of realisation. "It was a turning point in my life," she admitted. "I went through my whole life not really ever caring or wanting a father figure, but when the time came around and everybody started asking, 'Who's going to walk you down the aisle?', it saddened me that I didn't really have a good answer." She'd reasoned, however, that if she could perform to tens of thousands of people, then a short walk towards her husband would be child's play in comparison. She was mistaken. "It was emotionally overwhelming. I was shaking and thinking how amazing it would be to have that man that resembled this protector in your life, this man with those 'Don't hurt my little girl' kind of words and feeling the pain of never having that. I wanted to write about that because I thought, 'How many other women must feel this?'"

However, perhaps society placed undue pressure on couples to fall into step with an idealised norm – and Christina had never been one to blindly follow the pack. She'd stood out fearlessly when it came to other aspects of breaking the mould, so why pander now to an outdated tradition?

Months earlier, Christina had seen her personal trainer break every rule in the book when she'd married her girlfriend, in spite of disapproving parents. Taking her cues from the courage of the lesbian and gay community, many of whom didn't even have their families present at their big day due to the shadow of homophobia in their lives, she decided to embrace the absence of her father and focus instead purely on the love of her husband. 'The Right Man' spoke of leaving behind her past and allowing her future to mend the bad memories, but most of all it was dedicated to her future unborn daughter. Christina took comfort in the hope that when her child's wedding day came, she would be able to take Jordan's hand on the way down the aisle, safe in the knowledge that her mother had found the right man.

That marked the end of Christina's collaborations with Linda. The pair had been joined by the occasional co-writer in the studio – most notably Mark Ronson, who'd also worked with Amy Winehouse on *Back To Black* the same year – but for the most part, the flavour of the tracks was directed by Christina's synergy with Linda. Despite being an "extreme perfectionist" – apparently to the point of pulling out her own hair – Christina admitted, "On Linda's portion of the album, those were one-take songs where we took it all the way through... no matter what little crack of imperfection might come up."

For the rest of the album sessions, Christina would be working primarily with producers she had little to no experience with. Anxious that they wouldn't understand her vision, she sent a "producer's pack" out to her peers, featuring old-school sounds from Otis Redding, Billie Holiday and Nina Simone to James Brown, Eartha Kitt and Aretha Franklin, and asked all concerned to get their thinking caps on. "I compiled a two-disc CD, a compilation of 30 more soul-inspired songs that are throwbacks to more current-day, with a twist, all the kind of songs that have influenced me on some level in a soul, blues and jazz-driven way," she would elaborate. "I sent it out to producers that I thought might be able to get into this headspace with me because I didn't want another old sample that's totally recognisable and let's throw a beat over it. I wanted to get obscure pieces of music and get people who would really, really use their imaginations in reinventing the wheel. I didn't want any covers. I didn't want to do anything that would sound remotely recognisable."

Despite enclosing a handwritten note urging them to "experiment and chop things up, mix things around, reinvent and be inspired", the disappointing reality for Christina was that many modern-day producers were less than enthused by her project. They seemed alienated by her insistence on something that could in any way be construed as a soundalike. Additionally, many weren't accustomed to experimenting with vintage music, let alone fusing it with modern swagger.

Those who did make it onto the album had been willing to take musical risks – and previous collaborator Scott Storch wasn't among them. 'F.U.S.S.', produced by Charles Roane, was a middle finger salute to a certain person Christina regarded as disloyal – and by name-checking songs they'd worked on together, including 'Fighter', 'Loving Me For Me', 'Infatuation' and 'Can't Hold Us Down', she made it abundantly clear who the culprit was (the coded letters that named this short but not so sweet ditty stood for "Fuck U, Scott Storch").

In Scott's eyes, he'd been a crucial part of the production of seven songs for her and, in doing so, had helped her sell over 12 million copies of *Stripped* worldwide. Yet to Christina, this didn't entitle him to make what she perceived to be diva-like demands, such as a request that she footed the bill for a private plane. The heady rewards of fame and success seemed to have gone to Scott's head – but, according to him, every request was justified to honour his contribution. "I needed a private plane to get out to LA," he would tell *In Touch* unapologetically. "I had to bring equipment, clothes, my people. You want me to move my life from Miami to LA for six months and you can't get me a plane to do it? She didn't go to bat for me – and I truly cared about her as a person and a friend and as an artist."

An incredulous Christina thought otherwise, and 'F.U.S.S.' was her way of "burying" her experience with him. "We did great work on *Stripped*," she reminisced. "He was like a brother. Then he started working with other solo artists and I felt like there should have been a little loyalty. When I tried to work with him again, he made uncalled for demands. It was disappointing... I just think that some people get really affected by success." She added, "It's something I needed to get off my chest. It's a celebration song that I accomplished something without the help of someone that obviously didn't find it important enough to be a part of."

The photos on the page of the lyrics sleeve devoted to 'F.U.S.S.' captured this vengeful vibe. In one picture, she pouts argumentatively, a slight sadness etched across her face. The expression also oozes raw sexuality of a brand usually somewhat neglected during this more sophisticated Marilyn Monroe-inspired phase. Her bottom cheeks peek out provocatively from beneath a deliberately ill-fitting black negligee, while her breasts also struggle to be set free. She has the air of a shamelessly spoilt princess, sulking after she fails to get her way – and sure enough, a silver tiara takes pride of place on her forehead as if to validate the role. In another photo, she sticks out her tongue – playfully, but with intent.

Scott would later declare the track an "insult", adding, "It's pretty pathetic that she would do a song like this... Obviously she cares more than I do that I didn't do this album, but I can't blame her, with an album full of fillers, over-singing and lame Vegas-like cabaret music." Appearing to lack any shame for his role in producing Paris Hilton's novelty album *Paris* that year instead, he added caustically, "You should fire your management for letting me slip through your fingers."

'Slow Down Baby', produced by Mark Ronson, captured the same angry mood. If Christina's songs were to serve as an honest depiction of her real-life experiences, perhaps it was inevitable that this track would be born sooner or later. Her youth and often effortlessly pretty Barbie-doll looks had made her the object of unwanted solicitation ever since her teenage years, when men in the music industry would "hit on" her, despite knowing her age. Little had changed and, now that Christina had a ring on her finger, she was increasingly losing patience with the hangers-on. The track argued that although she presented a strong sensuality, it didn't mean she was up for grabs. The track, warning a suitor to get out of her space, portrayed all the anger of a feminist anthem and, although she hadn't been cheated on or abandoned, it had the air of a woman scorned nonetheless. With a nod to Gloria Gaynor's 'I Will Survive' and Whitney Houston's 'It's Not Right (But It's OK)', it made for an electric vengeance-style song.

Her other production collaboration with Mark was 'Without You' – in stark contrast, a tender love ballad thanking Jordan for being her "better half". Fittingly, the song's lyrics page depicts a softer, more modest side of Christina's sexuality than the public had seen for years. With her hair gently curled and her thighs bare, she gives the impression of a sexy yet virtuous wife who has just woken up with the man she loves. The picture is one of innocence and fragile femininity, giving the impression that – with Jordan's reassurance – Christina no longer needed the brash cover-ups and is finally comfortable with embracing her vulnerable side.

For 'Makes Me Wanna Pray', she enlisted the help of a surprisingly conventional producer, Rich Harrison, whose hit 'Crazy In Love' – produced for Beyoncé – had literally taken over music television in 2003. His work with Destiny's Child and Beyoncé and Kelly Rowland as solo artists had been held in high regard ever since. He was also a hit-maker for Amerie and Mary J. Blige, and he seemed the ideal person to reach the joyous, transcendental vibe Christina was searching for to convey how life had changed since Jordan had become a part of it.

For tracks like 'On Our Way' and 'Oh Mother', however, she reverted to less obvious producers again: the trio of Big Tank, Q and L. Boogie primarily worked with little-known hip hop acts, one of their biggest collaborators being Queen Latifah. They were invited to bring fresh ideas to a musical desert parched of them, a place where the favoured few produced prolifically across the pop genre – and they were up for the challenge. In 'On Our Way', the CD deliberately skips and flickers, as if nostalgically reliving the sound of an old, battered record player. Meanwhile 'Oh Mother', in spite of the unmistakable tinge of sadness in the background, boasted an almost triumphant gospel sound, an unselfconscious celebration of the escape her mother made.

The last time her mother had heard a song that reflected Christina's difficult childhood ('I'm OK'), she'd been reduced to tears. Yet this time the song lacked the bloodcurdling anguish of its predecessor. It was no longer a gut-wrenching act of musical therapy, but rather a tribute to her mother's strength. If anything, hearing it gave Shelly an insight into how much her daughter had understood of her struggle and how, in deciding whether to leave or to stay, her conflicts had divided her. When she finally heard the tribute, she called Christina to marvel, "I never knew that you knew how I felt going through all that." Indeed, only the picture alongside the lyrics betrays the reality of Christina's past of heartbreak and pain. Behind the eyes lingers a wistful expression, one of deep disappointment and genuine sadness. In that moment, she had truly channelled her feelings about the past. Yet while life might have scarred her, it had also given her the strength of character she knew today and, the self-modelled fighter that Christina was, she wouldn't allow that defeated expression to linger for long.

Her work with unconventional producers continued on 'Here To Stay', courtesy of Tony Reyes and Ben H. Allen. An anthem promising longevity on her own terms and dismissing haters as irrelevant, it was first heard as a sneak preview on her Pepsi advert.

Finally, she teamed up with Kwamé Holland, who was famed for his work with Mary J. Blige, on 'Understand'. With a voice reminiscent of Billie Holiday, Christina poured out an old-school ballad about an all-enduring love that had survived against the odds.

The remainder of the tracks were the responsibility of 'Ain't No Other Man' producer DJ Premier. One of the most controversial of those was 'Still Dirrty'. The song was a reaction to headlines Christina had read implying that she had toned her style down since marriage for the benefit of her more conservative husband. Fortunately she was in the studio when she cast her eyes over the inflammatory headline "From Crass to Class" – and she turned her outrage, indignation and sheer frustration at being misunderstood into a new song. "I was in my creative cave working on this record and I was hearing, 'Oh, now she's in love, she's cleaned up her act!'" she would recall. "I thought, 'OK, hold up there! I'm going to fall in love with someone who embraces all those qualities, not squashes them.' That's what that song is about, I can embrace it even more. I'm a happier person and those provocative qualities will never be erased."

After all, Christina had written 'Loving Me For Me' as an ode to a man who'd embraced not just her stage self but her inner qualities. Her sexuality wasn't simply a tool for entertainment, but "part of who I am as a woman". It felt natural to her to bring those aspects of herself to the forefront, not simply as a calculated move for publicity, but for self-expression. With all of this in mind, Christina would scorn claims that she'd changed, dismissing the gossip as "stupid clichés" and promising, "As if I would ever change who I am for anyone, let alone a man in my life!"

Christina also wanted to write a song that summarised and paid

Following a co-judging slot with Adam Levine on talent show *The Voice*, Christina lends her distinctive vocals to his group Maroon 5's track 'Moves Like Jagger'. Here Christina performs at the July 2011 video shoot for the song.

Boasting a dramatic floor-length black gown, Christina takes to the stage at the 2011 Grammy Awards with fellow performers Yoland Adams, Martina McBride, Jennifer Hudson and Florence Welch. MICHAEL CAULFIELD/GETTY IMAGES

Christina blows a kiss to the cameras at the 2011 Golden Globe Awards, held at the Beverly Hills Hilton, California.
STEVE GRANITZ/GETTY IMAGES

Stripped of her trademark makeup and dressed down in a simp and straw hat, Christina shows her tender side as she chaperone Max on a 2011 visit to the Animal Kingdom theme park at the Disney Resort, Florida. MATT STROSHANE/DISNEY VIA GETTY IM

With the American flag displayed behind them, Christina and *The Voice* co-star Adam Levine practise their Mick Jagger moves on set the 'Moves Like Jagger' video shoot. CHRISTOPHER POLK/GETTY IMAGES FOR A&M/OCTONE

Together with Jamie Foxx, a voluptuous Christina performs at the 2011 Michael Forever tribute concert at Cardiff's Millennium Stadium – an event organised in memory of Michael Jackson. SAMIR HUSSEIN/WIREIMAGE

Christina and her boyfriend Matt Rutler, whom she met during the filming of *Burlesque*, step out together for the launch party of 'The Elder Scrolls V: Skyrim' video game at LA's Belasco Theatre. JASON LAVERIS/FILMMAGIC

Christina celebrates her 31st birthday in Hollywood with an ostentatious bright pink cake. The woman depicted on it might be headless, but she poses behind it to complete the picture. JASON MERRITT/WIREIMAGE

ristina takes to the stage during NBC's Press Junket and cocktail reception in honour of 2012's autumn season of *The Voice*.

Christina performs at the 2012 American Music awards in LA clad in a star-encrusted leotard created by Gaga's favourite designing duo The Blonds. In an eccentrically choreographed set, her backing dancers would don bags over their heads emblazoned with logos such as 'Queen' and 'Freak'. KEVIN WINTER/GETTY IMAGES

Christina poses with her *The Voice* co-stars Blake Shelton, Adam Levine and CeeLo Green for a 2012 red carpet event honouring the show. FREDERICK M. BROWN/GETTY IMAGES

ving sobbed during rehearsals, Christina performs 'Blank Page' at the 2013 People's Choice Awards in LA—a song about wiping the
e clean and starting afresh. Later than night, when she won the People's Voice Award, she would thank God for her talents.
/IN WINTER/GETTY IMAGES FOR PCA

ristina shows off her new slim-line look onstage with Pitbull at the 2013 *Billboard* Music Awards in Las Vegas. The pair would
orm a rendition of the track they collaborated on, 'Feel This Moment'. ETHAN MILLER/GETTY IMAGES

Christina attends the 2013 Time 100 Gala in New York City, an event celebrating *Time* magazine's list of the 100 Most Influen[t]
People In The World. She was name-checked that night by Celine Dion as an artist who will "continue to amaze us for many, [r]
years to come". D DIPASUPIL/FILMMAGIC

homage to her vintage inspirations. Many of her tracks mingled classic sounds such as old-school jazz with a modern R&B twist, producing a result that differed from both musical styles individually – and she was ready to show where she'd got her soul.

She'd touched upon the subject on 'Intro (Back To Basics)', which opened like an introduction to a theatrical burlesque show, featuring a male voice marvelling, "That's what music should sound like!" In the heartfelt lyrics, Christina expressed her desire to step into the shoes of the vocalists she'd grown up hearing.

Then sister song 'Back In The Day' was born to complete the picture. Here, her voice had a depth usually acquired from a long lifetime of heavy smoking – or, at least, breathing the cigar-scented air of an after-hours jazz club every evening. As the record player of her imagination crackled and scratched away in the background, a male voice narrated the names of old-school legends such as Ella Fitzgerald and Miles Davis. Everyone mentioned had a special place in Christina's heart. Yet the most important tribute of all – at least, in her fans' eyes – was yet to come.

'Thank You' was her message to the supporters. She'd set up a contest via her website, encouraging fans to send recorded messages expressing how her music had touched their lives, promising that the most poignant ones would earn a spot on the album. Once she had decided the winners, DJ Premier sampled 'Genie In A Bottle', interspersing it with the voices of her fans.

It might have been counter-intuitive to think that this saccharine sweet memory of her repressive post-Mickey Mouse teenage years would be welcomed, but on the contrary, Christina was hooked as soon as she heard the beat. By reinventing the song she'd once resented and updating it to apply to the modern era of her career, she was finally in the driving seat. Singing her thanks that she was now in a position to choose her own musical destiny, this was her way of making peace with the song and all it symbolised and moving on to a new chapter – but she'd be taking her loyalists with her. Above all, the track was a token of appreciation for them, the people who'd stood by her through her many stylistic changes and battle to assert her identity, and had supported her evolution in all its stages.

The track ended, appropriately, with one fan enthusing that he couldn't wait to see what was coming next. Sometimes, with a life so fast-paced, that information was elusive even to Christina. However, there was one thing that she was adamant about – with so many songs to choose from, she wanted a double album.

But she faced intense opposition: to her label and management, the concept was career suicide. Double albums, unsurprisingly, cost twice as much to make, and, statistically, they sold fewer copies. Behind the scenes, the belief was that all she was heading for was double disappointment.

However, Christina was undeterred, and in her role as executive producer, she was ready to commit and take full responsibility for her dream. "Her label told her a double album was a big mistake," Linda Perry recalled. "And she said, 'I don't care.' So if the album fails or succeeds, she'll have to live up to that. But all I know is that the record sounds like nothing else out there – she definitely didn't go down the safe route. To me, the record has already succeeded."

For Christina's part, she would admit, "I'm really shooting myself in the foot to make a double record. It was a huge conversation, but [RCA label boss] Clive [Davis] felt I deserved this – so I got my way."

She was ready to shoulder the responsibility, come what may, but by August 15, the release day, she'd already exceeded all expectations. The album sailed straight to number one in 13 countries, including the UK and USA, making it her highest-performing album to date – and there could hardly be a more convincing case for following your heart.

While the images were a window into her soul, even the album sleeve would attract some attention, courtesy of celebrity photographer Ellen von Unwerth. The eccentric German with a taste for producing erotic and feminist art had already made waves for her work with the likes of Janet Jackson and would later create an infamous bondage photo shoot for Rihanna. Her manifesto was for artists – even those whose dirty underwear was perpetually on public display – to be seen as they'd never been seen before.

The shoot had been demanding: Christina had spent nearly an entire day peering out from behind the cage-like bars of a bed's headboard while Ellen snapped away in emulation of an iconic Marilyn Monroe shot – and that was just the beginning. They also took the method acting a step further with a visit to a recreation of a twenties burlesque club, Forty Deuce, in Hollywood, where she affected damsel-in-distress poses in the arms of a group of Swedish Navy sailors.

Research for the shoot was simple – Christina simply poured herself a glass of whisky and switched up the dial on Eartha Kitt's 'Champagne Taste'. Then she lost herself in the world of old movies, studying the glamour puss demeanour of Josephine Baker, Marlene Dietrich, Jean Harlow, Veronica Lake, Carole Lombard and Greta Garbo.

While Nelly Furtado, with her sex-themed album *Loose*, which included the mischievously titled 'Promiscuous', was following in the footsteps of the old Christina, the woman herself had already left that era behind. Her imitators were now wearing the second-hand styles she'd discarded at the metaphorical charity shop, because – as a proud Linda Perry had already foretold – as far as the pop market was concerned, there was nothing else like *Back To Basics* out there.

The New York Post would comment that the album was "a testament that she has more depth than Beyoncé and more staying power than Britney". Indeed her claim that she was different was no longer a protest that fell on deaf ears, the louder it became, but rather a vibe that preceded her and spoke for itself.

She portrayed further diversity when she kicked off the September 7 Fashion Rocks concert, a musical prelude to New York's Fashion Week, with a duet with Elton John. Later that night, she also gave her very first televised performance of 'Candyman'.

Meanwhile Christina, who performed a theatrical version of 'Hurt' at the 2006 VMAs, featuring Linda Perry on piano, then announced the ballad as her next single. A video followed, portraying her as a circus showgirl swinging from a trapeze and performing daredevil tricks and stunts. In her dressing room, surrounded by adoring aides, she receives a telegram announcing the death of her father. A shell-shocked Christina then has guilty flashbacks to her childhood, revealing him as the driving force behind her success. In one scene, a young Christina delights in the elephant pendant he presses into her hand as a gift while, in another, the pair see a tightrope walker together before, under his watchful eye, she trains herself to master the complex moves herself. The scene then switches to a present-day Christina who, consumed by her success, barely notices her proud father's presence in the audience any more. Dressed in a glittery corset and white gloves, she is seen emerging from the ceiling and jumping onto the back of a real-life elephant, to the wonderment of her audience. She is in high demand after the show, surrounded by autograph hunters and photographers. She hurriedly signs a few programmes before turning on her heel, leaving her forgotten father staring sadly after her.

Recalling her neglect of him, she runs outside the candy-striped circus marquee in tears, clutching the pendant her father gave her and sinking to the ground in despair. She reaches out to what appears to be the deceased standing next to her, but it turns out to be an illusion, her grief-stricken mind playing tricks. Meanwhile her lipstick has turned from bright pillar-box-red to a darker colour of the shade of dried blood, symbolising decay and grief. The plot was a cautionary tale warning of the all-consuming side of fame – those who get caught up in the adulation and ego-massages might lose sight of what is really important to them, realising their mistake only when it is too late.

The single was released on September 19 and, ironically, Christina would receive news of the death of her maternal grandmother just a month later. The 85-year-old Delcie Fidler died of natural causes on October 25. She had kept a low profile during her granddaughter's fame although, a traditionalist at heart, she had voiced concerns that her outfits were too risqué. Christina had laughed them off.

Meanwhile, although the plot of 'Hurt' was straightforward, the deeper meaning behind it was uncertain. Why would Christina – who had co-directed the video alongside Floria Sigismondi – choose to envisage the death of her father? She had been desperate from the start to write a track conveying the grief and regret of losing someone, but up until then she had never lost a major family member or close friend. Was she re-enacting the virtual bereavement she'd felt when her mother took her away from her father, despite knowing it was for the best? The sinister undertone seemed too personal to be a mere work of fiction; rather, the lyrics were tortured and stricken with guilt.

Perhaps 'Hurt' and the paternal-themed accompanying video reflected that – even if Christina herself didn't consciously realise it – a small part of her feared she was at fault for the past. However, music provided a therapy session and a profitable one at that: sales would reach over four million worldwide.

To her surprise, Christina also found herself in high demand in the rock camp – first Guns N' Roses performed 'Beautiful' at their show in California and then, on October 29, she was invited to join the Rolling Stones onstage in New York. While she belted out 'Live With Me', Mick Jagger put his hands on her hips from behind and gyrated with her. When, a few years later, she would sing that she had "moves like Jagger", unlike her vocal partner, Adam Levine of Maroon 5, she was talking from personal experience.

She was also popular in the rap camp, playing a guest role on Diddy's 'Tell Me', the second single, after 'Come To Me', featuring Nicole Scherzinger, to be released (on November 6) from his album *Press Play*.

For Christina, the collaboration was more a case of press rewind. Modelled into the shape of an archetypal rap star's arm-candy status symbol, she took on a look most thought she had discarded back in the 'Genie' days. Back were the long, blonde hair extensions she'd spent so long rebelling against, together with the soft and subtle make-up. It seemed as though she'd been transformed into a girl from one of Snoop Dogg's *Hip Hop Honeys* videos, playing it safe to appeal to mainstream hip hop and rap audiences.

Christina had always claimed she admired Madonna's brand of titillation – "being sexy without pandering to men" – and so it was difficult to imagine that the look Diddy sought appealed much to her personally.

Meanwhile her small, understated singing part gave the impression she was being sold on her image rather than her vocals. To add to the list of potential rap clichés, Diddy was sporting the almost obligatory hip hop uniform of a leather jacket and dark shades. In the USA, 'Tell Me' would become his lowest-charting single in over five years, while its biggest success was briefly reaching number two in Finland – not quite what his record label might have had in mind.

For Christina's part, she had bigger territories to conquer, and while, in 'Tell Me', her usual style had been obliterated by bling and conventional beauty, she'd be bringing "dirrty" back, along with a dose of originality, on her *Back To Basics* world tour.

Promising 800 pounds of confetti, 600 moving lights, pyrotechnics and circus fever, audience-participated S&M sessions, more costumes than she could count on both hands and a carousel house complete with its own built-in stripper pole, Christina was putting on a show like never before. "I don't think it would be fair to my audience to just sit on the stage with a mic," she reasoned. "If I play in an arena, I want my audience to look around and enjoy a show from all aspects... I really enjoy being taken out of my element for a moment and being able to use my imagination and enter this whole different world."

The tour kicked off in the UK in November, where support acts included the Pussycat Dolls, but Christina's take on burlesque made their usually sexy show seem as tame as a pensioner's bingo night by comparison. There was also an element of vaudeville. Her dancers had been to boot camp for intensive circus training – and it showed. During her set, they walked on stilts, swung from trapezes, performed acrobatics on ceiling swings and back-flipped all over the stage, even eating fire. Christina would somewhat understatedly describe the show as resembling a "mini Cirque du Soleil".

First however was the jazzy portion of the show, where giant stage projections of latter-day legends such as Gladys Knight, Marvin Gaye, Aretha Franklin, John Coltrane, Billie Holiday, Otis Redding and Louis Armstrong presented themselves as feasts for audiences' eyes. Each night, just as the crowd was getting lulled into a false sense of rhythm, Christina would change the pace totally by donning a pair of black lace chaps and draping herself over a rising piano for 'Still Dirrty'. This was the moment when blushing parents would affect looks of horror and cover their preteen daughters' eyes – but there was more sauciness to come. For 'I Got Trouble', Christina's silent home movie played out from behind the stage, featuring her writhing naked in a bath and proving just why she was worthy of that title. She also writhed on top of a stuffed dog, perhaps inspired by Madonna's *Sex* book. There was another link to Madonna as well: her former choreographer Jamie King, who'd also worked with Janet Jackson and Prince, was instructing Christina's dancers.

Then there was 'Nasty Naughty Boy', during which Christina would summon a member of the audience and beckon them onstage, purring, "I'm looking for a special naughty boy". They'd then be shackled to a burning "Wheel of Death", with a giant bull's-eye at its centre and knife-throwers strolling menacingly nearby. The uncomfortable exhibit would then be teased, titillated and humiliated for a few moments, a bondage-style leather belt tied tightly around the waist to strap him in. He'd be struck with a leather whip and fleetingly straddled by Christina, before fireworks exploded overhead and he was released back to his seat. Comically, the performance was considered controversial enough to necessitate each participant signing a release form indemnifying Christina from any psychological harm they might suffer.

Meanwhile, 'Lady Marmalade' made the song's official video seem like a rehearsal, with Christina reclining on a silky pink sofa and posing as a burlesque queen, while her compliant dancers waved feather fans around her. Those with an overactive imagination might visualise it as a lesbian scene between Christina and her maids – which, of course, was exactly what she had intended.

Even the old favourites had an element of surprise, with 'Come On Over Baby' reworked as a virtually unrecognisable jazz number, bemusing audience members so much that some would stop singing along. Meanwhile 'What A Girl Wants' transformed itself by way of an unpredicted reggae beat.

The night took on a sobering and momentarily sinister turn when 'Oh Mother' depicted projections of a woman covered in blood, begging for reprieve from a violent partner, but overall the show lived and breathed party mode. This was especially memorable in the circus portion, where knife-throwers and fire-eaters took control of the stage.

Costumes were provided courtesy of Italian fashion designer Roberto Cavalli and included a white tailored suit and matching fedora ('Ain't

No Other Man') and a replica of the white dress Marilyn Monroe wore in the film *Seven Year Itch* ('Let Me Stay').

However, some of her fashion choices were controversial and openly reviled by animal rights charity PETA. For example, her white forties-style satin tuxedo was not as pure and innocent as the colour implied – it came with accessories such as a white fox stole. Cavalli, who'd also dressed Michael Jackson for the World Music Awards, had sent out press releases boasting that the stole was made from the real fur of an Arctic fox.

Yet fur farmers stood accused of severe animal cruelty. Foxes kept in tiny cages with barely enough room to turn around traditionally turn to self-mutilation out of sheer frustration, even biting their own paws off or eating their cage-mates. Their lives end when they are electrocuted, causing an agonising heart attack while the animals are still conscious. It typically takes several minutes for them to die.

PETA contacted Christina's management enclosing the offending press release and a link to a video on its website featuring Stella McCartney giving some home truths about anal electrocution. A response came quickly, insisting that Christina "only ever wears fake fur" and had no knowledge that animals had been killed in the making of her accessories. The stole was swiftly replaced with a faux version.

The same month, on November 21, Christina would take time out for a rendition with Tony Bennett of his track 'Steppin' Out With My Baby'. The TV special on which they appeared was a tribute to Tony's new album, which saw him duet with artists such as Elton John and Michael Bublé. Christina was the only duet partner on the show who did not also appear on the album. However when Tony – who would later record with Amy Winehouse and Lady Gaga – heard her new style, which led him to reminisce over the sounds of Ethel Merman and Ginger Rogers, he knew instantly he wanted her on board. "She looks so dainty and everything and all of a sudden she belts out and hits the back of the wall like Ethel," he would marvel. "She has the biggest voice for a sweet little girl."

Perhaps he wouldn't see her as quite so sweet if he'd known her music was inspiring British bedroom antics. According to a survey conducted by the online sex-toy shop Love Honey to honour the launch of the world's first music-activated vibrator, 'Dirrty' was the song the majority of people felt best described their sex lives.

However, Christina had more than one side to her, just like the two CDs of her album, which she playfully referred to as "fraternal twins". The return of her serious side was demonstrated at the February 2007 Grammys when she performed James Brown's 'It's A Man's Man's Man's World' to a standing ovation. She would later reveal that she had been listening to and "taking notes from" six different versions of the track as research.

While her outrageous costumes and eye-popping stage show were a welcome part of a self-confessed visual artist's repertoire, they were increasingly considered a mere addition to the show and far from a gimmick invented to disguise a lack of ability. Indeed, the global media would noticeably soften towards Christina after this landmark Grammys performance. One newspaper, *The Battalion*, claimed, with a dig in no uncertain terms at Miss Spears, "Unlike many of her peers, Christina doesn't need panty-free nights out or a shaved head to draw herself an audience. Her powerhouse vocals shoot her to the spot of top diva of her generation."

CHAPTER 10

The Era Of Superbitch

Just a day after the tour hit North America on February 21, Christina's third single, 'Candyman', hit music TV. It saw three versions of her – a blonde, a brunette and a redhead – all doing the jitterbug in a tribute to forties culture. To achieve war-time era authenticity, she'd shot the video on the site of an airport hangar in Southern California. "We're saluting World War II, the bomber planes, servicemen and all those things," she'd revealed.

Meanwhile the triplets theme was a nod to singing trio the Andrews Sisters. To perfect the forties sex appeal of each, she'd been flicking through the books of vintage pin-up artist Alberto Vargas and recreating the poses. But the hardest task of all would be ensuring all three versions of Christina had identically matching choreography – something she confessed had been "painstakingly long to achieve".

While the single performed well, she would struggle to enjoy its success in the wake of a past flame on the war path, specifically producer Dallas Austin, and his slanderous attacks on her.

The pair's background was complicated. Dallas had been one of the many producers vying for a slot on *Stripped*, but although he'd presented Christina with several tracks, very few had made the shortlist. The only serious contender was a track called 'Cool', which Dallas had written about his enduring friendship with ex-girlfriend Chilli from TLC – and in the end, he hadn't been able to bear giving it away.

As one insider exclusively revealed to the author, "He took the song back at the last minute because the feelings it stirred up in him were too raw. It wasn't long since he'd broken up with Chilli and he still had strong feelings for her. He wasn't ready to hear someone else sing that track because it had so much personal meaning to him."

Eventually it would be prised away from him by Gwen Stefani, who'd released it in 2005.

Although Dallas hadn't been able to tempt Christina with any of his other tracks, they had briefly dated around that time – an experience that would result in nothing but bad memories for her. It was almost certainly Dallas to whom she had been referring when she spoke bitterly of an involvement with "a certain producer who didn't get any tracks on the record".

"That was the first time I smelled bullshit," she would recall, "my first dealing with a quote-unquote player. I found out later on he was… never really giving as much as I did."

She added, "I learned the hard way that people will say anything to get with you. Maybe if he had spent more time trying to make a record rather than trying to… he's got a bit of a reputation for trying to get with girls he makes records with."

Indeed, he'd seduced TLC's Chilli within hours of first meeting her. Dallas was the first producer she'd ever worked with and she'd fallen pregnant by him. Although the relationship continued for years, she felt the need to abort their baby, later revealing, "It broke my spirit… I cried every day for almost nine years."

This episode certainly didn't paint Dallas in a favourable light. His relationship with Christina had lasted mere months before she bowed out and the only good thing to come out of it, in her eyes, was that he'd introduced her to her future husband.

By his own admission, she'd tried to have Dallas banned from the 2007 pre-Grammys party – and conveniently, his outburst had come just days later. Thus, not only did it fail to dent Christina's credibility, but her life would suddenly change because the relationship between the couple remained strong. In fact, before long, she would announce that she was pregnant.

Ironically, the news came soon after she recorded a track for the charity album of John Lennon covers, *Instant Karma: The Amnesty International Campaign To Save Darfur* – and the track she'd chosen was 'Mother'.

It was for a worthy cause: John's widow, Yoko Ono, would be donating all royalties to Amnesty International's efforts to save war-torn and crisis-hit Darfur. Although the track was slightly dark, detailing how John had been abandoned as a child, for Christina the word now represented her own parenthood. Just as she felt she'd chosen the "right man" as a father, she could only pray she'd fulfil her maternal role perfectly too.

Yet the pregnancy, which saw Christina cheerfully refusing to scale down any of her work commitments, was perhaps more stress-inducing for her husband than it was for her. In the months leading up to motherhood, she would launch a new perfume, team up with Fredericks of Hollywood to design a corset for a children's charity auction, release 'Slow Down Baby' as an Australian-only single, appear at the Emmys for a live rendition of 'Steppin' Out With My Baby' together with Tony Bennett and, of course, continue her world tour. Given that the job description involved dancing in six-inch heels and, even worse, hanging precariously from a circus pinwheel, Christina was understandably "paranoid". She even took to wearing a carefully concealed heart monitor underneath her stage clothes. "There was no way in hell I was going to jeopardise my baby for my show," she asserted. "I didn't want to make the audience uncomfortable, like 'Pregnant lady onstage! Is she going to be OK?' but I had to announce it to my band and dancers because I wanted to make sure they had my back."

For a tense five months, they were the *only* people who knew – until an impromptu announcement by friend Paris Hilton spilled the beans. That September evening, Christina had hosted a private party at the LAX nightclub in Las Vegas's Luxor hotel and Paris had leapt onstage, squealing, "Congratulations to the most beautiful pregnant woman in the world. You're gorgeous!" Sporting a barely perceptible bump beneath a salmon pink dress which, at that moment, the entire room's eyes seemed to zoom in on, Christina visibly blushed before hiding her face in her husband's shoulder.

Yet once she'd been outed, it opened the floodgates for her to talk candidly. In November, she followed in the footsteps of Britney Spears and Demi Moore to pose naked, exposing her by now very large belly on the front cover of *Marie Claire* magazine. Revealing to readers that the pregnancy had been an accident, she divulged, "We were planning on starting to try after the tour and so I had gone off the Pill to prepare my body, because I didn't know how much time it would take. You've heard it takes some time – except with Power Egg and Super Sperm here!"

Not expecting to be carrying a baby during the gruelling world tour – which had taken her to Australia and New Zealand when she was already seven months' pregnant – she'd sometimes been overcome with exhaustion. However, her insatiable drive to make her unborn son proud kept her going. "I really was not alone – I had a little team-mate inside of me," she gushed. "On my worst days, when I was too tired, I felt like I had to do it for the little one in there and little one was egging me on. I felt like we were in it together every step of the way."

Yet there were limits even to her stamina – she'd been forced to turn down a starring role in a cinematic biography about Jeanne Carmen, the pin-up model, actress and burlesque dancer who counted Marilyn Monroe as her best friend. Despite the more experienced Scarlett Johansson hankering after the role, it was Christina's if she wanted it, but parenthood stood in her way. Tragically, Jeanne, who'd been a huge supporter of Christina's work, never lived to see herself symbolically immortalised on screen – she died that year, aged 77, from lymphoma.

Fittingly, 'Oh Mother' was the final single from the album. It was released on November 6 in selected European territories only, with a clip from the tour comprising the official video.

On January 12, 2008, Christina gave birth to her healthy – albeit small – baby son, Max Liron Bratman, who weighed in at just 6lb 2oz. The previous day had been celebrity delivery day at LA's Cedars-Sinai Medical Center when both she and Nicole Richie went into labour within hours of each other. Yet while Nicole had a complication-free natural birth and was soon back home, Christina's contractions stopped suddenly and even injections of a drug to induce them did nothing to assist. Still smeared with her trademark siren red lipstick, which an insider claimed she would meticulously reapply, she was eventually left with no other option but to undergo a Caesarean section.

Yet within weeks, a "sore" Christina had recovered enough to take part in her first TV interview as a mother, with Ellen DeGeneres. The openly lesbian TV presenter, never one to mince her words, looked admiringly at the prominent voluptuous curves spilling over her khaki dress, exclaimed, "You look great! Are you nursing?"

A blushing Christina would later reveal that, in honour of her son's Jewish roots, she'd not only given him the middle name Liron – Hebrew for "my song" – but she'd also organised a brit milah, a traditional Jewish circumcision ceremony to remove a baby boy's foreskin on the eighth day of his life. "Of course, we're such an unconventional couple that we had penis balloons everywhere!" she chuckled.

"They really have penis balloons [in the shops]?" Ellen asked incredulously. "You can just buy them?!"

Joking aside, Christina revealed that, despite her album sales tally reaching over 33 million, together with a string of Grammy awards and number one singles, it was nothing compared with the exhilarating achievement of creating life, flesh and blood. Every award, every accolade, paled into comparison to the high she received just from looking into her baby's eyes. "You think you've accomplished all these amazing things until you have your firstborn," she would reflect. "I was never more appreciative of what the female body is capable of doing." She added, "[Giving birth] is the best thing you will ever do in your entire life – it just lights up my whole world when Max laughs. Being a mother just gives you a whole new sense of purpose."

However, the situation – though a blessing – also created some conflicts for Christina. Even when Max had been just a few days old, she'd already begun to feel pangs of grief and uncertainty at the idea of being parted. As someone who was fully committed – and perhaps even addicted – to a fast-paced career, she was starting to feel torn. "How," she would muse aloud, "am I going to balance my love for creativity and performing with the ultimate of importance in my life – my child?"

The solution, initially, was to work from home. She'd recently purchased a mansion formerly belonging to the Osbournes, which had been the setting for the family's infamous reality TV show. However, needless to say, the gothic, garish décor favoured by her eccentric arch enemies was not Christina's idea of beauty and she had instantly set about stripping the house of "every gothic trace, every gargoyle and all the décor that she considered tasteless". While Christina would concede that it was "pretty stressful remodelling the whole place," she wanted to create her dream family home. With the exception of one bejewelled Moroccan-themed room, the rest of the house was transformed into "very old style vintage Hollywood with lots of chinois fabrics and crystal". Jack Osbourne's former bedroom became a walk-in wardrobe, a visual tribute to everything from sequinned corsets and the costume chaps that she threatened to bring out again when she hit her sixties, to high-fashion designer ball-gowns and diamond jewellery.

Best of all, however, was the home studio. "I don't need to leave my baby, I don't need to leave the house," she marvelled. "All I have to do to work is just walk over to the recording studio." In fact, the sprawling grounds were so expansive that Christina was reluctant to leave her cocoon, spending her days pushing Max's pram around, free from the paparazzi's prying eyes. "[They] actually pull up beside my husband and [say], 'When is she going to leave the house? I've been trying to get a picture of her for weeks!'" she would cackle later.

Yet while she prowled incognito around her $11.5 million home, the public's appetite for Christina never slackened. Her *Back To Basics: Live And Down Under* tour DVD, which captured her 2007 show in Sydney and included exclusive interviews with herself, Jordan, her musicians and dancers to name a few, debuted at number one on the US DVD charts following its February 4 release.

The next month, *Shine A Light*, a documentary dedicated to the Rolling Stones, was released, including footage of Christina dirty dancing with Mick Jagger and singing 'Live With Me'. Fellow band member Keith Richards was less than complimentary however, claiming that when he first caught sight of her, he'd thought she was an overzealous fan invading the stage. Implausibly, he added, "I still don't know who that is." Given that Christina had allegedly scolded a bellboy for not knowing her name nearly a decade earlier when she was in the first throes of fame, her reaction to a performer who'd shared a stage with her pleading similar ignorance might well have been unprintable.

Fellow band member Charlie Watts, however, had generous praise, marvelling, "We've had some great people [onstage with us] including our dear Amy Winehouse, although I don't think she was quite well – [but they] were never as good as Christina."

Meanwhile, mother and son would appear together on TV screens for the first time that summer when Christina cradled him and sang a lullaby version of 'America The Beautiful' in a bid to encourage US citizens to vote. Rock The Vote's inaugural ad campaign, back in 1990, had featured a naked Madonna wrapping herself in the American flag and threatening viewers that if they didn't vote, they'd get a spanking, which made a tender moment between mother and son seem almost tame in comparison. Yet the message was crystal clear – and the campaign was special to Christina as she felt a vote spelt empowerment. Despite the fact that, historically, women had once been denied the right to vote, in modern times, many shunned the freedom for which their ancestral sisters had fought. What was more, Christina had been one of them up until 2004 – and looking back, she was ashamed that she hadn't raised her voice sooner. Decisions were being made that affected Americans like herself almost every day and she'd grown to learn that taking no interest in the fate of the world around her meant political impotency – a lack of control over her own future. Now that she had a son, politics had become more important than ever as it gave her the opportunity to have a say in the world he would inherit. "I grew up in a house where politics weren't discussed," Christina recalled. "It was sort of a hopeless situation in my home. And as I grew up and became a woman myself and started caring about certain things such as domestic violence… I felt I can voice my opinion, I can change how the world is. You know, it takes one person."

She also fought back at public criticism that she'd chosen to expose her son, barely a few months old, to the world of celebrity. Some felt she was touting him for publicity, while she argued that invasive paparazzi meant press attention was inevitable and that his first public outing might as well be for a good cause. "[It's] a really intimate moment… symbolising what this song means in the sense that it's passing it on to the next generation," she told sceptical TV host Larry King. "It's trying to contribute in a way to make the future better for my son."

Christina was determined not to be suppressed by the nation's views on how a new mother should behave or indeed the appropriate way to raise a child – appropriate, she argued, was not a word in her vocabulary.

Her post-pregnancy comeback song, 'Keeps Gettin' Better', highlighted that, while many new mothers felt deflated and exhausted, she was empowered, energised and rejuvenated, all the stronger for the triumph of bringing life into the world. Contradicting every soft maternal cliché, she used the track to brand herself a "superbitch".

The superbitch persona was a rebellion against disapproving critics who had judged Christina for daring to take a night out on the town after putting her baby to bed, or who felt her career should hit a standstill – for reasons of misplaced moral righteousness – until her son was enrolled in school. The public largely expected a virginal image consistent with society's centuries-old stereotypes of motherhood, which made her all the more defiant. "I want to be the best mom I can be, but show my son who I am as a person," she explained, "not just this woman who changes diapers and breastfeeds."

She added to MSN, "After having my own child, [I realised] it's pretty amazing what females are capable of. We're Supergirl, we do it all – we give the love, we give the milk. On the other hand, I'm running a business. I'm running my career. That comes with being labelled a bitch. If that's what I'm gonna be called by being assertive and knowing who I am and what I want out of life, then so be it. I will wear that label proudly. For me, it's about turning that word in a positive, electro–pop beat."

That was another distinction about 'Keeps Gettin' Better' – while fans were told to expect almost anything from a chameleonic Christina's comeback, the sound that awaited them was the last thing they might have expected. She'd previously used countless interviews to scorn electronic music, branding it "over-produced" and claiming that, in stark contrast to the greats of yesteryear, technology-reliant beats had little soul or substance. She argued that fillers and effects stripped voices of their emotion and made it possible for a talentless, tone-deaf singer to fake a tuneful sound. She also saw the technology-fuelled tracks as dishonest and unrelatable – and also responsible for a wave of performers who were easy on the eye but, outside of the studio, offered little else.

In the early 2000s, electronic music had been prevalent only at techno clubs and raves and was part of a niche scene rather than a wider movement, as mainstream nightclubs generally veered towards pure pop. Yet performers such as the Black Eyed Peas slowly but surely spawned an electro-pop revival, bringing back a sound some listeners hadn't seen in prominent chart positions since the eighties, if at all – and now, of course, the technology was much better, too. However, just as she'd shunned the generic chart sound on her last album by opting for obscure producers, Christina took her inspiration this time not from mainstream electronica, but from artists that remained on the outskirts of the pop scene – the likes of Goldfrapp, Ladytron and Peaches. This dance music with a twist, with its intentionally electronic beats and robotic chanting proliferated by electronic effects, was just as likely to share her CD rack as the old favourites she'd previously claimed held the upper hand.

Consequently 'Keeps Gettin' Better' was no *Back To Basics*. "I wanted to go in a completely opposite direction – a very futuristic, robotic sound and computer-sounding vocals," she insisted. "I'm experimenting with my voice in ways I've never done before, almost like a technical, computer-generated sound, which is different for me because I'm the type of vocalist that just belts." Going a small way towards explaining her extreme transformation, she added, "I'm always inspired by new things because I get bored."

To Christina, repeating herself pointed to a lack of imagination and suggested to the public that she was running out of ideas. Besides that, her need to experiment, coupled with the enormous success of her vintage album meant that she'd now covered the genre and already taken it as far as she could.

Yet even someone who changed as often as Christina, leaving puzzled critics with no chance of pigeon-holing or defining her sound, was far from immune to accusations of copying the style of others. Sources such as MTV sniped that while Christina claimed to have been influenced by Madonna, she had in reality taken inspiration from "slightly more contemporary sources such as Lady Gaga".

Gaga had recently risen from obscurity, having spent the previous summer performing to a flagrantly uninterested and, at times, even abusive audience as an unknown at festivals such as Lollapalooza. Yet in 2008, she reinvented her look, dying her hair blonde to avoid the regular comparisons she received to Amy Winehouse, and had adopted a poker-straight style with a harsh fringe. Coincidentally, she took on the look at around the same time that Christina did and at the same time that 'Just Dance' hit radio play lists and she made her way to worldwide fame. Add to that both artists' affection for an electro-pop sound and it was a recipe for journalists to stir up an element of non-existent rivalry and feuding.

Kelly Clarkson would defend the mother of her hit 'Miss Independent' from the copycat accusations, pointing out that Christina had been around for a decade, while Gaga was a newcomer. Yet some critics countered that Christina was emulating her new rival in a bid to remain relevant and revive a popularity she felt was dwindling. After all, Christina's years were inevitably advancing and she'd become a mother – without a new tactic, they asked, how could the new generation of listeners take her seriously?

Yet perhaps the debate was superfluous – in reality, both artists had simply been inspired by similar icons from yesteryear. Paradoxically, the trend for a futuristic sound had been a huge part of the past and both Christina and Gaga had confessed to a love for acts such as Blondie and the Velvet Underground. "I was very inspired by the look and feel of that genre," Christina would clarify. "Your Jane Birkins, your Blondies, females who have come before, who have done this so many times and so well. It's almost a homage to them. Also Warhol, Nico from the Velvet Underground... it all kind of ties into a pop art feel and twist, with a mod look but a futuristic taste of what's to come."

Meanwhile, a strong sound commanded equally strong visuals – and Christina's paid tribute to a mixture of past and present pop art, including Andy Warhol, Roy Lichtenstein, D★Face and Banksy. Plus whenever she stepped out, Christina was a walking advertisement for the nouveau electro-pop movement: it was all about bold, vibrant, often neon colours and taking stylistic risks. Gone were the fifties film star style lashings of crimson lipstick, replaced by bright fuchsia or frosted candy pink. Plus, in the style of many a drag queen-inspired male musician in make-up, she was also rarely seen without several layers of long fake lashes. This bold, unorthodox slice of glamour was a stylistic choice but, equally, it seemed to be a gesture of defiance, a way of proving adamant assertions such as "I'm not going to go down the safe route because I have had a child. Motherhood hasn't changed me."

Like Gaga, Christina's look was at times a little unpalatable to followers of mainstream culture, because its emphasis wasn't on sex appeal, but rather making a statement. Christina's comeback arrived at a time when, more than ever, pop culture had become dominated by visual appeal and female entertainers were often judged by the public purely in terms of how they looked rather than their talents, as if looking pretty was their sole job description. The ever-increasing popularity of the internet proved this – readers were taking to forums or comment sections of online newspapers to add appraisals no more insightful than a belief that a featured performer was "ugly".

Yet Christina – and of course Gaga – were openly rejecting conventional ideals of beauty and refusing to pander to them. The former was no longer a visually perfect Barbie doll. Her look was now sharper and edgier with its clashing colours and provocative performance art played out on the face. Whether it was intentional or not, her look, which refused to cater to male-defined depictions of what was beautiful and what was feminine, was a victory for feminism. Although she hadn't conformed, she was still successful and, rather than being seedy and superficial, she hadn't achieved that success on her own terms. She'd been the beauty queen of teenage dreams already – now it was time for a change, a look that spoke a thousand words.

Viewers were introduced to that look formally with her single's promo video, a shameless celebration of her chameleon-like status and one that, now more than ever, visibly placed her at the centre of control. Futuristic fetish scenes flooded the screen while she would appear at a gargantuan mixing desk to view several prototype images of herself – a dark-haired 'Fighter'-era Christina, an angelic one reminiscent of her 'Genie' days, with white-blonde hair and a cowboy hat, and one that she was debuting for the first time, in bold black eighties eyeliner.

While she would peruse surrealistic scenes of an early Christina cycling through a field of flowers, it was the third, most forceful and dramatic version of herself that won in the end. A fierce cat-woman, with exaggerated drag-queen bright red shadow smeared across her eyes Bowie style, she would teasingly simulate shooting a gun.Hair glowing a futuristic shade of electric blue under the strobe lights, there was no doubt that this was her latest incarnation and, showing a side of her common to all of her personas, she would grip her car's steering wheel and drive. This metaphorical image of her in the driving seat hinted that she was now at a stage in her career where she could command absolute, uncompromising control. She was the executive producer of her work and if she who paid the piper called the tune, it seemed that she no longer needed to struggle with third parties to assert an identity over her sound. That was exactly what she was celebrating with her forthcoming greatest hits album and the futuristic taster song promised that, no matter what fans had seen so far, at the height of her creative control, she'd make sure it kept getting better.

The live debut of her new persona took place at the September 7 VMAs. That night, she made her grand entrance through the stage door in a golf cart, whooping and raucously cheering herself on all the while, just as keenly as the entourage behind her. She performed 'Keeps Gettin' Better' clad in a black leather outfit and a matching fetish-style eye mask. Yet the biggest surprise of the night was that she'd reinvented her first single with an equally futuristic tone, dubbing it 'Genie 2.0'.

The show's host was British comic Russell Brand but, in spite of their very different lives, it wasn't the first time Christina had seen him. Back in June, she, Katy Perry and frenemy Pink had all been offered cameos in *Get Him To The Greek*, a film in which Russell starred. The part was far from challenging – almost all that the three girls had to do was kiss him. "Christina was amazing," he later told *The Sun*, adding, slightly disrespectfully, "She is unbelievable – a perfect object. How could you ever talk to her about anything other than sex?"

When the film was released two years later, it had been heavily edited but Christina would nonetheless make an appearance. While Russell was a dubious "prize" to say the least, this moment seemed to be when Katy Perry went into direct competition with Christina. When she later married Russell, she admitted to the press that she couldn't match her rival's singing abilities. Instead, she chose to compete with costumes, recalling, "I asked some of the guys at MTV, 'So Christina Aguilera was a couple of shows back – how many outfit changes did she have?' They said 'Nine' and I said, 'Great, I'll have 12!'"

There was also a possibility that Katy's obsession with confectionery art, referenced in videos such as 'California Girls', had begun after seeing Christina pose inside a novelty ice-cream almost as tall as she was, or appear in magazines alongside jars of candy.

Yet there seemed to be no beating Christina at the VMAs. While Max wasn't allowed to watch TV yet, she had promised to "make an exception" for that night. Plus, at the after-show, she partied like a woman devoid of responsibilities at LA's Chateau Marmont hotel, the veritable fairy-tale castle, cut into the Hollywood Hills, towering over the glamour and hype of the legendary Sunset Strip below.

The hotel had history – it had been a favourite of Marilyn Monroe in her day, while troubled actor James Dean had auditioned for *Rebel Without A Cause* there, making his grand entrance by leaping in through a window. Resembling a perfectly packaged Disneyland castle or a Hollywood Neuschwanstein, it might have looked innocuous and innocent on the outside, but in reality it was more of a Transylvanian Dracula's lair. The home of an irresistibly magnetic decadence, it was a place where creative flames would both ignite and burn out, but it had a tragically strong reputation for the latter.

While the Red Hot Chili Peppers might have penned their hit 'By The Way' there, band member John Frusciante would take part in an interview in the lounge that would see him depicted him as a "skeleton with thin skin".

Jim Morrison lost "the eighth of my nine lives" there in a drunken fall from the roof – and the ninth would be spent soon after, as he suffocated in his bath tub in Paris.

Courtney Love had emerged from one of the property's rooms high on a self-made cocktail of alcohol and antidepressants before taking part in a slurred interview stark naked. With this in mind, it was little surprise that Linda Perry had talked Courtney out of releasing 'Beautiful', claiming she "wasn't ready" for Top 40. If one could be pinpointed, the charade in the Chateau Marmont was perhaps among the most humiliating moments of her career.

Meanwhile the legendary hotspot was the location of Amy Winehouse's first ever formal recording sessions, with her begging the producer not to go as they strummed guitar together in the lift. Her downward spiral had already begun.

It was described by one hotel review website as somewhere that may have seen "more celebrity excess and self-destruction than Caligula's boudoir", yet, fortunately for Christina, her ambitions shouted louder and she'd won her dance with the devil. "I don't get drunk," she would insist. "It's tempting, but there's too much left to achieve. My career is more important."

Two days after the VMAs, on September 9, 'Keeps Gettin' Better' was released to enormous public acclaim – and it made having the discipline to reject the world of excess all seem worthwhile.

Following that, her first major show was a headlining performance at the October 12 Africa Rising Festival at London's Royal Albert Hall. She took the opportunity to channel her inner "superbitch" with a futuristic fashion show comprising a Technicolor Pucci mini-dress with clashing prints, black leather trousers and purple YSL platforms. She looked the part, but it was the performance that really showed she hadn't become the frumpy mother that stereotypes dictated. Instead she leapt onstage in a leopard-print swimming costume to receive a spanking from her dancing troupe, who gamely descended on her with comically large feathers. Yet the X-rated material had been present from the get-go – before she'd even taken to the stage, screens projected a video segment of her naked in a bathtub simulating sex moves. Meanwhile shocked parents, grumbling that the video was "like porn", covered their children's eyes in horror. While the "little darlings" might have downloaded far worse on an iPhone in the playground, the indignation continued. Yet motherhood or no motherhood, love her or despise her, you couldn't hold Christina down.

The exception to this rule, however, might have been her debut concert in the Middle East later that month, at Abu Dhabi's Emirates Palace hotel. The deeply religious Emirate upheld Islamic values, forbidding the consumption of alcohol and even condemning kissing in public – both of which were potentially punishable by a jail sentence. Meanwhile pornography was blocked across the Emirate's entire internet network, making it impossible for anyone to access it even illegally.

Consequently Christina's everyday dance routines would probably masquerade as full-blown obscenity in Emirati eyes. She switched the dial from naughty to nice to accommodate the occasion, instead appearing at a press conference with a saccharine-sweet candy theme to prove it. The media would describe the event as "a scene from *Charlie And The Chocolate Factory*, with giant jars of chocolates, jelly-beans, liquorice and other sugary treats as far as the eye could see".

"It was all I could think about while I was pregnant," she would announce to puzzled Emiratis by way of explanation – before Katy Perry's 'California Girls', confectionery and music had rarely, if ever, appeared together. She would add, "I wanted sugar and all things sweet and didn't know when to stop" – and it was the sweet side of her demeanour that she would reveal to 15,000 fans at that night's show. It seemed that, even when her performances were stripped of sex appeal, they were anything but ordinary.

The following month, on November 9, she lent her support to protests against Proposition 8, a new law which had overturned the right of same-sex couples to marry earlier that week. Protesters placed the blame on the Mormon Church, congregating outside the city's temple in their thousands – and for Christina this meant a backlash against her parents' religious background. Yet she agreed with furious citizens, who accused the church of spending millions of dollars on door-to-door flyers and even TV ads that incited hatred, urging the public to vote to put a stop to gay marriage. The advertising campaign strongly implied that homosexuality was not compatible with a virtuous lifestyle, or even belief in God.

Why, asked protesters, were the Mormons using their influence – and wasting their vast financial fortune – to spread hatred and prejudice? Surely these actions went against the religious teachings they'd been raised to obey. What was more, wasn't there a more appropriate use for their wealth, such as feeding the homeless?

For Christina, the situation was simple – her life was filled with gay muses, from fashion designers and stylists to dancers and friends. To her, Proposition 8 was nothing short of barbaric. "[It's] discrimination," she told MTV, "and I don't understand how people can be so closed-minded and so judgmental. We chose an African-American president, [so it's] a time in history of great change and open-mindedness. Why is this different? It just doesn't make sense to me. Why would you put so much money behind something stopping people from loving each other and bonding together? It's hard for me to grasp."

The timing was a little unfortunate, as her album, *Keeps Gettin' Better: A Decade Of Hits*, was due for release on November 11. "Mormons aren't gonna buy my album," she would wryly acknowledge, "but you know, what are you gonna do?"

The album release was promoted by an advert featuring Christina in a bright red superhero costume and its top-charting debut proved to the naysayers that she was still relevant in the music world. There were new versions of hits such as 'Lady Marmalade' and 'What A Girl Wants', while – according to *Entertainment Weekly* – "The real curiosity is a 'Beautiful' redo that imagines how John Lennon might've sounded if he'd lived in the age of electro." Then there was a new and unheard track hiding away – 'Dynamite'.

As her album generated a buzz in the charts, Christina was doing another disappearing act, hitting her home studio to record album number five. Of course, the public would see her occasionally – for instance, in July 2009, she hit the headlines in her role as a global spokeswoman for World Hunger Relief. Announcing that over a billion people worldwide were going without food and that, somewhere, a child's life ended every six seconds due to starvation, she appealed to the public to put a stop to the global crisis.

Not content with merely regurgitating press releases, however, she made her own journey in September – along with Jordan – to the deprived highlands of Guatemala, where up to 80 per cent of the villagers suffer from chronic starvation. "I wanted to see with my own eyes what hunger means," she explained, adding, "As a mom, my heart just breaks."

It wasn't pretty – children and adults alike were emaciated, near lifeless and far below average height due to malnourishment. Yet the pictures of Christina, devoid of her usual trademark make-up, paying her respects, was likely the equivalent of a thousand press releases in commanding the public's attention. It was another example of how she was veering away from the superficial, using her profile to raise awareness of global issues.

It was an interesting, if sinister, dichotomy that, just weeks after visiting children starving to death from lack of food, she would appear on *Project Runway*, a show championing the Western fashion industry, where some models were starving themselves by choice. The show featured would-be fashion designers competing for a career-altering contract and Christina would appear as a guest judge to help decide their destiny on October 15. The competitors' task was to design a costume that Christina would be proud to wear onstage with an improbably small budget of just $150. They had to impress both Christina and her intimidatingly fashion-savvy partner, veteran designer Bob Mackie. She'd worked with him several times before – as had Cher, Diana Ross and Tina Turner – and standards on both sides were uncompromisingly high. It wasn't going to be easy.

The brief was to envision "a goddess from some mythological kingdom", but according to a characteristically outspoken Christina, one of the creations made her look more like a "cave-woman". Meanwhile, some of the contestants barely knew Christina's trademark style at all, with one opting to clothe her in a long white gown shadowing as a misshapen wedding dress. In the end, it was Carol Hannah Whitfield who won the challenge with a strapless black gown festooned with feathers and glitter. She and she alone, it seemed, had tapped into the heart of Christina's stagecraft.

Although Christina was also occasionally seen around LA wearing T-shirts emblazoned with provocative slogans such as "Auto-Tune is for Pussies", her hiatus continued well into early 2010. In fact, it was her longest absence from the music scene yet. Apart from the occasional tantalising news snippet announcing that she was working with Ladytron or Sia from Zero Seven, but revealing little more, no one really knew what Christina had been doing – she'd largely disappeared from public view. Yet this absence preceded her biggest, most dramatic musical evolution yet.

CHAPTER 11

The Rhythm Of The Future

"When she sings 'Tonight I'm not the same girl'," *Entertainment Weekly* enquired, "are you concerned she means in terms of quality control?"

It was April 2010 and the electro-pop sound Christina had debuted on 'Keeps Gettin' Better' was back in full force for 'Not Myself Tonight' – but not everyone was a fan. As her biggest selling point was a formidable vocal prowess that most pop stars simply didn't possess, wasn't resorting to electronic music to disguise it overshadowing her raison d'etre?

"Christina gave up her famous belting because she said she was bored of it," a friend told the author, "and that was the downfall of her career." Yet she had constantly reinvented herself, seeing each album as an opportunity to play a brand new role.

Focus, a producer who would work with Christina on the album which 'Not Myself Tonight' preceded, mused, "The moment they know your style, you *have* to reinvent yourself. Once you get set in your style, it's hard to break down what you've been doing and rebuild up to what everyone else is doing."

Indeed, this seemed to be Christina's problem. For the current generation, electronic music was a fairly new trend, but unfortunately not one that she had started – and according to many critics, she was merely a poor imitation, jumping on the bandwagon of newer and fresher rivals. "For an artist with a voice like Christina's," *Neon Limelight* lamented, "quite possibly one of the best voices of our generation, it does nothing to showcase her as a vocalist and it's a step in the wrong direction. A direction where she feels she has to compete with artists like Britney Spears and Lady Gaga, who do dance music well."

Comments like these represented just how much the music scene had changed in Christina's short absence. A decade earlier, she'd been one of a kind – at that time, girl groups had prevailed over solo artists and of the latter, very few had offered Christina's message of sexual and societal liberation and feminist empowerment. Yet now she was no longer alone – her example had paved the way for the likes of Rihanna, Lady Gaga and Fergie. For example, with 'Dirrty' and 'Beautiful', she'd delivered the message that body confidence should be celebrated and that doing so did not necessarily equate to arrogance, a theme which Fergie took further in the defiantly immodest 'Fergalicious'. Meanwhile in Christina's era, one of family-friendly "sugar candy" pop, she'd brought back an outspoken sexuality to music, one that had barely reared its head since Salt-N-Pepa's 'Push It' back in the eighties.

Yet now everyone was doing it. And critics now felt that, in a bid to remain relevant, she was emulating the sound and attitude of newer artists and losing herself in the process. "Hopefully next time," *Rolling Stone* griped, "she'll be more herself and less like everyone else."

Her biggest visual influence seemed to be Lady Gaga, with 'Not Myself Tonight' bearing numerous similarities to 'Bad Romance'. For example, in both videos, each singer wore an identical pair of Carrera sunglasses, but in different shades – Christina's black and Gaga's white. Both wore tops featuring long silver chains looped around their bodies, too. Although she hadn't been on the scene too long, Gaga's eccentric style was unmistakable – and critics weren't about to let Christina forget it. While she'd tried her best to ignore the comparisons that had crept in since the release of 'Keeps Gettin' Better', she had eventually been provoked into a response. "This person was just brought to my attention not too long ago," she would snap back defensively. "I'm not quite sure who this person is, to be honest. I don't know if it's a man or a woman.

215

I just wasn't sure. I really don't spend any time on the internet, so I guess I live a little under a rock in that respect."

Perhaps that was true and it was solely her video director, Hype Williams, who was responsible for the Gaga-isms. Unfortunately, either way, the comparisons weren't stopping any time soon. Akon, a producer for Gaga and rapper in his own right, claimed that Christina was trying to "do the exact same thing" due to "insecurity", before adding, a little patronisingly, that her fears were unnecessary as she'd been successful already long before Gaga had come along.

His comments were just the tip of the iceberg and Christina soon found herself defending her artistry yet again. "[It's] not even worth wasting the breath to comment on," she hit back. "I've been around for over a decade and I think my work speaks for itself." She would later add to *Billboard*, "I'm in it for the long haul and… I have nothing to prove. To anyone who wants to be negative, it's like, 'I'm obviously relevant enough to you for you to care and to talk and to evoke negative feelings inside of you.' At this point in my career, I'm over any and all weird comparisons."

Gaga, on the other hand, was delighted, playfully threatening to send flowers to the woman whose outraged denials had put her "on the map". "Even though I've only been on the commercial market [for a short time], I've really burned graphic images of my visuals onto the irises of my fans," she marvelled. "They saw a huge Grammy-winning star who's been around for years and they recognised Lady Gaga. That, to me, is quite an accomplishment." In a sly bid to attain the upper hand, she would continue that her image was not a mere tool for entertainment, but a lifestyle in itself. "People say, 'Your look is the same'," she explained, "but this isn't my look. This is my life, I dress like this all the time. You're not gonna ever catch me at the grocery store in flip flops."

Aside from comparisons with Gaga, singing about kissing both boys and girls seemed to be an attempt to get on the bisexuality bandwagon. Katy Perry had kissed a girl and liked it – or, at least, liked the publicity – while a formerly straight Lindsay Lohan had begun a relationship with Mark Ronson's sister Sam. Rihanna had released her video 'Te Amo' about a woman who was infatuated with her. Then Gaga's 'Telephone' video had even seen her recruit the staunchly religious Beyoncé, who had previously stated that girl-on-girl kisses were against God, for an implied lesbian love affair.

The trend had perhaps begun when the USA's perception of homosexuality slowly became more tolerant. Following changes in the law in certain states to allow gay marriage, same-sex crushes were no longer considered a shameful, illicit secret but in fact a marketable asset, a tangible measure of sex appeal. Whether this flirtation with sapphic romance was an offensive exploitation of the gay community for profit or merely a way to raise awareness for a misunderstood minority group was open to debate. Perhaps some of the girls were genuinely bi-curious and society's increasing tolerance towards gay lifestyles had merely awakened their latent desires or given them the courage they needed to express them.

Only Madonna had dared to flirt with and embrace lesbianism in public, regardless of how many fans it might lose her. As someone who'd also linked sex with religion in numerous incendiary ways, she was an artist with very few boundaries. Even her name seemed to liberate her from the rules that applied to the rest of society and, with her penchant for fearlessly flaunting all things taboo, she represented total, uncompromising artistic freedom. That was precisely why so many new artists aspired to be like her – and again, perhaps those matching Christina to Gaga needed to look further back to a source that had inspired both women.

Sure enough, before long, Christina revealed that Madonna – and more specifically her 1989 video 'Express Yourself' – had been the central inspiration for 'Not Myself Tonight'. "[It's] one of my favourite videos ever," she told MTV. "[It] came across as really strong and empowering, which I always try to incorporate through my expression of sexuality. I love the direct reference I made to Madonna [in my video] with the eyeglass movement and the smoke and stairs. I was paying tribute to a very strong woman who has paved the way before." For good measure, she'd also emulated the video by adding a scene where she, like Madonna, lapped milk out of a pet bowl on the floor.

Yet while 'Not Myself Tonight' was littered with references to Christina's ultimate icon and fantasy lover, it wasn't just 'Express Yourself' to which it gave a wink and a nod. Her penchant for leather and S&M guises was something Madonna too had portrayed in 'Human Nature'. Meanwhile the church location resembled that of 'Like A Prayer'.

Despite an initial explosion of interest, the single declined in popularity quickly. It wasn't what her fanbase was accustomed to hearing and, as many listeners challenged that the sound and vocals lacked originality and failed to stand out from the crowd, she failed to gain many new supporters, either.

Moreover scenes featuring Christina drinking from a cat or dog bowl also proved controversial. They gave rise to a debate: was this truly an empowering statement of sexuality or had it crossed the line into something demeaning, a cheap publicity stunt that cared more about scoring shock value points than retaining integrity? Although Christina counterbalanced these moments with playing the dominatrix role, to the feminist quarter, the imagery was deeply unsettling and at odds with the public figure they thought they'd known. Yet Christina would freely admit that she was "hard to define" – and this moment was no exception.

The ripples had barely settled when it was time for her album to be unveiled. *Bionic* hit the shelves on June 8, to mixed reactions. As with 'Not Myself Tonight', there was an initial hype, but it was unsustainable. It debuted in album charts at the top spot, but – with just 24,000 copies sold that week – it became the lowest selling number one in eight years. By the following week, it had made chart history – but for all the wrong reasons. It would suffer the largest drop for a number one album since records began. Meanwhile in the USA, it debuted at number three with 110,000 copies sold, but that paled in comparison with *Back To Basics,* which had achieved more than three times as many sales in its first week.

The enormous drop in popularity so soon was the most concerning aspect for Christina – it suggested fans had initially purchased the album with high hopes because it had her name attached to it, but that the word had spread quickly that it didn't live up to their lofty expectations.

Why? First, there were widespread complaints that the computer-generated vocals masked the very sound that fans were buying into.

Additionally, in contrast to the heartfelt, relatable and emotion-heavy atmosphere of *Stripped*, most of the tracks on *Bionic* lacked a personal meaning. Rather, they were more of an abstract celebration of the electro-pop movement and Christina's infatuation with it. Much of her previous work had been borne out of pain but, as a wife, mother and enormously successful career woman, Christina simply wasn't that angst-ridden young woman any more. She'd mellowed – her songs were fun and flippant rather than deep and meaningful. She no longer needed musical therapy and escapism and consequently, her work was simply less heartfelt.

A third obstacle that seemed to stand between Christina and mainstream success was her unusual choice to devote much of the album to collaborations with obscure artists, something which arguably elevated their profile more than hers. For instance, Sia Furler of Zero Seven had lacked a significant chart presence for years, but as soon as she linked herself to Christina via a quick mention on Twitter, she gained 5,000 new followers within minutes. Better known for her dreamy easy listening sound than conventional pop, she had lacked a voice in the pop world until writing with Christina. The floodgates opened, allowing her to subsequently work on tracks such as David Guetta's 'Titanium' and Rihanna's 'Diamonds'.

However, before Sia had garnered demonstrable pop credibility, Christina was taking a risk in collaborating with her. This was perhaps another problem that had prompted her downfall – she wasn't in the mindset of making a hit. "There was a song that the label really wanted me to record," she recalled, "and I just said no, because it didn't fit on the album – it wasn't creatively inspiring to me. They said, 'It's a hit, it's a hit!' and absolutely, it's a hit for someone. But it's not for me because when it jeopardises my integrity too much, I can't do it. The hit thing… 'Who Let The Dogs Out' was a fucking hit, you know what I mean?!"

It was admirable that Christina was following her heart instead of coldly calculating a way to have audiences eating out of her hands, regardless of whether the material was truly representative of her. Yet she might have had to sacrifice some long-standing fans to retain her identity. Sia had insisted, "She can afford to take risks. She's at a place in her career where she could do a line-dancing record and it'd sell a bazillion copies because it's her singing… Christina could shit in a bottle and her fans would still love it!"

Unfortunately, Sia's confidence was misplaced, but the pair enjoyed their creative sessions together nonetheless. They spawned the electro-ballads 'Stronger Than Ever', 'You Lost Me', 'I Am' and 'All I Need', an ode to Max. "It's a total collaboration," Sia would later reveal. "There are some artists who walk in and say, 'I want to write a song about a stiletto' and then walk out again. You write the song and they take a third. That's not at all what it's been like working with Christina. Often she saves the day when we're stuck."

Then there was Christina's work with Le Tigre, an electro-punk group with feminist roots and a niche sound. These girls were more likely to occupy Courtney Love's iPod playlist than Christina's, so the collaboration came as another surprise – but according to band member Johanna Fateman, the chemistry was undeniable. "While the giant sound of her stacked vocals and the pop sheen she lends to the tracks might seem at odds with Le Tigre's aesthetic roots, it really works," she revealed. "The songs have a lot of elements we're known for, like a garage guitar sound and schoolyard chants, new wave-y synths, electro beats and somehow it all sounds crazily right with Christina's unbelievable voice."

Their shared ambition was to create "upbeat danceable tracks" that celebrated "female friendship, strength and partying" – and the song that best fitted that description was 'My Girls'. Devoted lyrically to nights out on the town with a gang of close friends, it featured vocals from the long-standing queen of electro-pop, Peaches. This would be the first time that a guest vocalist had appeared on one of Christina's albums, but with the tongue-in-cheek 'Fuck The Pain Away' and 'Fatherfucker' already under her belt, Peaches' straight-talking demeanour suited her down to a T.

Another collaborator who definitely wasn't shy was MIA. The daughter of a Sri Lankan freedom fighter who almost lost his life for the cause, much of her work held powerful political messages beneath the surface. When she got together with Christina, it was a meeting of two intelligent minds. The track that resulted, 'Elastic Love', might not have been politically motivated, but it was witty, using an array of stationery-related metaphors to describe love and sex. It had so much of MIA's flavour that many first-time listeners thought she was not just co-writing but singing along with Christina; on the contrary, just as she had done on the title track, 'Bionic', Christina emulated MIA's distinctive vocal sound, claiming that she didn't need to overcompensate with Mariah Carey-like warbling to prove she had an impressive range and could truly sing. Now that she was stronger, she wasn't afraid to let her vulnerability show, and a new, softer and more experimental side to her voice was shining through.

Ironically, MIA had been thoroughly disappointed. "I really thought I was going to be able to go in there and get her vocals on the next level," she lamented, "but she didn't want to do it. She was like, 'You might think that's great because it's not what you do, but to me, I'm really bored of it.'" Christina had insisted to her bemused co-writer that she'd wanted to reach a place of "less singing" and have some fun without the need to prove herself.

She continued the theme on 'Woohoo', a less than subtle ode to oral sex. The track had been released to radio only shortly before the album, on May 25, and featured an obscure sample from the 1972 Hungarian song 'Add Már Uram Az Esöt' by Kati Kovács. The co-writer and co-performer was equally alien to music fans' ears. Back then, unless underground mix tapes counted, Nicki Minaj hadn't yet released an album and hadn't infiltrated the mainstream at all. Ironically her popularity would later overshadow Christina's, something that neither artist might have expected when Christina invited Nicki to liven up the track as an unknown. Her usual material was a curious mixture of rap, dance and hip hop, but – as tantrum after tantrum in front of the media would subsequently reveal – Nicki was "definitely not pop" and refused indignantly to be defined as such. During one interview, she would threaten to walk out after a journalist uttered the offensive word, arguing that the pigeon-hole meant they hadn't listened to her music. "Not pop" was exactly the way Christina now yearned to be categorised, and the fact that Nicki hadn't built up cool credentials yet meant nothing to her.

Yet the public wasn't quite so keen – Music OMH had sneered that while 'Woohoo' might be about the delights of oral sex, it was "about as sexy as going to the dentist", while The AV Club dismissed it as "already-passé electro-trash". Nonetheless, it received a warm reception at the June 6 MTV Movie Awards, when Christina and her dancers peeled off leather capes at the end to reveal strategically positioned bright red hearts on their groins.

The track was filled with the type of sexually straight-talking lyrics that were slowly becoming commonplace in music but which, coming from women, some listeners found crude and intimidating. Love it or hate it, the theme featured heavily on *Bionic*, perhaps due in no small part to Esther Dean's co-writing slot.

Esther, who'd also been one of those responsible for Rihanna's 'Rude Boy', had co-written a number of tracks for the album, including 'Not Myself Tonight', the withering 'I Hate Boys' (which compared the male gender with bananas good for only one thing) and finally 'Vanity', an unabashed poem of self-love during which Christina would sing of turning herself on and a growing desire to become her own "legally wetted" wife.

Other sexually charged songs on the album included 'Morning Dessert' and 'Sex For Breakfast'. On the sleeve, the lyrics page devoted to the latter song screamed Gaga. Not only did Christina's leather bra, metal neck choker, blonde tousled hair and make-up choices resemble some of Gaga's own, but the picture featured neon yellow crime scene tape emblazoned with the word 'Caution' – exactly the same as the tape Gaga had wrapped herself in for the 'Telephone' music video earlier that year.

Again, she had invited the Gaga comparisons she loved to hate, but other parts of the album gave reference to someone with whom she'd rather be associated – Madonna. 'Glam', co-written with Christopher 'Tricky' Stewart and Claude Kelly, was her version of 'Vogue', detailing the pleasure of striking poses in glamorous couture and unleashing the inner diva with the help of costume. 'Desnudate', a Spanglish story of liberation and sexual abandon and 'Primadonna', an ode to the simple pleasures of non-stop partying, were co-written by the same duo.

Claude had formerly worked with Whitney Houston, Backstreet Boys, Akon and Jessie J to name a few, while Christopher's back catalogue included work with Beyoncé, Ciara, Janet Jackson, Katy Perry and Mariah Carey – and both had worked with Britney.

Christina returned to the obscure by collaborating with Ladytron. The group had previously been admired by the likes of Nine Inch Nails, Depeche Mode and Placebo, but no one like Christina. They inhabited their own world of ice-cold mechanical beats, in which pop didn't have a place, but Christina, ever the adventurer, wanted to join them. She would work with them on a cover of Ladyhawke's 'My Delirium' as well as new co-creations such as the sentimental 'Little Dreamer', but it was one solitary track, 'Birds Of Prey', that made the final cut on the deluxe edition of the album.

As harsh as it seemed, Christina had to delegate an unfinished track with Alison Goldfrapp to the metaphorical bin, too – there simply wasn't enough room to accommodate every track from the prolific songwriting sessions. This time around, even Linda Perry had worked on just one track, the optimistic-in-times-of-trouble ballad 'Lift Me Up'.

However, Christina did manage to squeeze in collaborations with singer, writer and producer Santigold for the deluxe album. An obscure, genre-defying, uncategorisable friend of Mark Ronson's, she'd added electricity to 'Bobblehead' – Christina's answer to Pink's 'Stupid Girl' – which criticised those who "played dumb" as a strategy to get what they wanted. Meanwhile, 'Monday Morning' boasted a Gwen Stefani-inspired sound infused with electronica, which wouldn't sound out of place on No Doubt's *Rock Steady* album. However, there was that added futuristic feel, as Christina played the role of a rebellious teenage party girl, refusing to turn her music down when the neighbours complain, triumphantly countering that Monday morning was the last thing on her mind.

To Christina, the album was the sound of the future, but as record sales continued to plummet, it became evident that, largely, the public didn't agree. She had hoped for more success with the June 29 release of 'You Lost Me'. She'd had her own take on her sudden fondness for all things electronic, telling Sirius XM Radio, "I was completely inspired by a lot of electronica when my son was born and we both were listening to it a lot together. Having a child makes you think of the future and the next generation and I got really inspired by electronica which is so no-holds-barred with its sound and technology... [Max] definitely inspired a playful side of me that I didn't have prior to having him."

Yet, as the public hadn't taken to the whimsical party girl lyrics, futuristic beats and synth-heavy sounds of the majority of *Bionic*, she was now choosing to release as a single a deep and dark track with more emotional meaning, something which channelled the Christina of old. 'You Lost Me' was about a partner choosing the temptations of illicit love instead of remaining faithful to her and the pain that followed the inevitable separation. The accompanying video demonstrated the fragility of loss, featuring Christina sobbing hysterically and pushing a male figure away from her before peeling off her clothes to rid herself of the toxic relationship. "When I take my shirt off," she revealed, "it's a moment when I'm saying, 'I'm taking control of the situation, I'm shedding the skin.'"

Yet in spite of a compelling video, this track also failed to ignite as a chart hit.

The final single, 'I Hate Boys', was an Australia and New Zealand-only release which, after hitting the airwaves on September 3, briefly peaked at a paltry number 28 on the Australian Airplay chart. Finally, the album also dropped out of the charts all over the world and promotion ground to a resounding halt – it was time to shelve *Bionic*.

Unsurprisingly, Ladytron blamed the flop on the fact that their own collaboration with Christina had been relegated to the deluxe editions of the album. "She was on the right track but the record label fucked up everything," insisted band member Reuben Wu. "All the good stuff got pumped into disc two. I think that with what she had in mind she could have sidestepped all the kind of potential comparisons with Lady Gaga, which... was a nightmare for her. She would have done it in the smart way and she would have been renowned now, but her record label instead wanted to put her against Gaga."

Meanwhile Christina maintained that the album hadn't gelled with the public because it had been "ahead of its time". She added, "You had to really be a music lover to really appreciate that record. It's just a special piece in my body of work that will forever live on." She also remained defiant about her own strength, asserting, "People expect me to cry – but I just laugh when things go wrong."

That was just as well because the worst blow was yet to come: as if 'You Lost Me' had been an eerily self-fulfilling prophecy, the backbone of her private life was about to come crashing down, too. Jordan, the father of her child and love of her life, would become history.

The couple had mutually misjudged their compatibility with each other. Christina would tell *People*, "I will not have my son grow up in a tension-filled home."

With two-thirds of all American marriages ending in divorce, Christina's own new beginning was no more than a statistic shared by millions of others – but the difference for her was that her failure was news-stand fodder. What was more, everyone who read the showbiz pages seemed willing, if under-qualified, to pass judgment. "I knew there would be a negative reaction in the press," she acknowledged, "but I am not going to live my life because of something someone might say. That goes against everything I sing on my records. I have to be myself."

So, just five short years after she'd tied the knot, Christina was filing for divorce. She was keeping it amicable, applying for joint custody of Max, and it seemed both parties were united in the goal of making life as stress-free for their son as it could be. As Christina would announce to *People*, "I felt torn about splitting our family up [but] when you're unhappy in your marriage, your children are the ones who suffer. That's the last thing I wanted for my son."

In the midst of her divorce, Christina was secretly adding the finishing touches to a collaboration with gangsta rapper T.I., who had been in and out of prison several times during his career. The single was 'Castle Walls', a track detailing how, to outsiders, a celebrity life in a fairy-tale castle seemed idyllic, but that behind the scenes, it was anything but. For T.I., the metaphor was obvious – his castle walls were suffocating, impenetrable and impossible to scale as, in spite of all his fame, he was trapped in a prison cell. Yet Christina had more in common with the notorious convict than met the eye – she wasn't the princess in an ivory tower that onlookers envisaged either. Her own life, too, had started to resemble a prison sentence.

That October, she and T.I. were scheduled to film a video to accompany the song, with production by Alex Da Kid, who'd also brought to life Eminem and Rihanna's 'Love The Way You Lie' – but it wasn't to be. T.I. was arrested and stood accused of violating a previous probation, as well as drug possession. The latter charge was later dropped, but he still faced a substantial jail term. The video was put on hold indefinitely. The news was symbolic of yet another of Christina's dreams turning to dust.

The saving grace after a chain of negative events was the November 24 release of her first ever feature film, *Burlesque*. The film charted a small-town girl with enormous hidden talents who breaks away from a troubled background, singing, strutting and stripping her way to the top at an LA burlesque club. The film was directed by Steve Antin, the brother of Pussycat Dolls founder and choreographer Robin. At first Christina was far from convinced and asked that they rewrite aspects of the role. "There have been a lot of attempts at making movies like this that haven't turned out so well and I definitely had to think it over to do *Burlesque*," she confided to *Collider*. "They had to rewrite the character because I was just like, 'This girl doesn't have a lot of drive. She doesn't have a lot of meat. I think you should give [the role] to someone else.' I had an initial meeting with [the producers] and I said, 'I just don't think she's for me. I want someone with more bite and more passion for what she wants in life' – and so they rewrote it."

The result was a girl who, in many ways, was the spitting image of Christina in her younger years. "Ali has a rough past," she would elaborate. "Her mother dies when she's very young and she's been in foster homes. I could relate to that pain. That gave me great motivation to provoke my tears for the scenes where I had to really pass it on... I felt it deeply, to go through a lot of those things that brought up a lot of painful memories."

The film begins with Ali begging an exploitative boss she works for as a bar-girl to pay her two months of overdue wages. When nothing is forthcoming, she snatches a few banknotes from the till, assuring a co-worker she's taking only what she's owed, and vows to use it to start a new life in LA. Moments later, alone there in the bar, Ali suddenly breaks into the Etta James classic 'Something's Got A Hold On Me' – just as a young Christina would have hummed along to her *Sound Of Music* favourites to soothe her troubles. The only difference, of course, was the specific soundtrack to her liberation. Moments later she arrives at the train station asking for a ticket to LA. "Return or one way?" the clerk asks. Christina shoots him an incredulous look, hitting back, "You've got to be kidding, right?"

Before long, she's escaped from the sleepy Midwest town that's been holding her back from her dreams and is instead pounding the pavements of LA to the tune of Marilyn Manson's frenetic 'The Beautiful People', her dreamy wide-eyed expression standing out a mile among the streetwise and savvy city dwellers.

By the time night falls, her eyes are drawn inexplicably to a glittery glow-in-the-dark sign spelling out 'Burlesque Lounge' and the grinning, scantily clad showgirl leaning out over the balcony. Her rush of excitement is palpable – the nightspot has a certain magnetising 'je ne sais quoi' and, without even realising it, it's what she's been searching for her whole life.

This is where the rewritten script comes into play – Ali presents as an almost implausibly tenacious woman with an animalistic hunger for showbiz so all-consuming that it hurts. "I'll practise 'til I bleed!" she screams in desperation, with the demeanour of a toddler in the throes of a tantrum, when she's passed over for an opportunity. "I swear to God!" She approaches staff with a sense of entitlement, demanding an impromptu audition, and when she gets the cold shoulder, she makes it clear she won't take no for an answer. Instead she recruits herself as a waitress to get her foot in the door and ingratiate herself more fully into the burlesque world. Admittedly this scene lacks authenticity – the synchronicity of Ali marching in at the very moment when, despite there being a performance in full swing, there is no waitress on hand to serve revellers, seems too miraculous to be true. That said, she takes her chance like a pro. Pushy, thick-skinned and voraciously determined, she's confident that her chance to prove herself will come. Yet the bosses are condescending – on the surface, she lacks the glamour of the sequinned, bejewelled dancers she aspires to join and still has the deceptive guise of a shy small-town girl. She's beautiful, but, outwardly, at least, not burlesque material.

Her next chance to prove otherwise comes when the club hosts an audition for a dancer to join the troupe – without telling the lowly amateur, of course. Nonplussed, Ali waits in the wings. Club owner Tess – who in real life is singer Cher – turns to her companion and asks despairingly, "Where did all the *good* dancers go in LA?" Her fellow judge witheringly remarks that they're probably on *Dancing With The Stars*. Enter Ali. She gatecrashes the audition and starts to dance herself and, when Tess rolls her eyes and turns her back, orders, "Listen to me!" Insisting that she knows every song, she eventually breaks her down and persuades her to give her a part, which marks the beginning of the working relationship between the pair.

As it turned out, no acting was required to conjure up affection between the pair, Christina was already in awe of Cher due to her decades of experience in the industry. Recalling their first meeting, she told *Collider*, "I was on my way to dance rehearsal. I was in sweat pants and flats and I had my baby on my hip. [Producer] Clive [Culpepper] came up to me and said, 'You've got to meet Cher. She's right over there in the next soundstage' and I was like, 'Clint, you can't put me on the spot like that. I have sweat pants on and I've got my baby on my hip. I need my high heels. I'm going to meet Cher. What are you thinking?!' And he was like, 'No, she doesn't care about that. Just come meet her.' I was like, 'But she's so tall and I'm so short. It's not going to be right.' I wanted to look good. Lo and behold, he twisted my arm and I went."

Cher was under no illusion about how Christina felt either. "After I found out Cher was a possibility to star in the movie with me," she continued, "I wouldn't let Clint take no for an answer in getting her to sign on to the film. I was like, 'Go stalk her. Sleep outside her door. Do whatever you need to do to get Cher to do this film with me because I can't see anyone else being Tess.' He told her, 'Christina loves you. She wants to be in this movie with you. She would drink your bath water. She's in love with you.' Then she signed on. As I walked up to meet her, all shy, I just went for it and put my hand out and said, 'Hi Cher, I'm Christina. I'm the one that wants to drink your bath water.' She laughed and opened her arms up to me and it was a bonding love fest from that day on."

Likewise, while there were some tense moments where Ali's tantrums upgraded her to a diva-in-training role, her onstage relationship with Tess was very much the same as it was in real life. Tess nurtures the new girl with an almost maternal affection, taking on a mothering role for a girl who, due to bereavement, lacks one of her own. Ali repays her kindness by looking up to her as a veteran influence to learn from – a singer herself and an astute businesswoman, too. The pair's relationship blossoms during intimate, emotive conversations in the dressing room while, in the make-up department, Tess' decades of experience in artistry combined with Ali's blank canvas of beauty and youth allows the older woman to transform her protégé into a dazzling beauty, a veritable goddess with bold black eyes and bright red lips. Swooning in the mirror at her makeover, she later sings out onstage, "Where have I been all my life?"

With her mundane life in Iowa now just a distant memory, Ali secretly hankers after the lead role she knows is within reach – and sure enough, it isn't long before she gets it. When another dancer, Nikki, makes the fatal mistake of breaking the no-alcohol-at-work rule, she is sent home and Ali is drafted in as her replacement. Consumed with jealousy, Nikki creeps backstage, tricks the sound technician into leaving her alone at the controls and pulls the plug on Ali's microphone – a low blow that backfires in spectacular form. Shocked into silence for a matter of a few short seconds, Ali soon recovers and launches into an a cappella routine without the music, her first belting singing role of the film. When she breaks into 'Tough Love', the look on her face is of someone who relishes her role so much that she's no longer acting. An incredulous Tess looks on with amazement, realising Ali's full potential as if for the first time.

After she blushingly receives a standing ovation, Tess calls a meeting to announce that she'll be rewriting the entire show to create one based around Ali as the star. A furious Nikki, who realises she has unwittingly masterminded her rival's promotion, despite trying to achieve the exact opposite, snipes, "They don't come to hear us sing!" Tess turns to her and replies, "They'll come to hear *her* sing." While Nikki is telling anyone who'll listen that Ali is "a slut with mutant lungs", her major track of the night tells the last story – 'You Haven't Heard The Last Of Me'.

As the film continues, tales of Tess' growing financial difficulties and the romantic tension behind Ali's friendship with the bartender at the club are interspersed with full-length numbers onstage at the Burlesque Lounge. While many of the *Back To Basics*-era tracks Christina belted out were cover versions, she was involved with the writing of three – 'Express', 'Bound To You' and the grand finale of the film, 'Burlesque'. Her co-writers included a few faces from the past: Christopher Stewart, Claude Kelly and Sia Furler. Creating the songs turned out to be a form of method acting within itself. "When I went in to write the music, I wasn't just writing from my own point of view," Christina recalled. "I had to look at Ali and see what makes her tick and what makes her feel this way, in this moment. I had to look at all those bullet points and write it from her perspective."

As well as getting to grips with the songs, the role also called upon her to master some punishing dance routines. "I had so many bruises every day," she confided to *Collider*, "especially when I was whipping that long strand of diamonds around for 'Diamonds Are A Girl's Best Friend'. I smacked my leg so many times in rehearsals before I got it right. Getting down on my knees for some of the movements bruised me. I bruise easily, but it looked like I got in a car accident some of the days!"

That was just one of a number of awkward moments, but she persevered until the cliffhanger scenes at the end. Together with Ali, a nearly bankrupt Tess hatches a plan to save the club from going into administration with just 24 hours to spare – and it's a happy ending all round.

There'd been so many reasons Christina hadn't wanted to do the movie. She'd been expecting a gargantuan challenge due to the many roles of acting, dancing, writing, singing and memorising lines – not to mention juggling that with childcare, family commitments and her existing career. The demanding 18-hour days took her away from writing music for her own projects, not to mention preventing her from answering nature's call: the primal, magnetic pull she felt towards Max. For months, outside of weekends, she'd been barely able to spend time with him at all. Although he was a regular visitor to the studio, the punishing schedule meant she'd be working full speed ahead at those times.

Christina had also initially felt some anxiety about working with Steve Antin. "I had a few reservations about him," she admitted, "as I'm sure everyone had a few reservations about me acting in my first film." However, one step into his office and her confidence in him began to build. "I looked at all of his mood boards that were strewn all over his walls and they were referencing *Cabaret* and beautiful women and you could tell this man appreciated a woman's beauty, her body and the way it moves, in the way he wanted it to be lit and the way he wanted it to be shot. There are many ways that you could perceive or interpret burlesque and I wanted to make sure he had the right idea involved [but] he appreciated the art form so much that I knew it was going to be a perfect fit."

Then there had been the developing friendship with Cher to motivate her. "Her emails of encouragement and support are like unwrapping little pieces of candy and getting the best sensation from it," she would reminisce fondly. "I feel like we're old girlfriends and we'll talk and talk and talk and she just has stories for days... I really, really adore her."

Overall, Christina was glad she'd taken on the movie – and after the flop of *Bionic*, she was pinning all of her hopes on it being a box office success. Yet again, however, the reality was a different story, About as humiliating as Mariah Carey's appearance in *Glitter* or Britney Spears' starring role in *Crossroads*, it disappeared from notoriety as quickly as it had arrived. In the eyes of the public, it was no *Showgirls* or *Moulin Rouge*, and it lacked the love-or-hate-them tawdry thrills. Steve Antin's vision had been of something classier, more elegant, but ultimately less exciting, and many might have felt it passed up on abundant opportunities for electricity, drama and sex appeal.

Then there was the script, with its interpretation of Ali and Co. that could have been accused of propping up an unrealistic plot.

Viewers were less reluctant to engage with the music, however. After two taster singles featuring Christina were made available for digital download – 'Express' on November 3 and 'Show Me How You Burlesque' on November 19 – the main attraction, the soundtrack album, was released on November 22. It went on to sell a million copies.

While the film itself had been less successful than expected, there was a silver lining: she'd developed a lasting friendship with her set assistant, Matthew Rutler. In fact, after she filed for divorce, the couple began to step out in public as boyfriend and girlfriend. Some might say she had moved on alarmingly quickly, or even that she was callous and insensitive, that the impact of losing the father of her son had barely dented her. Yet the reality was that, regardless of all other issues, she'd simply outgrown her love for Jordan. Perhaps her marriage hadn't been so much about passion but rather she had clung to her husband as a security blanket. Maybe she had even viewed him as an unconventional father figure. After all, in the early days, he'd offered something that most people might receive only from a parent: unconditional love and support. Instead of reacting jealously to her erotic photo shoots and sexualised dance routines, he'd been her most ardent cheerleader, encouraging her every step of the way. As he hadn't been the archetypal looker – with many members of the public even insisting he was "ugly" – and he had, in comparison to her, a very poorly paid job, it seemed as though she'd been attracted to his ability to nurture her, removing the pressure from being the boss in everyday life. With Jordan, she'd found someone she'd trusted enough to surrender her control to – a rarity for her – and as a result, she'd experienced a liberation so relieving that it became addictive. However, it seemed there was no grand passion, no adult love affair; instead had Christina been looking for a man to fill her father's void? As she'd grown up, as brutal as it might have sounded, maybe she no longer required that security blanket. "When I first met my husband," she would clarify to Q, "I needed that helping hand to take the reins and look after me. After the movie, I grew out of being that little girl: I became more of an adult."

As such, Matthew was her new love, symbolic of a new era in her life. She didn't rule out a second marriage either, claiming, "Wholeheartedly, I know one day I'll be able to feel that again for someone. That idea will never die."

It was love that would carry Christina through the most humiliating moments of her career. Her spate of bad luck ran right into 2011, when her invitation to sing the National Anthem at the February 6 Superbowl turned into a disaster. As she'd sung 'The Star-Spangled Banner' countless times in her childhood, recreating a moment that was widely seen as a forgettable footnote in her career (one so insignificant that it was barely worth mentioning) should have been child's play. Yet as an incredulous nation looked on, she sabotaged herself. Instead of singing: "O'er the ramparts we watch'd, were so gallantly streaming", she offered the unusual alternative, "What so proudly we watched at the twilight's last reaming." The bizarre, nonsensical lyrics instantly made Christina a laughing stock and prompted many critics to sneer that she'd been intoxicated. Yet her explanation was more simple. "I got lost in the emotion of being there," she admitted, "and I messed up the lyrics."

However, she turned to her first line of defence in times of trouble – laughter. "I went to dinner after the Superbowl with Matt and I laughed about how I'd made myself into a Trivial Pursuit question," she chuckled to *W* magazine. "In 2011, what female singer fluffed the lyrics to the national anthem?"

Yet the persistent rumours that she'd been drinking the pain away due to a traumatic divorce unfairly intensified at the February 13 Grammys ceremony, when she tripped and stumbled during a tribute to Aretha Franklin. "When I nearly collapsed, I was thinking, 'Are you kidding me?!'" Christina reflected. "I've always been really good with my heels. Even pregnant, I could perform in heels. Note to self: never wear a train onstage. My heel got caught in my train and if it wasn't for Jennifer Hudson, who picked me up as I went down, I would have fallen to the floor." She added jokingly, "It was just like, 'What else, God? What else?!' I threw my hands up in the air and started smiling, because what else could go wrong?"

She had to wait a mere matter of days to find out. March 1 should have been a day of celebration for her – she'd just signed the contract to become a guest judge on TV talent show *The Voice*. Based on a reaction to so-called superficial contests such as *American Idol* and *The X Factor* where would-be singers often seemed to be judged not just on how they performed but also how they looked, *The Voice* aimed to reverse the injustice. In a sea of nearby acts and Auto-Tuned beauty queens, the show offered a format which left no room for bias; judges would listen to an audition while their chair faced the opposite direction, and only when they pressed a button to indicate interest in an act, their chair would swivel round, allowing them to see the face behind the voice. This way, first impressions were based entirely on performance, giving every contestant a fair and equal chance of competing in the talent stakes, regardless of whether or not their face fit the bill. The breakout success of artists such as Susan Boyle, however, raised questions about whether talent shows were as guilty of looks-related discrimination as producers of *The Voice* implied. Nonetheless, the idea was well-intended.

Christina and her co-judges, Blake Shelton, Cee Lo Green and Maroon 5's Adam Levine, would each pick eight acts to mentor. They'd work with them closely in rehearsals, building up to a weekly performance that pitted them against rival acts. The ultimate winner would be crowned 'The Voice' and go on to earn a recording contract.

Christina couldn't wait for the battles to begin – it finally seemed as though things were looking up – and she'd been in high spirits at dinner that night. Yet to her horror, the night of celebrations would end in a jail cell. At around 2.45 a.m., police cars surrounded Matt's vehicle, accusing him of "driving erratically" and claiming that both he and Christina appeared to be "extremely intoxicated". In fact, tests would subsequently reveal that Matt had been under the legal blood alcohol limit for driving. Nonetheless, police arrested, fingerprinted and detained them, not to mention taking their mug shots. The following day, Christina was released and even though the police had no intention of prosecuting her she was unhappy about the situation. A police spokesman said: "She was not capable of taking care of herself," adding she was "very co-operative, not belligerent in any way".

It hadn't been Christina's year, but by April 15 her divorce was finalised and she was ready for a new chapter in her life. Within a couple of weeks of signing her divorce papers, *The Voice* premiered to an impressive audience of 11.8 million viewers. Clearly they liked what they saw, as the following week's viewing figures were even higher. In fact, for the under 50s demographic, it had quickly become the top programme of the night.

As the series progressed, Christina eventually found herself performing with Maroon 5 for their single 'Moves Like Jagger'. The fun-loving pop track, which interspersed a studio performance of the song with footage from Mick Jagger's heyday, was released on June 21 to enormous public appeal.

Coming as a breath of fresh air after the poorly performing singles from *Bionic*, it was Christina's first number one on the US *Billboard* chart for a decade, following 'Lady Marmalade'. Yet her appeal wasn't entirely down to such prolific TV exposure – it shot to number one in over 20 other countries, selling a grand total of more than eight million copies worldwide and being certified as one of the best-selling singles of all time. The wheel of fortune had finally turned in Christina's favour and she'd been given a chance to show the world what really mattered: the voice.

CHAPTER 12

Setting The Lotus Free

"When you've been on this show, that's your chair for life," *The Voice* producer Mark Burnett asserted. "There will never be anyone getting replaced, ever."

After months of mentoring, he'd finally set Christina free. As much as she loved to play the senior pop star, coaching and critiquing the next generation of talent all the way to the top, seeing their hunger was a constant reminder of the craving she too had to be onstage. Reassured by the knowledge that anyone who took over her judging slot would purely be a stand-in, there was nothing else standing in her way.

"Album title: *Lotus*," she wrote cryptically on Twitter. "Representing an unbreakable flower that survives under the hardest conditions and still thrives." These words sounded like the war cry of an indefatigable fighter, someone who hadn't let the failure of *Bionic* break her. The humiliation had cut like a knife – especially for someone who, prior to that, had never truly experienced failure. Once the US tour couldn't go ahead it proved the death knell for the ill-fated album.

However, Christina had found her silver lining. She'd taken on the *Bionic* project knowing it was anything but commercial, but had reached the stage in her career where, instead of pandering to the charts, she could produce an album purely for herself. Instead of anxiously calculating what the next big trend might be and then applying the formula, she'd poured out her passion to create something that, in that moment, whether it was loved or hated, truly represented herself. To follow this path took courage, single-mindedness and tenacity, plus the strength not to be swayed by other people's opinions. It was empowering for her to have survived the backlash – and her next offering aspired to prove that she could bounce back even stronger.

The big comeback took place on September 17 with 'Your Body', an uptempo slice of anthemic dance-floor pop. It was everything *Bionic* wasn't and, with Max Martin on board – a Swedish producer renowned for slushy bubblegum pop – it sounded like a hit.

To choose something so overwhelmingly pop, when she'd started her career desperately trying to get away from that genre, seemed counter-intuitive, but that was the tease about Christina – never predictable, she took pride in continually confounding people's expectations.

She admitted that she'd avoided Max like the plague when she'd first entered the industry because he was "a classic hit-maker" who appeared "all over radio". Back then, she'd been focused on producing a distinctive, iconic sound that, without reference to any other artist, screamed her name alone. "I'm not sure we would have been able to create the same music had we connected earlier," she confessed. "He did all the Britney and 'N Sync songs and I was doing something a little more daring." Yet after years of watching each other from afar – on Christina's part, with the occasional hint of contempt – she'd come "full circle" to a place where she embraced the classic iconography of the pop star. The difference between then and now was that she was no longer being pressed into a commercially friendly mould – she was embracing pop in her own way and on her own terms. What was more, unlike the teenage girl all those years earlier, she maintained full control. She recalled that Max stepped back and gave her "creative freedom".

The demo of 'Your Body' had featured "fuck" in the chorus in place of the word "love" but, once Christina had realised the song was a potential single, she'd had to re-record a more family-friendly version to ensure it would be played on radio. Yet the brazen, forthright energy of the track, detailing her desire for a one-night-stand, remained – and the video was equally colourful.

While Christina's gradual passage to womanhood could easily be charted through her music, the journey showed on her body, too. She now boasted a veritable Marilyn Monroe figure, a voluptuous hourglass silhouette with a defined waist, womanly hips and shapely thighs. Measured against the superficial values and stringent physical ideals of some anorexia-fuelled fashionistas, she was "fat", but in the eyes of others, she was shapely.

Regardless, this was the incarnation of Christina that would feature on 'My Body'. A tongue-in-cheek sign would appear at the start of the track reassuring that "no men were harmed in the making of this video", which set the tone for what was to follow.

For Christina, sex appeal had always equalled power – she'd enjoyed the control she could exert over someone due to her looks and had once confessed she wanted to portray a "cruel sexuality, one that men can never reach". In keeping with that, the look she coveted was a formidable, intimidating brand of beauty. It was fitting, then, that Christina was in the driving seat in the video of 'Your Body', seducing lovers and then killing them. She had become a siren – a mythical beauty that, according to popular legend, would captivate sailors by distracting them as they cruised away and, consequently, lure them to their death. Christina's misdemeanours, however, were a little less subtle, seeing her bludgeon one unfortunate admirer to death in a bathroom stall and set another lover's car alight in a blaze of electric pink flames.

However, maybe there was more to the video than there seemed. Taking into account Christina's long-standing fury about double standards in society, perhaps it served as a parody of male views on women. Some seemed to portray the fairer sex as evil temptresses hellbent on sabotaging and distracting men from their purpose, not to mention manipulating them via the effect they had on their groins. If it was a parody of this attitude, however, it was a playful one. When snippets appear in between murders of Christina casually sitting at home, laughing innocently – if a little maniacally – at cartoons, it seems it's all been a light-hearted joke.

The single peaked at number 34 on the US *Billboard* chart, while in the UK it reached a respectable number 16 but, regardless of statistical measures of popularity, it seemed the public was behind her. Co-judge Adam Levine jokingly, but admiringly, told her, after hearing the song, "I hate you because it's so good." Meanwhile, according to *Pop Crush*, "2012's club banger" would see Christina managing to "walk the tight-rope between electronically enhanced dance music and pretty pop and she does it while wearing six-inch stilettos. Nice work, girl!"

Of course, all of the hype provided a perfect build-up to the release of *Lotus*, which hit shelves on November 9. Just as she had done with each of her other albums, Christina had totally reinvented herself, even omitting the previously ever-present Linda Perry from writing duties this time around. The only link she retained to the past was a new collaboration with Sia Furler, 'Blank Page'. In this heartbreak ballad, Christina's lyrics were infused with the painful resignation of saying goodbye to a marriage she'd hoped was forever. To her, the song was "so valuable and so empowering" that it reminded her of 'Beautiful'. "It's about being OK with saying you're sorry and the fact that you might have regrets," Christina elaborated, "but it's about finding closure and making peace with yourself and the situation."

By linking vulnerability with power, she'd highlighted that it wasn't always an exterior of toughness and total self-control that provided empowerment – on the contrary, it took a strong person to let go of their fears and admit that, sometimes, they were weak. That conclusion suggested a new maturity, one that, as Christina entered her thirties, was entirely fitting.

On 'Empty Words', she repeats the theme, freely admitting that someone's words cut her like a knife, but promising that they won't break her. Similarly on 'Best Of Me', she strips away the illusion that she's "tough as nails", revealing that, in reality, in spite of the lofty superstar pedestal on which she'd been placed, her heart aches like anyone else's. Behind her words is a challenge to the assumption that, due to her wealth and internationally relevant career, she is immune or untouchable by human cruelty. In fact, perhaps for her the burden of scrutiny is even heavier. She'd been experiencing the same rites of passage as many other young women – divorce, heartbreak, trouble at work and human change – but humiliatingly publicly, with every wrong move recorded, analysed and accessible at the click of a button on any Google search. Yet as she's grown older, she's grounded herself in that which is truly important – her son, family and friends and her artistry – and no matter what the world throws at her, she will "rise undefeated". For Christina, the true indicator of security and comfort in one's own skin was an ability to shake off the pain of others' opinions and live for herself instead – the ultimate measure of liberation and empowerment.

Christina's work on *The Voice* had put her back in touch with the younger generation – fiercely ambitious aspiring singers desperate to succeed, who reminded her a little of her younger self – and she felt obliged to share her "stay strong" manifesto with them, too. That was the inspiration behind 'Army Of Me'. "All these six-year-olds who know me from pushing my button and turning around in a big red chair who weren't around for the actual 'Fighter', this is my chance to recharge it, rejuvenate it and do something modernised for them," she stated in reference to the 2003 single that had prefaced it. Labelling 'Army Of Me' as 'Fighter 2.0', she added, "I feel like every generation should be able to enjoy and have their piece of 'Fighter' within."

The lighter piano ballad 'Sing For Me' had also been inspired by her experiences with young contestants on *The Voice*. "You really come face to face with a lot of people that are predominantly younger," she mused. "That's inspiring because they come up to you and they're such big fans and they share with you what song touched them the most and how they had to learn every single ad-lib and dissect it. As a vocalist it brought me back to, 'Yeah, that's what I used to do to my Whitney Houston record and my Mariah Carey record and my Etta James record.' It brings you back to a place where it becomes your personal responsibility to infuse the next generation with more information about learning every intricate note. That's why 'Sing For Me' is a special song. It's one of those singer's songs where, if you're not a vocalist, you can't mess with that song." If, as she'd lyricised, everyone needed a melody to set their souls free, this was one for the budding singers out there aiming to follow in her footsteps.

This wasn't the only track heavily influenced by her judging slot on *The Voice*. Having already collaborated with Adam Levine, she'd set about teaming up with her other co-judges too – Blake Shelton and Cee Lo Green.

A collaboration with Blake, a veteran country star with a sound straight out of Nashville, seemed almost comical. Yet Christina took the initiative of starting a performance with a cover snippet of his song 'Hillbilly Bone', only for him to tweet publicly that he was "speechless". The pair then flirted with the idea of a joint song on Twitter, with Christina writing, "Now we need to team up for a country duet, Blake. I'm down!"

What had initially seemed like a jokey exchange of messages soon morphed into 'Just A Fool', an archetypal country love ballad to which Christina's voice seemed surprisingly suited.

Then there was the uplifting 'Make The World Move', an already written track with a space for a soulful addition. "There was a part for a potential male vocal on the chorus and I just heard immediately Cee Lo's voice on it, his signature Cee Lo, and it was fun collaborating with him and having him on my record and just joining forces together," Christina marvelled. "As in every record, it's my heart. It's a labour of love. It's not just [a song] to me, [it's] blood, sweat and tears and stuff from the heart."

Meanwhile, to return the favour, Christina collaborated with Cee Lo on the classic Christmas track 'Baby, It's Cold Outside' for his own album, *Cee Lo's Magic Moment*. A third track they'd worked on, 'Nasty', had been shelved for a future opportunity.

'Make The World Move' had been an Alex Da Kid production, courtesy of her earlier work with him on T.I.'s 'Castle Walls'. He also lent his magic to 'Best Of Me', the uplifting 'Light Up The Sky' and the light rock-infused 'Ceasefire', about breaking away from self-destructive fighting in a relationship and liberating oneself as an enemy-free army of one.

Alex Da Kid also produced 'Circles' and 'Shut Up'. 'Circles' saw Christina take on the guise of a female Eminem, with an additional cross-breed of Rihanna and Lil' Kim. It was feisty, outspoken and full of attitude, aiming to make the middle finger demeanour typically associated only with wealthy superstars accessible to the wider public.

In the same vein, 'Shut Up' asks detractors to kiss Christina's ass and suck her metaphorical dick. "That's for my fans to blast in their cars," she explained mischievously. "I know a lot of them get heated and pissed off whenever they hear some bullshit rumour or bullshit story and it's a great venting song for anyone that is having a bad day or not liking their boss. It's playful and tongue-in-cheek."

Of course the album wouldn't have Christina's stamp on it if there weren't a few candid sexual references – and sure enough, they were in abundant supply on 'Around The World', a track in which Christina invites international love. From Puerto Rico to the Congo and from Tokyo to Milan, she's getting down around the world. Then there was the Max Martin-produced 'Let There Be Love' and the equally pop-infused 'Red Hot Kinda Love'. Yet the latter took its influence from a myriad of genres, including samples from Mark Radice's 'The Whole Wide World Ain't Nothin' But A Party' and the vintage dancehall-style '54-46 That's My Number', originally performed by Toots & The Maytals.

Finally there was the title track – the intro and perhaps the most symbolic and significant out of all the songs on the album. A decade on from *Stripped* – the moment when she'd finally broken out of an externally manufactured shell and showed the music-buying public the real Christina – she'd finally come full circle. Enhanced by the maturity that her thirties had provided, she was now setting her inner self, the lotus, totally free.

It was no mistake, of course, that she'd chosen the resilient lotus as her definitive avatar, a flower that experiences year-round bloom. She wasn't someone who could only survive laboratory conditions. The economic and musical climate was irrelevant and even the latest trends failed to dent her. Her beauty burned just as brightly whatever the weather. "This album represents a celebration of the new me," Christina would explain, "and to me, the lotus has always represented this unbreakable flower that withstands any harsh weather conditions in its surroundings, that withstands time and remains beautiful and strong throughout the years."

Living up to her self-created name, she was undeterred when her duet with Blake Shelton – released on December 3 – peaked at just number 71 in the USA. Taking risks and experimenting, regardless of the outcome, was all just an integral part of her artistry.

She crossed another genre boundary by appearing on rapper Pitbull's 'Feel This Moment', a single from his seventh album, *Global Warming*. Pitbull had frequently been called into question due to his potentially misogynistic lyrics, which some felt sexually objectified women and set a bad example to listeners. However he was like a pussycat when it came to praising Christina's vocals, marvelling, "To work with [her] is an honour [and] a blessing. [She is] someone that I highly respected." The track, released on February 4, 2013, was a moderate hit, performing highest in Austria where it reached number seven.

Christina had also recorded a Spanish language track, 'Casa De Mi Padre (House Of My Father)', for the Matt Piedmont-directed film of the same name. She would make a brief appearance in the movie to sing it but, in the style of *The Rocky Horror Picture Show*, the footage featured just her lips.

With all of these achievements under her belt, Christina was diversifying, and, while she wore the occasional costume created by Lady Gaga's preferred designers, the Blonds, she was now far beyond the point of any comparisons. The evocative cover art of her album, featuring a naked Christina rising up from a pale pink lotus flower, said it all, but as strong and triumphant as she now was, there were still battles to be won, and this was why Christina was a perpetual fighter.

One such battle was the public's reaction to her weight gain. While she was still under the average weight for a western woman, she stood out in contrast to the stature of her younger self and indeed the industry-defined norms of a female singer. The chants of the public screamed "FAT", although in reality, she was anything but. The episode culminated in the publication of some controversial quotes in *US Weekly*, which Christina subsequently stated were false. She had allegedly told the magazine, "[In 2002], I had gained about 15 pounds during promotion and during my *Stripped* tour. They called this serious emergency meeting about how there was a lot of backlash about my weight." She had allegedly added,

"I told them during the *Lotus* recording, 'You're working with a fat girl. Know it now and get over it.' They need a reminder sometimes that I don't belong to them. It's my body… my body is just not on the table that way any more."

The first hint that the quotes were fabricated came from their factual inaccuracy even on well-known trivia; for example, in one, she defined herself as "a Puerto Rican girl", when it was common knowledge that her Latin roots were Ecuadorian. The suspicions of a faux interview were confirmed when Christina herself spoke out against the quotes. The feature was subsequently removed from the *US Weekly* website altogether, apparently owing to "an error about the source".

Christina could simply roll her eyes contemptuously, but of more concern was the national obsession with slimming that the situation highlighted, which sometimes had tragic consequences. In the UK, anorexia causes more deaths than alcohol, drug addiction and depression put together, with thousands of young women hospitalised for the condition every year. Thus for Christina, the handling of these quotes – which were repeatedly copied into every celebrity magazine and tabloid newspaper – highlighted the perils of a society that defined full-figured girls like Christina as fat. She could laugh off the snubs, but what about the young, impressionable girls that couldn't? She had to be their voice and it was time to fight back. Standing against dubious role models such as Kate Moss, who irresponsibly boasted, "Nothing tastes as good as skinny feels" as a defining catchphrase, Christina wanted her body to be a symbol that skinny didn't necessarily equate to successful and that self-starvation was a symbol not of triumph and self-discipline but of oppression. She wanted her voice to shout louder than Kate et al in the battle against the typically western culturally transmitted disease that was low body image – and if her figure was demonstrative of the possibilities for fuller-figured women, then that was even more reason for it to stay.

Yet it wasn't the first war she had waged on society – and it wouldn't be the last. As she would wryly acknowledge, "There's always going to be a fighter in me, getting through some obstacle and some hurdle."

That fighting stance had served her well. She'd once been an insecurity-plagued, malleable, easily manipulated teenager desperate to get her foot in the door at all costs for a singing career, but when she arrived, instead of enjoying the fame and fortune, forgetting her original passions and striving no further, she'd turned the industry and its values and steadfast formulas upside down.

She'd fought structural sexism, the trend for manufactured artists and the many injustices of a corrupt society. For over a decade now, she'd been reaping the fruits of her labour.

She'd been bruised and broken, objectified, stifled and overpowered – but now she was a symbol of female strength the world over.

This lotus would wear its bullet wounds with pride, because it had taken a lifetime of fights to reach this point – one where she felt truly "unbreakable".

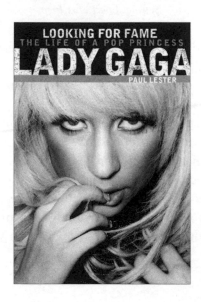

LOOKING FOR FAME
LADY GAGA
By Paul Lester

This electrifying biography explores Stefani Germanotta's rapid rise to global stardom in the guise of the outrageous Lady Gaga. Hers has been a triumph achieved with the help of wild image-making, infectious pop hits and a teasing strand of ambiguous sexuality that has turned her into a gay icon. At heart it's the story of a unique self-made phenomenon — a Madonna for today.

As an adoring fan of Freddie Mercury and David Bowie, Lady Gaga took the essence of eighties glam and reinvented it for the digital age. Commercially successful and critically accepted, she shot from obscurity on Manhattan's Lower East Side club scene to worldwide fame in just a couple of years. This is the story of her high-speed rise in the fame game, told with a mix of admiration and sharp journalistic insight.

Paul Lester is the author of acclaimed biographies of Gang Of Four, Wire, and Pink. He contributes to numerous magazines as well as The Guardian *and* The Sunday Times.

ISBN: 978.0.85712.466.1
Order No: OP53438

CRAZY IN LOVE
THE BEYONCE KNOWLES BIOGRAPHY
By Daryl Easlea

Crazy In Love explores the life and astonishing career trajectory of Beyoncé Knowles, the Texan teenager who rose from performing in her hometown backyards to headlining shows all over the world. Daryl Easlea's biography details her time with Destiny's Child – the troubled group that launched her – and her subsequent spectacular rise to a particularly modern kind of fame.

Beyoncé now spans movies, albums, product endorsements and the obligatory celebrity marriage. Hitched to Jay-Z, she kept changing her hairstyles and was accused of changing her complexion to a lighter shade for a L'Oréal commercial. She even changed her name to Sasha Fierce for one album. Making sense of the chameleonic career that prompted Michelle Obama to declare Beyoncé 'one of my favorite performers on the planet' the author has produced a biography that is both exciting and revealing.

Daryl Easlea was the deputy editor at Record Collector, to which he remains a regular contributor. His work can be found in Mojo *and* bbc.co.uk; *and has appeared in* The Guardian, Uncut, Dazed & Confused *and* The Independent. *He is the author of the critically acclaimed* Everybody Dance: CHIC & The Politics of Disco *and* The Story Of The Supremes.

ISBN: 978.085712.723.5
Order No: OP53988

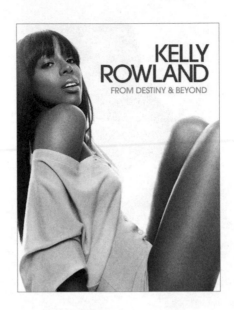

FROM DESTINY & BEYOND
KELLY ROWLAND
By Chloë Govan

From Destiny and Beyond charts Kelly Rowland's rise from painfully shy child to successful backing vocalist and internationally acclaimed solo act. Fleeing a broken home and an alcoholic father, she entered the tough world of show business via what would become one of the best-selling girl groups in the world, Destiny's Child.

A brutal rehearsal regime and a love-hate relationship with the group's manager - bandmate Beyoncé's father Matthew - meant that life was still far from easy. Kelly's eventual emergence from the shadow of Beyoncé to grasp stardom in her own right makes for a truly inspiring story. Biographer Chloë Govan tells it all, from childhood loneliness to success as a solo performer and UK *X-Factor judge*.

Chloë Govan has written about travel, lifestyle and music for a variety of publications around the world including Travel Weekly, The Times *and* Real Travel, *where she has a monthly column. She is also the author of* Katy Perry: A Life of Fireworks *and* Rihanna: Rebel Flower, *also published by Omnibus Press.*

ISBN: 978.1.78038.553.2
Order No: OP54824

WHO'S LAUGHING NOW
THE JESSIE J STORY
By Chloë Govan

This extraordinary biography tells how Jessica Ellen Cornish from Ilford in north east London overcame being 'not really that good at anything' to reinvent herself as Jessie J and record one of the biggest selling albums of 2011.

Success came in the face of extraordinary setbacks. Childhood bullying, an irregular heartbeat, a serious fall from the stage and a minor stroke at the age of 18 all threatened the health and career of the BRIT school student who first pursued fame through dance and the musical theatre.

Author Chloe Govan has interviewed record producers, school classmates, friends, dance tutors and many others to unearth the real stories behind Jessie J's improbable road to fame.

Chloë Govan has written about travel, lifestyle and music for a variety of publications around the world including Travel Weekly, The Times *and* Real Travel, *where she has a monthly column. She is also the author of* Katy Perry: A Life of Fireworks *and* Rihanna: Rebel Flower, *also published by Omnibus Press.*

ISBN: 978.1.78038.313.2
Order No: OP54505